# The Return of the Ring

# Proceedings of the Tolkien Society Conference 2012

## Volume I

Edited by
Lynn Forest-Hill

Copyright © 2016 by The Tolkien Society
www.tolkiensociety.org

First published, 2016 by Luna Press Publishing™, Edinburgh

ISBN-13: 978-1-911143-02-4

Cover photograph by Pamela Chandler © Diana Willson
Cover design © Jay Johnstone 2015
Return of the Ring logo by Jef Murray

All contributors to this volume assert their moral right to be identified as the author of their individual contributions.

Each contribution remains the intellectual property of its respective author and is published by the Tolkien Society, an educational charity (number 273809) registered in England and Wales, under a non-exclusive licence.

All rights reserved by the Tolkien Society. No part of this publication may be reproduced, stored in a retrieval system, or transmitted in any form or by any means, electronic, mechanical, photocopy, recording or otherwise, without prior written permission of the copyright holder. Nor can it be circulated in any form of binding or cover other than that in which it is published and without similar condition including this condition being imposed on a subsequent purchaser.

www.lunapresspublishing.com

# Contents

| | |
|---|---|
| *Foreword*<br>Shaun Gunner | v |
| *Introduction*<br>Lynn Forest-Hill | vii |
| Abbreviations | ix |

## BIOGRAPHY

| | |
|---|---|
| *Tolkien's Birmingham*<br>Robert S. Blackham | 3 |
| *J.R.R. Tolkien's 'second father' Fr. Francis Morgan and other*<br>*non-canonical influences*<br>José Manuel Ferrández Bru | 9 |
| *Tolkien's Oxford*<br>Robert S. Blackham | 19 |
| *J.R.R. Tolkien and the origins of the Inklings*<br>Colin Duriez | 25 |

## WAR AND ITS EFFECTS

| | |
|---|---|
| *Robert Quilter Gilson, T.C.B.S.: A brief life in letters*<br>John Garth | 43 |
| *Tolkien: the War Years*<br>Robert S. Blackham | 59 |
| *Sauron Revealed*<br>LeiLani Hinds | 69 |

ii

*Clean Earth to Till:A Tolkienian Vision of War*     85
Anna E. Thayer (née Slack)

*The Importance of Home in the Middle-earth Legendarium*     99
Sara Brown

PHILOSOPHY AND ETHICS

*Tolkien versus the history of philosophy*     111
Franco Manni

*Tolkien's Boethius, Alfred's Boethius*     131
Gerard Hynes

*Teaching Leadership and Ethics through Tolkien*     141
Laura Miller-Purrenhage

RELIGION AND ITS DISCONTENTS

*Tolkien - Pagan or Christian? A proposal for a 'new' synthetic approach*     155
Claudio A. Testi

*A Latter-day Saint reading of Tolkien*     165
James D. Holt

*Tolkien's Magic*     175
Ronald Hutton

THE MYTHIC DIMENSION

*Cyclic cataclysms, Semitic stereotypes and religious reforms:*     191
*a classicist's Númenor*
Pamina Fernández Camacho

*From 2012 AD to Atlantis and Back Again -*     207
*Tolkien's Circular Journey in Time*
Xavier de la Huerga

*The Notion Club Papers: A Summary* 219
David Doughan

*Myth-Making: How J. R. R. Tolkien Adapted Mythopoeia from Old* 227
*English*
Zachary A. Rhone

*J. R. R. Tolkien's Mythopoeia and Familiarisation of Myth:* 241
*Hobbits as Mediators of Myth in The Hobbit and The Lord of the Rings*
Jyrki Korpua

*White riders and new world orders: Nature and technology in* 251
*Theodor Storm's Der Schimmelreiter and J.R.R. Tolkien's The Lord of the Rings*
Larissa Budde

List Of Contributors 262
Index 265

# Foreword

The Tolkien Society has a heritage going back nearly 50 years. Since its foundation in 1969, the Society has consistently sought to promote – and encourage research into – the life and works of J.R.R. Tolkien. From our humble beginnings as an advert in *The New Statesman* we have grown to become a worldwide community that fosters Tolkien scholarship whilst giving our members the opportunity to become part of our global fellowship. We do all of this in honour of a man who is one of the world's best-selling and most-loved authors whose contributions have helped to shape modern literature, our understanding of the history of the English language, and even 21st century cinema.

The aims of our Society were recognised by Tolkien himself, who consented to be our honorary president (a title he retains *in perpetuo*) whilst his daughter Priscilla is today our honorary Vice-president. In that 50-year history the Society has published over 400 journals, bulletins, books and proceedings in order to advance our aims, which includes our bimonthly bulletin *Amon Hen*, our annual journal *Mallorn*, and our regular shorter academic books in the Peter Roe series. Through our events, publications and community, we are proud that our support has gone into nurturing some of the best-known Tolkien scholars.

In August 2012 the Society held a five-day conference celebrating Tolkien and marking the 75th anniversary of the publication of *The Hobbit*. Around 500 people from across the globe came to this 'Return of the Ring' event which followed our successful conferences in 1992 and 2005, which respectively marked the centenary of Tolkien's birth and the 50th anniversary of the publication of *The Lord of the Rings*.

What made 'Return of the Ring' so unique was that it brought together several distinct strands of the Tolkien community. Academics and scholars such as Tom Shippey, Verlyn Flieger and Dimitra Fimi delivered their latest thoughts in the realm of Tolkien scholarship. Artists Ted Nasmith, Cor Blok, Jenny Dolfen, Anke Eißmann and Jay Johnstone were in attendance offering an unparalleled exhibition of Tolkien artwork, whilst Alan Lee and John Howe – still tied up in New Zealand working on *The Hobbit* films – sent us a video message. Tolkien Society members delivered papers, enjoyed banquets, took part in workshops, and danced in ceilidhs in the warm spirit of fellowship that the Society helps to foster.

As Chairman I get to avoid doing real work by delegating to more able people. These volumes have been very ably edited by Dr Lynn Forest-Hill. Lynn has been on the Tolkien Society's education team for over ten years ensuring that, as a charity, we are fulfilling our objectives in helping scholars with their research into the life and works of J.R.R. Tolkien. Lynn, a medievalist with a PhD from the University of Southampton, has expertly fielded thousands of requests from primary and secondary school children, radio journalists, doctoral students and public libraries across the globe. On top of that, she has contributed to the journals *Mallorn* and *Tolkien Studies* as well as chapters in the books *Tolkien's Poetry* and the Society publication *The Ways of Creative Mythologies*. These two volumes of *The Return of the Ring: Proceedings of the Tolkien Society Conference 2012* are a testament to her professionalism and determination and I have no doubt that you will agree.

The first volume primarily covers Tolkien's life and explores the themes of his stories: readers will recognise authors Robert S. Blackham, Colin Duriez and John Garth writing about Tolkien's friends and experience in war, whilst Professor Ronald Hutton brings his unique perspective to bear in 'Tolkien's Magic'. The second volume places Tolkien in a wider context with the likes of Nick Groom's 'Tolkien and the Gothic' whilst the rest of the volume covers a diverse range of other subjects. My own favourites are Murray Smith's 'Legal bother: Law and related matters in *The Hobbit*' and Christopher Kreuzer's 'Colours in Tolkien', both of which explore some niche, but interesting, topics in Tolkien's stories.

*The Return of the Ring: Proceedings of the Tolkien Society Conference 2012* is being published to enable attendees of the event to have a copy of some of the scholarship that was on offer during the conference, but, more importantly, to give everyone else a chance to access research and ideas they will not find anywhere else. I am proud that the Tolkien Society has published such a compelling collection of articles, and I hope that you find these two volumes as thought-provoking as I do.

Shaun Gunner
*Chairman of The Tolkien Society*
February 2016

# Introduction

These proceedings are a record of papers presented at the Tolkien Society's most recent major conference 'The Return of the Ring: Celebrating Tolkien in 2012', which was held at Loughborough University from the 16th to the 20th August 2012. The number of papers collected here, and their range of subject matter has resulted in two volumes. Volume I (this volume) covers Biography, War, Philosophy and Ethics, and further considerations of Tolkien's use of mythology.

The essays in the first part of this volume enable comparisons to be made between major aspects of Tolkien's life and their influence on his creativity, so Robert Blackham's contribution on Tolkien's early life in Birmingham sits alongside José Manuel Ferrández Bru's sympathetic analysis of the Spanish dimension of Father Francis Morgan's family background, while Blackham's essay on Oxford sets the scene for Colin Duriez's essay on the development of the Inklings.

Inevitably, any biographical work on Tolkien leads to a consideration of the effect of war on him and his creativity, but John Garth expands this in his revealing biography of Robert Quilter Gilson, thereby illuminating Tolkien's experience of war and friendship from a different perspective. Blackham's contribution under this heading provides a detailed overview of practicalities before LeiLani Hinds reviews one example of bad leadership during the First World War as a context for understanding Sauron as commander of armies. Anna E. Thayer takes a wider view of war in literary forms, while Sara Brown considers the effect of the Second World War as a context for Tolkien's particular use of images of homeliness.

In the later part of the volume Franco Manni positions Tolkien's work in the context of philosophical influences known and potential. Gerard Hynes reconsiders the significance of the Anglo-Saxon *Boethius* while Laura Miller-Purrenhage discusses the usefulness of Tolkien's work in the teaching of ethical descision-making. Claudio Testi introduces the controversial topic of the balance of Christian and pagan elements in Tolkien's writing while James D. Holt reads the *legendarium* in terms of the beliefs of the Church of Latter-day Saints before Ronald Hutton continues his survey of the various forms of magic that he finds in Tolkien's major works.

In this volume's final section the Mythic Dimension includes contributions on matters such as the fate of Númenor with Pamina Fernández Camacho's consideration of the cyclical nature of motifs of drowning, as well as Xavier de la Huerga's discussion of circularity and the Atlantis myth. David Doughan

viii

revisits *The Notion Club Papers*. Zachary A. Rhone finds Old English providing a pattern for Mythopoeia, while Jyrki Korpua addresses the need for hobbits to serve as mediators for the mythic dimension in the major works. Finally, in this volume, Larissa Budde moves beyond well-known nineteenth-century influences to present a comparison between a classic work of German fiction and Tolkien's vision of the White Rider.

Some of the contributions included here have already been published elsewhere and where this is the case acknowledgements are given in immediate proximity to those essays. Their inclusion here reflects the comprehensive scope of the Return of the Ring conference, its value as a forum for honing research, and demonstrates yet again the extent to which Tolkien's works encourage diverse critical approaches and breadth of participation.

I would like to record my thanks to Troels Forchammer, Olga Akroyd for help with the editing process. I must also pay tribute to Daniel Helen and Francesca Barbini for managing the production, design and lay out of these volumes - without their hard work these proceedings would not exist. As always, I owe grateful thanks to my family for their tolerance and understanding during the editing process.

Lynn Forest-Hill
*Editor*

# Abbreviations

| | |
|---|---|
| *The Lord of the Rings* | *LotR* |
| *The Fellowship of the Ring* | *FotR* |
| *The Two Towers* | *TT* |
| *The Return of the King* | *RotK* |
| *The Hobbit* | *TH* |
| *The Silmarillion*<br>[when unitalicised refers to the unpublished variants] | *TSil* |
| *Unfinished Tales of Númenor and Middle-earth* | *UT* |
| *On Fairy-Stories* | *OFS* |
| *Farmer Giles of Ham* | *Giles* |
| *Smith of Wootton Major* | *Smith* |

# BIOGRAPHY

# 'Tolkien's Birmingham'

## Robert S. Blackham

*Tolkien lived for much of his early life in and around the industrial city of Birmingham. This paper covers the places from that time and today where he lived, played, worshipped and went to school. The talk starts with Tolkien's arrival in England in spring 1895 and follows him to Birmingham and his other homes in the area. It covers his school days and his meeting of his future wife, Edith Bratt and finishes with him leaving Birmingham for Exeter College, Oxford. Many of these places emerged later in the fictional world of Middle-earth. The roots of Middle-earth can be traced back to his childhood and teenage years here in Birmingham. New material about this period of Tolkien's life is still coming to light.*

John Ronald Reuel Tolkien, who preferred to be called Ronald, lived for much of his early life in and around Birmingham but was born in Bloemfontein in the Orange Free State in southern Africa on the 3rd of January 1892. His father Arthur Tolkien came from Moseley and his mother Mabel came from King's Heath, at that time not part of Birmingham. They married in Cape Town in 1891.

Ronald's brother Hilary was born on the 17th of February 1894 and Mabel and her two sons returned to England in the spring of 1895 and stopped with her parents in Ashfield Road, King's Heath. In the November of 1895 Arthur Tolkien became ill with rheumatic fever, he remained in poor health for some months and had a severe haemorrhage on the 14th of February 1896 and died the next day.

In the summer of 1896 Mabel Tolkien and the two brothers rented 5 Gracewell Cottages on Wake Green Road in the small hamlet of Sarehole on the rural edge of Birmingham. This was a golden time in Ronald Tolkien's life, he was taught by his mother and there were wonderful places to see and explore in the countryside around the hamlet.

In a rare interview in 1966, reproduced in *The Guardian* in 1991, Tolkien described how important the little hamlet of Sarehole on the rural edge of Birmingham had been in the development of his fictional vision:

> It was a kind of lost paradise … There was an old mill that really did grind corn with two millers, a great big pond with swans on it, a sandpit, a wonderful dell with flowers, a few old-fashioned village

houses and, further away, a stream with another mill … I could draw
you a map of every inch of it. I loved it with an (intense) love.

Further on in the article he re-emphasises the importance of his childhood memories of the area: 'I was brought up in considerable poverty, but I was happy running about in that country. I took the idea of the hobbits from the village people and children.'[1]

This love of a more simple life was so much to Tolkien's liking that when writing about the heroes of his books, the Hobbits, he said:

...they love peace and quiet and good tilled earth: a well-ordered and well-farmed countryside was their favourite haunt. They do not and did not understand or like machines more complicated than a forge-bellows, a water-mill, or a hand-loom, though they were skilful with tools. (*LotR*, 'Prologue', 13)[2]

This is on the very first page of the Prologue to *The Lord of the Rings* written many years after his time in the hamlet of Sarehole.

While living at Sarehole Mabel, Ronald and Hilary would have walked to King's Heath to see her parents in Ashfield Road and they most likely walked up Green Hill Road in Moseley. The memory of these walks may have been in his mind when writing the 'Three is Company' chapter in *The Fellowship of the Ring* in which the three hobbits, Frodo, Sam and Pippin pass through Green Hill Country on their journey to Crickhollow.

## MOSELEY AND KING'S HEATH

In 1900 Ronald passed his examination for King Edward's School in New Street in Birmingham city centre but travelling from Sarehole was a problem. So Mabel decided to move to Moseley Village to get connected with the tram system – trams at that time were steam powered. So they packed their belongings up and most likely loaded them onto a horse-drawn cart or even a handcart and travelled up Wake Green Road to Moseley Village.

The house they rented was on the hill leading out of the village towards King's Heath and was on the route of the steam trams ploughing back and forth in and out of the city centre. The houses on the tram route were blighted by the noise and smoke the trams produced but the rents were lower. This was not a bad thing

1. John Ezard, 'Tolkien's shire', *The Guardian*, Saturday 28 December 1991 <http://www.theguardian.com/books/1991/dec/28/jrrtolkien.classics> [accessed 15 October 2013].
2. J.R.R. Tolkien, *The Lord of the Rings*, George Allen & Unwin, London, 1954–55.

for Mabel who by this time had been a widow for nearly four years and money must have been tight with two young sons to bring up. She had converted to the Roman Catholic religion just before leaving Sarehole. The church at St Anne's, Alcester Street, was a short tram ride away.

Ronald did not like the house in Moseley, he thought it 'dreadful' and Moseley, with the noise, smoky chimneys, horse-drawn traffic and lots of people, was such a change from the rural surroundings of Sarehole. Wherever he had moved to in the Victorian Birmingham suburbs, in the type of housing Mabel could afford, he would have had the same reaction.

After a very short time in the house in Moseley they moved to King's Heath, to Westfield Road on the Grange Estate. This house backed on to the railway line and looked across fields to two grand mansions, Highbury and Uffculme. Coal was king in those days and coal trucks from the South Wales coalfields were coming and going from King's Heath Station a short way from their house. The strange sounding names on the trucks led to Ronald discovering the Welsh language.

The Tolkiens were attending the small Catholic church of St Dunstan's on the corner of Station Road and Westfield Road in King's Heath. The church was a small iron building with a pine-board interior opened in 1896. It was destroyed by bombing in the Second World War. The new church is on Institute Road, King's Heath.

In the 1930s Tolkien's school, King Edward's moved from the city centre to Edgbaston Park Road just over the road from Birmingham University. King Edward's had played an important part in Tolkien's early life and he became a school governor at the new school. The school is not now open to the public but can be viewed from the pavement outside the school.

Birmingham University was to play a small part in Tolkien's life in Birmingham as he was a patient there in 1916 when it was the First Southern Military Hospital during World War 1. He was treated for trench fever, a common illness of soldiers on the Western Front.

## EDGBASTON AND REDNAL

For reasons only known to Mabel, in 1902 they moved to Oliver Road in Edgbaston. The Tolkiens attended the Birmingham Oratory Church which was a short walk from Oliver Road. This was the first English community of the Congregation of the Oratory, the order started in Rome by St. Philip Neri in the sixteenth century. This community was founded by John Henry Newman in 1848 and moved to the present site on the Hagley Road in 1852. The house in Oliver Road has long gone as the road has been redeveloped.

While still living in Oliver Road Mabel, Ronald and Hilary became friendly with Father Francis Xavier Morgan who was the local parish priest. In 1904 Mabel became ill with diabetes and spent some time in hospital. Back in the early part of the twentieth century many illnesses that today can be controlled or even cured could be fatal and one of the best prescriptions for recovery after an illness was fresh air. So they moved just out of Birmingham and stayed in Woodside Cottage in the large grounds of Oratory House in Rednal. Oratory House stands on the wooded slopes of Rednal Hill, part of the Lickey Hills and was used as a retreat by members of the Oratory community.

But after a wonderful summer in the woods and fields of the Lickey Hills and the glorious colours of the trees in the autumn, Mabel's diabetes overcame her and she died in the November. After a short time Ronald and Hilary returned to Edgbaston to live with their aunt Beatrice Suffield in Stirling Road, a short distance from the Oratory. Living on the other side of the road was the widow of the locally famous surgeon Dr Joseph Sampson Gamgee. He had founded the Birmingham Hospital Saturday Fund in 1873 which helped members with hospital bills as it still does today. He also invented Gamgee tissue, cotton dressing used for dressing wounds, which is still used today. Although he died in 1886 his name became that of Frodo's companion and fellow ring bearer on the *LotR* quest, Sam Gamgee. There is a plaque located on the Repertory Theatre building in Centenary Square in the city centre, the site of Dr. Gamgee's home.

At the end of Stirling Road stands a tall chimney, one of many that once formed a forest of chimneys on the Birmingham skyline. But this is not your common circular brick chimney but a beautiful Italianate style red brick chimney with ornamental cream brickwork built in 1862. Standing next to the chimney was the boiler house, engine room and workshops of the Edgbaston Water Works that was pumping water day and night to supply water to Birmingham and Aston from bore holes. This would have been a busy site at the time when the Tolkien brothers lived in Edgbaston in the early 1900s, with much horse-drawn traffic coming and going from the site. The carts would have been carrying coal, most likely from the canal a short distance away to feed the ever-hungry boilers that supplied steam for the beam engines that pumped the water. Inside the boiler house rows of boilers supplied steam to the engines. From outside the great chimney would have sometimes been seen belching black smoke and the sound of the engines pumping would have been felt and heard. In the engine house men oiled the great engines as the connecting rods moved up and down and beams rocked like giant see-saws. The spinning weights of the engine governors would flash in the light as they controlled the speed of the engines.

A short distance further down the aptly named Waterworks Road, just before the junction of Monument Road, stands a second tower but this is a true tower in every sense. This beautiful jewel of architecture was built in brick in 1758 for Humphrey Perrott next to his hunting lodge. The tower known as Perrott's Folly has a spiral staircase of 139 steps with small rooms on each floor and the roof of the tower is stone-embattled parapet with the height of the tower being 96 feet. In the later part of the nineteenth century the tower became one of the world's first weather stations under the guidance of the pioneering meteorologist A. Follett Osler. The two towers are locally believed to be Minas Morgul and Minas Tirith but Tolkien himself was very ambiguous about which pair of towers the second volume of *LotR*, *The Two Towers*, is named after.

While living in Stirling Road Ronald would most likely have walked past a Victorian public house on the corner of Monument Road and the Hagley Road as he went to and from school in the centre of Birmingham. This public house is called the Ivy Bush and this would reappear many years later as the Ivy Bush Tavern in Hobbiton.

In 1908 Ronald and Hilary moved from Stirling Road to Duchess Road to Mrs Faulkner's boarding house. Living there at the time was Edith Bratt, also an orphan, and romance started to blossom between Ronald and Edith. They most likely would have gone for walks around Edgbaston Reservoir, a short walk from Duchess Road, which in those days was like an inland seaside attraction. It had a band stand, rowing boats for hire and even beaches. Their relationship was frowned on by Father Francis Morgan, the boys' guardian, and he had Hilary and Ronald moved out of Duchess Road into a house in Highfield Road just over the road from the Oratory. This was the last place Ronald was to stay in Birmingham. While living at this house Father Francis Morgan banned him from carrying on with his relationship and Edith moved away from Birmingham to live in Cheltenham. But before Edith left she and Ronald had a chance meeting one lunchtime at The Prince of Wales Theatre on Broad Street. Ronald had been to see *Peter Pan* there in April 1910 and had been greatly impressed by the performance, in which Pauline Chase had played Peter Pan; seeing her 'fly' on stage was a wonder of the age.

This tale now moves away from the Birmingham area as Ronald went to Oxford University. At the age of 21, while still at Oxford, he made contact with Edith, who was about to get married to someone else, and restarted the spark of romance with her. Ronald finished at Oxford in the summer of 1915, by which time the First World War was raging. He joined the Lancashire Fusiliers and he and Edith married in the spring of 1916. The couple returned to Birmingham in June 1916 and stayed at the Plough and Harrow hotel just over the road from the Oratory. They stopped for one night only. Ronald was most likely on embarkation leave as he was shortly to go the Western Front and it would be nice to think that they were returning to the places of their childhood sweetheart days. They stayed in room 116 in the Plough and Harrow where there is now a Blue Plaque recording their short stay.

# 'J.R.R. Tolkien's 'second father'
## Fr Francis Morgan and other non-canonical influences'

## José Manuel Ferrández Bru

*Father Francis Xavier Morgan Osborne was a Catholic priest of the Birmingham Oratory born in Spain, although his ancestors were a mixture of Spaniards, English, Germans and Welsh. The Tolkien family met him in 1902 when they moved near the Oratory and joined this parish. He became the guardian of J.R.R Tolkien since the death of his mother in 1904 and he played this role until his coming of age, although the contact between both continued. His importance has not always been properly appreciated by Tolkien's critics and biographers probably because of his initial attitude to Tolkien's relationship with Edith Bratt, but a significant intellectual streak (and maybe an indirect influence on Tolkien) can be identified.*

## INTRODUCTION

Tolkien did not like biographies or, more properly, he did not like their use as a form of literary criticism. For him a biography was the worst way to understand the creation of an author. But in Tolkien's works we can find an influence between some elements of his life and his fiction. Without going any further, clear examples are his own life as an orphan, which was certainly reflected in the complex personality of Frodo; his romance with Edith which inspired the great love story of Beren and Lúthien; or in another context, the landscapes of The Shire were definitely inspired by his early years in contact with nature in a vanished rural environment; while his terrible experiences in World War I are reflected in the desolation of Mordor. This paper will try to reflect other influences which may be outside the canonical (and better known) biographical aspects of Tolkien. It will focus especially on the hardly-known 'Spanish connection' through Tolkien's tutor, Father Francis (Curro) Morgan, and other people of Spanish origin.

Tolkien's relationship with Father Francis was especially important during his early life. He undoubtedly became a strong point of reference for Tolkien and his adaptation to the turn-of- the-century changes not only in the social field, but also to important cultural transformations:

In the late nineteenth and early twentieth centuries, historians, sociologists, politicians, and writers of different religious and political persuasions were as polarized on the fundamental issues as ever before or after, but they thought about them in the same period in specific terms: evolution vs. degeneration, individualism vs. collectivism, organic vs. mechanical, patriotism vs. cosmopolitanism, the common man vs. the elite, modern mass society vs. traditional localized community, and so on. Not all of these apply to Tolkien - no single person could have embraced all the existing cultural strands in their diversity - but it is possible to demonstrate just how much he shared in the received habits of thought.[1]

But despite all these issues, the development of his own views on religion, linked to the impact of his conversion to Roman Catholicism, is probably the main cosmogonic landmark of this period for the young Tolkien. In this process he was accompanied first by his mother, but also by people like Father Francis Morgan, who became Tolkien's guardian after the death of his mother in 1904. Unfortunately, Father Francis is primarily remembered and judged for his opposition to the romance between Tolkien and Edith, actually not an act of intolerant authority, rather, from the point of view of Father Francis, a way to protect Tolkien from himself when facing the possibility of losing the opportunity to be educated at Oxford.

Nonetheless the consequences of the love affair had a creative impact on Tolkien. The identification he made between his own story and that of his quintessential lovers is well known: Beren and Lúthien, protagonists of a tale originated in the mind of a tormented young man, forced to overcome the separation from his lover in the purest romantic tradition. Continuing the parallelism, the role of Father Francis seems to correspond to Thingol, the possessive father of Lúthien who commands Beren to fulfill seemingly impossible tasks to win her hand.

However, as in the fiction, Tolkien (and Edith) had no resentment towards his guardian. In fact there is an unquestionable statement of respect and deep admiration to him in the Gnomish Lexicon (circa 1917). Tolkien added the entry 'Faidron or Faithron = Francis' as a reference to his guardian. Until then only proper names are capitalised in the Gnomish Lexicon and the sign = is used to match names in different languages. Furthermore, *Faidron* and *Faithron* are clearly related to the entries that appear next to them: 'fair: free, unconstrained', 'faidwen: freedom', faith: liberty' and 'faithir: liberator, Saviour'.[2]

---

1. Anna Vaninskaya, 'Tolkien: A Man of his Time?' in Frank Weinreich and Thomas Honegger, eds, *Tolkien and Modernity 1*, Walking Tree Publishers, Zurich, 2006, 1–30, pp. 6–7.
2. Christopher Gilson, Carl F Hostetter, Patrick Wynne, and Arden R Smith, 'Gnomish Lexicon', *Parma Eldalamberon* 11, 1995, p. 33.

His admiration for his guardian can be seen as well in a couple letters written by Tolkien in his maturity:

> I remember the death of Fr Francis my "second father" (at 77 in 1934) ... In 1904 we (H[ilary] & I) had the sudden miraculous experience of Fr Francis' love and care and humour.[3]

And also:

> He was an upper-class Welsh-Spaniard Tory, and seemed to some just a pottering old snob and gossip. He was – and he was not. I first learned charity and forgiveness from him; and in the light of it pierced even the 'liberal' darkness out of which I came.[4]

However, this esteem is not shared by some biographers of Tolkien. In fact it is interesting to note the animosity against him. To cite a few examples, Humphrey Carpenter says that 'Francis Morgan was not a man of great intellect'.[5] Charles A. Coulombe ventures: 'Described as a Welsh-English Tory, surely as Ultramontane a combination as one could wish for'.[6] This reveals a deep ignorance of his life and his ancestors.

Francis Xavier Morgan was born in Spain in 1857, into a family with British roots and links with the sherry trade. He was related to a significant social environment both in Spain and in the United Kingdom. In fact, he was a member of a wealthy family that is still very important in Spain: the Osbornes. Regarding his education, after his first years in Spain, he was educated at the Birmingham Oratory School, briefly at the Catholic University College in Kensington and finally at the University of Louvain in Belgium. When he returned to the Oratory, as a novice, he served as personal secretary to Cardinal Newman and even accompanied the Father Prefect of the Oratory School to Rome, to a private audience with Pope Leo XIII.

Both the families of his father and his mother had important social positions and a very notable history in the world of literature. The two brothers of his

---

3. Humphrey Carpenter, ed., *The Letters of J.R.R. Tolkien*, with the assistance of Christopher Tolkien, Allen & Unwin, London, 1981, Letter 332, pp. 415–16. Tolkien is mistaken. He actually died in 1935 at age 78.
4. Op. cit., Letter 267, p. 354.
5. Humphrey Carpenter, *Tolkien: A Biography*, Houghton Mifflin, Boston and New York, 1977, p. 34.
6. Charles A Coulombe, '"The Lord of the Rings" – A Catholic View', in Joseph Pearce, ed., *Tolkien: A Celebration*, Fount, London, 1999, p. 74.

father, also named Francis Morgan and representative in Spain of the *Morgan* wine-trade importing company from London, wrote several works. The eldest, called Thomas, was author of several articles on archaeology and a specialised book. The other brother, Aaron Augustus, wrote two works of some impact: *The Mind of Shakespeare* and a famous translation of *Ecclesiastes*. Their interest in culture was probably inherited from his grandfather, Aaron Morgan, the patriarch of the family, who in 1795 wrote the admired *History and Antiquities of the Parish of St. Saviour's* which described both the neighborhood and this Anglican parochial church, now Cathedral, in London (where he has a memorial).

Father Francis's mother, María Manuela Osborne Böhl de Faber, was the eldest daughter of the owner of the trading house of sherry *Osborne*, formerly known as *Duff-Gordon*. Several members of this family are among the most prominent nineteenth-century Spanish authors, especially Juan Nicolas Böhl de Faber (grandfather of Father Francis), a famous scholar, and his great-aunt Cecilia Böhl de Faber, who used the *nom de plume* Fernán Caballero, one of the most prominent novelists of the century.[7]

Cecilia Böhl de Faber is the main representative author of the modern Spanish novel of customs: the *Costumbrism*. She attempted to claim the tradition, which led her to try to revive popular folklore, hence she continuously extols the countryside and strongly censures the city and the industrial progress. She wrote several novels and short stories and also collected folk-tales and native poetry. Interestingly, Cecilia Böhl de Faber published several collections of riddles (and also of proverbs and sayings) aimed primarily at children and young people, and some of them have an unusual similarity to the riddles of Tolkien in *The Hobbit*. In particular, a riddle she uses to describe the wind should be noted:

*Vuela sin alas,*
*silba sin boca,*
*azota sin manos,*
*y tú ni lo ves ni lo tocas.*[8]

This can be translated into English as:

---

7. Moreover the Osborne house was rich and notorious, so that the presence of distinguished guests was usual as, for instance, the American author Washington Irving, who developed close friendships with Juan Nicholas Böhl Faber and Cecilia. Irving had family in Birmingham (his sister Sarah, her husband, Henry Van Wart, a leading merchant and banker in the city, and their sons). During Irving's stay in Birmingham, he visit Aston Hall and he was so impressed by the house that he used it for one of his novels: *Bracebridge Hall*. On the other hand, the parents of Father Francis spent their honeymoon there, maybe with the mediation of Irving.

8. Fernán Caballero, *Cuentos, adivinanzas y refranes populares*, Sáenz de Jubera, Hermanos, Madrid, 1921, p. 180.

Wingless it flies,
mouthless whistles,
*handless lashes,*
*and you neither see nor touch.*

And Tolkien used the following in *The Hobbit*:

Voiceless it cries,
wingless flutters,
toothless bites,
mouthless mutters. (*TH*, 'Riddles in the Dark', 79)[9]

Surely it is a coincidence but certainly this similarity should be discussed, as Tolkien had access to Father Francis's books and it is likely that among them he would have found the works of his relatives. In fact, Tolkien confirms that he had access to his guardian's books and that he used them, for example, to develop his high esteem for the Spanish language. His love for Spanish is evident from his first creations, *Naffarin* (one of the first of his invented languages), and as he admitted:

> Spanish was another [language which gave to Tolkien linguistic-aesthetic satisfaction]: my guardian was half Spanish, and in my early teens I used to pinch his books and try to learn it: the only Romance language that gives me the particular pleasure of which I am speaking.[10]

The mark left by Morgan on Tolkien can also be felt in more mundane aspects. So when he took over their guardianship he privately increased with his own goods the legacy that Tolkien and his brother had received from their mother. Likewise, his financial assistance was instrumental to Tolkien when he began his studies at Oxford. Tolkien belongs to one of the first generations of young Catholics who could study at Oxford and he entered Exeter College in 1911, with a partial scholarship which was supplemented by Father Francis. Oddly enough, money from the wine trade partially paid for the education of Tolkien.

Obviously from his relationship with Tolkien, it is easy to develop a list of situations and facts that clearly indicate the real influence of Father Francis both, personal and as literary inspiration, on Tolkien. In fact, in the oral tradition of

---

9. J.R.R. Tolkien, *The Hobbit*, Allen & Unwin, London, 1983.
10. Op. cit. [3], Letter 163, pp. 213–14.

the Tolkien family there are several anecdotes that serve to portray the intensity of the relationship they had with Father Francis. Tolkien used to recount to his children what happened on a visit by Father Francis to Leeds, where the Tolkien family moved at the beginning of 1921 when Tolkien was appointed as Reader of English. The presence of the old priest was noticed and a little girl remained looking at him fixedly. Realising it, Morgan was amused and swept off his large wide-brimmed hat, and bowing to the girl he told her '*good afternoon*' with great ceremony. At this, the girl ran off in panic, surely surprised by this unexpected action.

There is a parallel between the girl's reaction and what happened to the Troll of Tolkien's poem *Perry-the-Winkle* (presented in the collection *The Adventures of Tom Bombadil*). The Troll wants to find friends among the Hobbits but his appearance scares them:

He looked around, and who did he meet
But old Mrs. Bunce and all
With umbrella and basket walking the street;
And he smiled and stopped to call:
"Good morning, ma'am! Good day to you!
I hope I find you well?"
But she dropped umbrella and basket too,
And yelled a frightful yell.[11]

This poem, together with most of those published in this book was composed between 1920 and 1930 and contrary to most of the other poems in the book no information exists on its origins. Perhaps a part of the inspiration of the trolls (or a little of the troll of the poem) could come from the Father Morgan's anecdote. In any event, it is demonstrates the humour of the old priest who was almost seventy years old when the encounter happened.

Tolkien recalled another anecdote that happened in Leeds. Father Francis travelled home on the tram with Edith after having bought a present for Tolkien. It was a Camembert cheese, a gastronomic delight that Tolkien liked a lot but a luxury in those times because it was an especially expensive product. This type of cheese is best when mature, although at that time its aroma is extremely strong and not too pleasant. The cheese in the story was particularly mature and, hence, especially pungent; to the extent that its aroma was potent and so unpleasant that the rest of passengers on the tram abandoned it. Only Edith and Father Francis remained, who returned home with the whole tram to themselves.

---

11. J.R.R. Tolkien, *The Adventures of Tom Bombadil*, Allen & Unwin, London, 1962, pp. 41–42.

This innocent anecdote remained in the memory of the Tolkien family and was repeated throughout the years. In fact I got it from Priscilla Tolkien, who was not born when it happened.

In summary, Father Francis had a more profound intellectual and social background that was known for the Tolkien family, and as a human being he was very influential on Tolkien. Priscilla Tolkien stated of her father:

> I remember him saying how terrible it would have been for Father Francis if he had been alive after de onset of the Spanish Civil War. The whole period of the Civil War cast a great shadow over my father's life and is a powerful and lasting memory from my childhood.[12]

In addition, it is likely that through Father Francis, albeit indirectly, Tolkien met other people of Spanish origin who are mentioned in his biographies. This could be the case in regard to two important characters, Francis de Zulueta and Pablo Martínez del Río. The first, the prestigious professor of Roman Law (Regius Professor of Law at All Souls College between 1919 and 1948), Francis de Zulueta, was the godfather Priscilla Tolkien. Born in 1878, although naturalised British subject and living in Oxford for most of his life, he had Spanish-Irish ancestors. His father, Pedro de Zulueta, was son of the second Earl of Torre-Diaz, a Basque businessman settled in London. His mother was sister of Father Denis Sheil (a priest of the Birmingham Oratory who Tolkien knew). He was also cousin of Cardinal Merry del Val, Secretary of Vatican State during the papacy of Pius X.

De Zulueta was a prominent Catholic in Oxford (only the second Catholic professor since the return of Catholics to Oxford) and chairman of the Newman Society. Despite his academic prestige in Oxford, many colleagues disapproved of his support for the Nationalists during the Civil War (and, after the war, his support for the Franco regime). In fact, a black legend developed around him, describing de Zulueta as a fascist aristocrat who considered his Oxford colleagues as plebeians. However, some facts contrast with this description, for example his help given to several German Jewish professors persecuted by the Nazi regime, including Fritz Schulz and especially David Daube, who developed a deep friendship with Zulueta.

Meanwhile the relationship with Pablo Martínez del Río was born in the summer of 1913 when Tolkien took a job as a tutor of two Mexican boys who

---

12. From personal correspondence with Priscilla Tolkien. Father Francis died thirteen months before the Spanish Civil War broke out. His last years were marked by his suffering for Spain, immersed in political and social tensions since the establishment of the Republic in April 1931.

travelled to Paris. It is likely that the genesis of this employment would be in a contact made through an acquaintance in Oxford. It was probably in Oxford, maybe in the Newman Society, that Tolkien met, a young Mexican aristocrat (although half Spaniard), the same age as him, member of one of the most important families of that country, who studied History at Oriel College.[13]

Pablo Martínez del Río y Vinent studied at Stonyhurst and from 1910 was at Oriel College. In 1914 he returned to Mexico but came back to Europe in 1922 to marry with the Spanish lady Maria Josefa Fernández de Henestrosa, Marquise of Cilleruelo. He was Professor of Ancient, Medieval and Modern History at the Faculty of Arts at the Universidad Nacional de México and he developed an extraordinary career as a scholar, researcher and archaeologist. His interests always dealt on the origins of the American man.

Tolkien was employed to accompany to Paris two young cousins of Pablo Martinez del Rio who were studying at Stonyhurst. In Paris they would meet with two aunts and with their youngest brother who came from Mexico, probably in order to start his studies at Stonyhurst after the summer. The boys were Ventura, Jose Pablo and Eustaquio Martínez del Río y Bermejillo and their aunts were Angela and Julia, sisters of their late father who lived in Paris. The trip lasted for a month and a half and was marked by a fatal accident, when Angela Martínez del Río was struck by a car.

Until now I have noted biographical material, more or less verifiable. To conclude I will develop a highly improbable, or at least rather unprovable, speculation about certain parallels between the background of Father Francis and Tolkien's work. So, in *LotR*, in the chapter 'The Scouring of The Shire', the resistance of the Hobbits to the invasion of The Shire is similar to the behaviour of the Spanish people against the occupation of the powerful Napoleonic army. Morgan's family directly witnessed the Napoleonic invasion of Spain and wrote about it, and even created some commemorative drinks.

On the other hand, Tolkien demonstrates an extraordinary knowledge of cellars and the fluvial transport of the wine in the chapter 'Barrels out of Bond' in *The Hobbit*. Interestingly, until the construction of the railroad, fluvial transport from El Puerto de Santa María, the home town of Father Francis's family on the coast in the province of Cádiz, to the interior areas of the country was important. Perhaps the reference in the text to the kinsfolk of the south who had vineyards, is not completely casual. In fact, there are some curious coincidences between the southern part of the Middle-earth in the Third Age and the area of Cádiz in the south of Spain. For example, the Anduin and its navigability recall the

---

13. The details of the relationship with Pablo Martínez del Río will be known when his correspondence with Tolkien becomes public.

main Andalusian river, the Guadalquivir, which is navigable as far as Seville, the famous capital of the region. Both names mean literally 'Great River'. Gualdalquivir comes from the Arabic expression *Oued-the-kabir* and Anduin is directly the conjunction of the words *river* and *big* in Sindarin. Moreover, these rivers are known colloquially by the title of *the great river*, so much in the imaginary Middle-earth is like real Andalusia.

In addition, the White Towns which are in the Cádiz region are a group of towns so called because all their houses have white facades. Arcos de la Frontera – a town where Father Francis's relatives often stayed on vacation – is one of their most outstanding. It is a beautiful place, built on a crag. Its sheer streets, from the foot of the town up to its higher levels, where the tower of a castle still stands, are narrow and many arches indicate different heights or levels. Pushing the speculation even further, maybe Arcos was the inspiration for Minas Tirith and Gondor could be in Andalusia?

# Tolkien's Oxford

## Robert S. Blackham

*Tolkien spent most of his adult life in and around the city of Oxford. This paper covers the period from 1910 when he came to Oxford to take his entrance examinations at Corpus Christi College through to his retirement in 1959 and his final time living in Merton Street in the 1970s. Topics covered include; His student days at Exeter College, working on the Oxford English Dictionary and his return from Leeds University as a professor at Pembroke College in the 1920s; home life in Northmoor Road where he wrote most of his famous books; and his friendship with C. S. Lewis and other academics.*

## INTRODUCTION

Tolkien spent most of his adult life in and around the city of Oxford. This talk covers the period from 1909 when he came to Oxford to take his entrance examinations at Corpus Christi College through to his retirement in 1959 and his final time living in Merton Street in the 1970s.

## EXETER COLLEGE

Tolkien's first experience of Oxford colleges was in early December 1909 when he stayed at Corpus Christi College on Merton Street to take his University scholarship examination. He failed to gain a scholarship award and returned to Birmingham in low spirits. He returned to Oxford in December 1910 having prepared hard for his examination and this time he passed and on the 17 December he heard that he had been awarded an Open Classical Exhibition, worth £60.00 a year, to Exeter College, Oxford.

At the end of the second week in October 1911 Tolkien and another former student of King Edward's School, L.K. Sands, were taken to Oxford by motorcar by R.W. 'Dickie' Reynolds, who had taught English Literature at King Edward's School. At Exeter College Tolkien had a bedroom and sitting room in the college building known as Swiss Cottage that fronted onto Broad Street but Tolkien's rooms looked out onto Turl Street. Tolkien played rugby for the college but did not take up rowing. The all-male college life style suited Tolkien as he was happy in the company of like-minded students. In the Junior Common Room Suggestions Book, Tolkien wrote that the college needed to purchase a good English dictionary; most of the other students' comments were usually about college food.

In 1912 Tolkien became a student of Joseph Wright studying Comparative Philology. I think that readers of Tolkien's books have a huge debt to this man for inspiring Tolkien. Joseph Wright was living proof that you could make it up the ladder from the very bottom; he started work in a mill in Yorkshire aged six. He taught himself to read and write at the age of fifteen and later on went to Heidelberg University and studied many old Northern European languages before returning to England to become Deputy Professor of Comparative Philology at Oxford.

Tolkien became bored with Greek and Latin, his main interest was Germanic literature. In 1913 he took his Honour Moderation examinations but failed to achieve a First. The head of Exeter College, Dr. Farnell, knew that Tolkien was interested in Germanic languages and Old English and arranged for Tolkien to study at the English School in 1913 where he specialised in Old Norse.

In 1913 Tolkien was twenty-one and got in touch with Edith Bratt and they eventually became engaged and married in Warwick on the 22nd March 1916 at St Mary Immaculate Church. He took his final examinations for the Honours School of English Language and Literature at the Sheldonian Theatre on Broad Street in June 1915 and achieved a First Class Honours.

## AFTER THE WAR

After service in the British Army during World War One, Tolkien returned to Oxford in 1918 and became an assistant lexicographer on the Oxford English Dictionary working on the W section and it is nice to think that when you look up a word starting with 'W' you are using some of Tolkien's early printed work. The work was being undertaken in the Old Ashmolean Building on Broad Street next door to Exeter College.

He got rooms at 50 St John Street not far from his rooms when he was out of halls in his later period at Exeter College. Edith and their baby John who had been born in November 1917 joined him in the November of 1918. In the summer of 1919 they rented a small house in Alfred Street, now Pusey Street, just round the corner from St John Street. Ronald was also working as a private tutor in Anglo-Saxon, mainly for the young ladies from the women's colleges such as Lady Margaret Hall as because he was a married man living with his wife the young ladies could attend tuition at his house without a chaperone. By the spring of 1920 this work was bringing in enough money to allow him to give up his work on the dictionary but things were about to change. His second son, Michael, was born in the October of 1920 and Tolkien was appointed to the position of Reader in English Language at Leeds University and he and his family were off to live in Leeds till 1925.

## PEMBROKE COLLEGE

Tolkien had been elected Rawlinson and Bosworth Professor of Anglo-Saxon by the casting vote of Joseph Wells, the Vice-Chancellor of Oxford University. The appointment was to Pembroke College which is located around Pembroke Square and Beef Lane off St. Aldates, opposite Christ Church College. The appointment to Pembroke College was to give Tolkien college support and the social side of college life but he was to teach on a faculty basis and taught students from many Oxford colleges. He was at Pembroke College till 1945 and during this period Tolkien wrote *The Hobbit* and most of *The Lord of the Rings*.

Tolkien sometimes lectured at Pembroke College and at the Examination Schools on the High Street, giving very popular lectures on subjects like the epic Anglo-Saxon poem *Beowulf* and the Middle English poem *Sir Gawain and the Green Knight*. It is said that he made his lectures come to life and, in the case of *Beowulf*, took his students back to the mead halls and feasting of the poem. He was a quietly spoken lecturer possibly due to his rugby accident at school when he almost bit his tongue off.

Tolkien was contracted to give at least 36 lectures a year but usually did 72 to 136 in order to fully cover the topics of Anglo-Saxon and Middle English, and he was also holding tutorials for his students.

Tolkien bought number 22 Northmoor Road in the north of Oxford as the new family home. The house is close to the River Cherwell, University Parks and Lady Margaret Hall. The family returned from Leeds in early 1926 to move in and they lived there till 1930 when they moved next door to number 20, staying at this address till 1947. Number 20 was lived in by Basil Blackwell the owner of Blackwell's Book shop before the Tolkiens moved in.

Tolkien met C.S. Lewis at an English faculty meeting in 1926 at Merton College and the two men become great friends. Lewis joined the literary group founded by Tolkien called Coalbiters (Kolbítar in Icelandic meaning 'men who lounge so close to the fire in winter that they bite the coal') in 1927. The group met at Balliol College to read Icelandic Sagas out loud to one another. In the early 1930s the Coalbiters stopped meeting and a new literary group was formed by an undergraduate, Edward Tangye Lean, from University College, Oxford. This group was called the Inklings but after Lean left Oxford in 1933 the group folded though the name did not die.

Tolkien and Lewis started having meetings, with other like-minded academics, in Lewis's rooms in the New Building, Magdalen College. They carried on calling this group the Inklings. It was made up of mostly Christian men and during the meetings readings and discussions of members' current and unfinished works would take place. This is where Tolkien first aired *LotR* to the Inklings.

During the Second World War Tolkien, C.S. Lewis and Charles Williams were now drinking in the White Horse on Broad Street, just over the road from Tolkien's old college, Exeter. Tolkien would read chapters from the ever growing *LotR* to the two in the bar of the White Horse. It must be said that the place is charming but very small and it would not be hard for other members of the clientele to overhear these readings.

Then later the Inklings met informally on Tuesday lunchtimes in the Eagle and Child public house, also known by the group as the Bird and Baby or just The Bird. Meetings were held in the pub landlord's sitting room, known as the Rabbit Room, which is now incorporated into the pub and is like a shrine to the Inklings with pictures of Tolkien and other Inklings on the walls.

The Inklings also later met sometimes in the Lamb and Flag; the two pubs face one another across the broad St. Giles Street in Oxford. The Inklings as a group continued into late 1949 usually meeting on a Thursday evening in Lewis's rooms in the New Building, Magdalen College.

Tolkien was once again attending St. Aloysius Church on the Woodstock Road. He had attended this church while at Exeter College, and sometimes cycled there with his sons to mass at 7.30am and then returning home for breakfast. While living at Northmoor Road Tolkien would hire a punt each year and the family would go on punting expeditions up and down the River Cherwell.

## MERTON COLLEGE

In 1945 Tolkien was elected Merton College Professor of English Language and Literature becoming a Professorial Fellow of Merton College. The college fronts onto Merton Street and the back of the college looks out onto Merton Fields over a section of the old town wall and beyond this is Christ Church Meadow with the River Thames or Isis flowing at the bottom of the meadow. He had rooms in the Fellows' Quadrangle overlooking the meadows. Tolkien liked Merton College; it was more relaxed and less formal that Pembroke College.

Tolkien was to give new lectures in the history of English language and English Literature to the period of Chaucer as well as having to undertake his work at Pembroke College till a new Rawlinson and Bosworth Professor of Anglo-Saxon was elected.

In the March of 1947 the Tolkien family moved out of Northmoor Road to one of Merton College's houses, number 3 Manor Road. The house was very small compared to their previous home and still living at home were Christopher and Priscilla and to make matters worse Tolkien had a small study in an attic room. After a short time they realised that the house was too small for their needs and the college agreed to move them into a larger house when one became available.

By this time Rayner Unwin was a student at Oxford; he had read *The Hobbit* for his father Stanley Unwin in 1936 at the age of 10 and recommended the book for 5 to 9 year old children and had been paid the princely sum of one shilling for the reading. In the summer of 1947 Rayner Unwin, who had become friendly with Tolkien, was given an almost complete typed copy of *LotR* to read. He enjoyed it but was a little uncertain if it was a book for children or adults. He felt that his father's printing firm Allen and Unwin should publish it but it should be divided into three books. Was this the birth of the trilogy that we take for granted today?

Also around this time Tolkien was revising the chapter 'The Riddle in the Dark' in *The Hobbit* so that the Ring and Gollum flowed seamlessly into the sequel – *LotR*. He was still honing and refining *LotR* but the end of what had become a huge manuscript was in sight. He then typed the whole manuscript up in his attic study and this was completed in the autumn of 1949. In 1950 the Tolkien family moved round the corner to number 99 Holywell Street, the house is close to the end of the street and the town wall can clearly be seen running along Long Wall Street at the end of Holywell Street.

In 1953 Tolkien and Edith moved out to the North Oxford suburb of Headington to number 76 Sandfield Road and finally in 1954 the start of *LotR* trilogy was being published. *The Fellowship of the Ring* and *The Two Towers* came out that year with *The Return of the King* coming out in 1955. The books came out to mixed reviews but were selling very well and were reprinted many times in the coming years and translated into many languages. Tolkien retired from Merton College in 1959 aged 67 but his relationship with the college did not end there. When he and Edith had been married for 50 years in 1966 they celebrated their anniversary at Merton College.

## RETIREMENT, FAME AND STORY'S END

Retirement and Sandfield Road had its good and bad points for Tolkien. The house was well out of town and a good walk from a bus service so to get about he needed to use taxis. His book sales were very good and he no longer had any money worries, in fact he had become quite wealthy and he used his wealth to help his growing family. He treated himself to colourful waistcoats and for a man who for years had prided himself on being a plain dresser this must have been a big change.

Because it was the 60s and because the term 'pipe-weed' was used for tobacco in Middle-earth Tolkien was to become a leading figure in the counter-culture of the time, probably something he disliked. Even the Beatles became involved with *LotR*, planning to make a film of it in which Paul McCartney was to play Frodo, John Lennon – Gollum, George Harrison – Gandalf and Ringo Star – Sam. The telephone was becoming a problem for Tolkien in the middle of the night with stoned Hippies phoning from the west coast of America to talk to him completely unaware of the time difference. In 1968, by which time Ronald and Edith were both in their late 70s, they moved to Poole to live a more peaceful life.

They lived in a bungalow at 19 Lakeside View and from all accounts lived a peaceful happy life for around three years but in the November of 1971 Edith became ill and she died in hospital on the 29th of November. After Edith's death Merton College stepped in and asked Tolkien to become a resident honorary Fellow of the college and offered him a flat in one of the colleges houses, 21 Merton Street. He moved to 21 Merton Street in the March of 1972, travelling up from Bournemouth with the removal men in their lorry. The flat was made up of a lounge, bedroom and bathroom and the building's scout/caretaker Charlie Carr and his wife cooked him breakfast and lunch or an evening meal if he was not going to a college for lunch or dinner.

In late 1972 Tolkien started to feel unwell and was put on a diet to reduce his weight and told not to drink wine and by the summer of 1973 the diet had worked and his weight had been reduced. But he was starting to show his years and he was very lonely even though he had a constant stream of family and friends visiting him. He was especially lonely when the students who shared 21 Merton Street with him were away on holiday.

In late August of 1973 he went to Bournemouth to stay with Dr Tolhurst and his wife. Dr Tolhurst had been his and Edith's doctor while they were living in Bournemouth. Tolkien became unwell at a family party and the next day was taken to hospital where he developed a chest infection and died on the 2nd of September 1973 at the age of 81.

He and Edith are buried in Wolvercote Cemetery in the north of Oxford. There are two trees planted in his memory beside the River Cherwell in University Parks and also a bench with a memorial plaque on it.

# 'J.R.R. Tolkien and the origins of the Inklings'

## Colin Duriez

*Various suggestions have been made about the origins of the group of literary friends which included J.R.R. Tolkien and C.S. Lewis. This paper is an attempt to throw light on the origins of the Inklings, and how its origins defined the character of the group. The paper will include discussion of the duration of the group, the date of its beginning, and why it had similarities and important differences from other Oxford literary groups attended by members.*[1]

### ABOUT THE INKLINGS

The Inklings were a literary group of friends which included J.R.R. Tolkien and C.S. Lewis as its most famous members but was not exclusively made up of academics. It existed in Oxford during the nineteen thirties, forties and fifties, and petered out with Lewis's death in 1963. Tolkien occasionally referred to them in his letters, once describing the club as an 'undetermined and unelected circle of friends who gathered around C.S. L[ewis] and met in his rooms in Magdalen.... Our habit was to read aloud compositions of various kinds (and lengths!).'[2] Almost 30 years earlier Tolkien wrote to his publisher, Stanley Unwin, about Lewis's science-fiction story, *Out of the Silent Planet*. He speaks of it 'being read aloud to our local club (which goes in for reading things short and long aloud). It proved an exciting serial, and was highly approved. But of course we are all rather like-minded.'[3] It is clear from his letters that the Inklings provided valuable and much-needed encouragement as he struggled to compose *The Lord of the Rings*.

Another member, Classics don Colin Hardie, wrote of the Inklings, and its literary character, in 1983, around fifty years after its inception: 'Oxford saw the informal formation of a select circle of friends, mostly writers or "scribblers" (reminiscent perhaps of the 18th century Scriblerus Club, whose members were Pope, Swift, Gay, Arbuthnot – author of the *Memoirs of Martinus Scriblerus* –

---

1. The material in this paper derives from *The Origins of the Inklings* © Colin Duriez, 2013.
2. Humphrey Carpenter, ed., *The Letters of J.R.R. Tolkien*, with the assistance of Christopher Tolkien, George Allen & Unwin, London, 1981, Letter 298, p. 388.
3. Op. cit., Letter 24, p. 29.

26                                    COLIN DURIEZ

and others).'[4] Hardie became a member towards the end of the Second World War.

## ORIGINS AND DEVELOPMENT

In the first years of its life, from around 1933,[5] the Inklings was, from what little we know, a gathering in Lewis's college rooms intent on listening to work read out, and commenting upon it, though this would not rule out the friends sometimes gathering in pubs just to talk at times. It is quite likely, because of the rhythms of Oxford academic life, that readings to the group were mostly a term-time affair. We know, however, that readings did also take place between Tolkien and Lewis sometimes out of term time. At around the beginning of World War Two, parallel pub gatherings were established, usually on Tuesday mornings, with the reading club normally on Thursday evenings, but sometimes other evenings. The reading group seems to have concluded in the autumn of 1949, coinciding with Tolkien's completion of the main writing of *LotR*. During the next thirteen or so years, from the end of 1949 to Lewis's death in November 1963, there appear to be no recorded Thursday night meetings in the college rooms of either Lewis or Tolkien specifically to read work in progress. The pub gatherings continued, however, moving from Tuesday to Monday mornings to accommodate Lewis when, after 1954, he commuted to Cambridge during term time, leaving Oxford on Tuesdays and returning later in the week. A few days before his death Lewis referred in a letter to the group in diminished terms: 'Once a week I attend a re-union of old friends at one of the Oxford taverns. (Beer thank goodness is not on the list of things denied me.)'[6] It might be significant that he does not name the group as Inklings.

   After the ending of the reading group *per se* in 1949, the Inklings therefore still continued as a talking group. Even to portray it thus is somewhat simplistic – lots of conversation took place within the reading sessions (in fact, in later years of the reading group, H.V.D. 'Hugo' Dyson, who decidedly preferred talk to writing, tended to exercise his veto as a member against Tolkien reading yet another episode of, to him, the interminable story about Elves). Similarly, there would have been many references to writing in progress by members, or books

---

4. Colin Hardie, 'Inklings at Oxford and Germans at Aachen', *Inklings-Jahrbuch* 1 (1983), 15–19, p. 16.
5. Some believe the Inklings began earlier or later than 1933, but in my view the context and nature of the group, as outlined in this paper, as well as what little documentation we have, gives this year a strong plausibility.
6. Letter to Mrs Jones, 16 November 1963, in C.S. Lewis, *Collected Letters*, vol. 3: *Narnia, Cambridge and Joy*, 1950–1963, ed. Walter Hooper, HarperCollins, London, 2006, p. 1481.

just published, in the conversational, rowdy setting of the pub.

As a specific club for reading, 'the Inklings proper,' as C.S. Lewis's brother Major Warren Lewis once called it in his diary, lasted therefore from around 1933 to 1949, over fifteen years, a little over half of the existence of the Inklings in its one form or the other. The other form, subsidiary to the 'proper' Inklings, was that of the even more informal meetings. One of the most favoured haunts was 'The Eagle and Child' public house in St. Giles (known more familiarly as 'The Bird and Baby'). Many a discussion or friendly argument was washed down with draught beer or cider.

The 1930s saw readings of such works in progress as Lewis's *Out of the Silent Planet* and various pieces by Tolkien, including readings from the unpublished *The Hobbit*, but the Inklings group then was very small. In 1936, when Lewis invited Charles Williams to visit the club from London, it seemed to have few regular attendees (Lewis only mentions four who have read Williams's *The Place of the Lion*). The Inklings' most important years became the 1940s, especially the Second World War years when Charles Williams was resident in Oxford and added his distinctive presence to the group. Williams attended frequently and was often in the company of Tolkien and Lewis outside of Inklings meetings, when sometimes Tolkien would read additional chapters of *LotR* fresh from drafting. Poet and novelist John Wain was a member for a time following the war. After Charles Williams's death in 1945, he recalled, the two most active members of the group became Tolkien and Lewis. In his autobiography, *Sprightly Running*, Wain, in broad brush strokes and no doubt with some irony, describes the Inklings as 'a circle of instigators' encouraging each other 'in the task of redirecting the whole current of contemporary art and life.' He writes that

> While Lewis attacked on a wide front, with broadcasts, popular-theological books, children's stories, romances, and controversial literary criticism, Tolkien concentrated on the writing of his colossal "Lord of the Rings" trilogy. His readings of each successive instalment were eagerly received, for 'romance' was a pillar of this whole structure.[7]

## DEFINING THE GROUP

The Inklings as a group has always presented a daunting challenge to those who seek to portray it. This is because of its being an informal, somewhat loose group

---

7. John Wain, *Sprightly Running: Part of an Autobiography*, Macmillan, London, 1965, pp. 181–82.

of friends that functioned both as a reading and as a conversation group. As one of Tolkien's descriptions quoted above suggests – where he speaks of the club as 'undetermined' and 'unelected' – there is somewhat of a problem of definition. Furthermore, at many meetings clearly no readings took place. The group called the Inklings was so informal and casual that very little common entity at first seems to remain. As Tolkien pointed out, 'the Inklings had no recorder and C.S. Lewis no Boswell.'[8]

Glimpses of meetings, however, may be seen in the letters of Tolkien, Lewis, Charles Williams, and in the diaries of Lewis's brother, Warren. There are also reminiscences from and interviews with some other Inklings members or those who attended meetings. Owen Barfield wrote down some brief memories of the group. After his brother's death, Warren Lewis lamented: 'Had I known that I was to have outlived Jack I would have played Boswell on those Thursday evenings, but as it is, I am afraid that my diary contains only the scantiest material for reconstructing an Inklings' (from his unpublished biography of C.S. Lewis). Memoirs by Warren Lewis and John Wain also provide information. Curiously, furthermore, we have a fictional portrayal of sorts in Tolkien's unfinished and profound *The Notion Club Papers*, in which some of the characters reflect aspects of actual members.

Lewis's editorial preface of *Essays Presented to Charles Williams* is also informative. This volume, originally intended as a *festschrift* to mark Williams's return to London after the ending of the war, was brought out instead after his untimely death. Interestingly, the Inklings come over, from the fragmented documentation that we have, as an all-male club, characteristic of Oxford groups of the time. However, in the Preface, Lewis includes Dorothy L. Sayers, one of the six contributors, as part of a distinctive circle in which Charles Williams read and heard other members reading out their pieces. He takes no pains to distinguish this circle from the Inklings group of male friends. Lewis has, it seems, no rigid idea of what the Inklings circle included and excluded which he was concerned to gatekeep. Lewis's tone is far from the misogynous or at least exclusive-club attitude that some wrongly perceive in him. In the same preface, he does however write of Inklings' meetings being full of 'the cut and parry of prolonged, fierce, masculine argument'. It is clear that Lewis is not out to give a precise portrait of the circle. He does not seem to mind leaving an impression that a woman was part of the circle. (Maybe, in his mind the Inklings sometimes overlapped with a wider circle of friends, perhaps because it was intentionally a relatively unstructured group?)

C.S. Lewis provides a rare window into the Inklings in this preface. He points

---

8. Op. cit. [2], Letter 298, p. 387.

out that three of the essays in the collection (including Dorothy L. Sayers's) are on literature, and, specifically, one aspect of literature, the 'narrative art'. That, Lewis says, is natural enough. He explained that Charles Williams's

> *All Hallows Eve* and my own *Perelandra* (as well as Professor Tolkien's unfinished sequel to *The Hobbit*) had all been read aloud, each chapter as it was written. They owe a good deal to the hard-hitting criticism of the circle. The problems of narrative as such – seldom heard of in modern critical writings – were constantly before our minds.[9]

## THE SHAPE OF THE GROUP

The Inklings undoubtedly embodied the ideals of life and pleasure of Lewis, and, to a great extent, Tolkien, and centred on an appreciation of the continuing power of myth and romance stories which embodied glimpses or more of other worlds. Such stories, they believed, were adult fare. Expressing Lewis's tastes, the 'bill of fare' could include imaginative theology (for instance, he read his treatise, *The Problem of Pain*, to the club). Both Tolkien and Lewis were clubbable – Tolkien in his youth had been in the T.C.B.S. group of friends and in the Coalbiters (along with Lewis) in previous years. The Inklings was based upon a network of friends and professional acquaintances. The group also had an edge to it in that most had experienced combat in World War One. Several, such as Lewis and 'Hugo' Dyson, had been wounded. Tolkien had been emotionally scarred by his experiences in the Battle of the Somme.

Naming is an important marker of the group. Lewis prior to the Inklings had a circle of friends, indeed several coteries. Tolkien was associated with one group of linguistically-inclined colleagues, the Coalbiters. Naming a group calls forth an identity. Because of lack of documentation it is impossible to know exactly when the Inklings began as a named group. The date of 1933, it seems to me, is most likely. (As the Inklings formed out of a pre-existing group of friends, Barfield for instance offers this date as the year the group was named, even though he saw a group of friends, including himself, as predating the yet unnamed Inklings right back into the twenties.) Others give alternative dates, earlier or indeterminately later. The name, according to Tolkien, was transferred to C.S. Lewis's circle of friends from an undergraduate club, which folded with the graduation of its prime mover, Edward Tangye Lean, which was in 1933.

---

9. C.S. Lewis, ed., *Essays Presented to Charles Williams*, Oxford University Press, London, 1947, p. v.

Interestingly, Tolkien writes of this on two occasions, a year apart, with some of the same specific details.[10] In one of the letters, he mentions that 'this association and its habit would in fact have come into being at that time, whether the original short-lived club had ever existed or not'.

The Inklings was already well established in 1936 when C.S. Lewis, writing to Charles Williams, characterised the club as having informally evolved the qualifications for attendance as Christianity and 'a tendency to write' in a letter which included the first documented use of the term 'the Inklings'.[11] The members were Christians, Lewis records – indeed Tolkien and Hugo Dyson had been highly influential in C.S. Lewis's conversion to Christian belief in 1931. Unlike earlier groups to which pre-Inklings had belonged, which were made up of university dons and sometimes undergraduates, the Inklings included professional people like Dr. Robert Havard and Lewis's brother Warren. Warren Lewis came on the scene in December 1932, having just retired from service overseas with the British Army. Like his brother, he had returned to Christian faith in 1931. While not exclusively for dons, the Inklings was consciously Christian in character, and was made up of people aspiring to write. It had a broader climate, also, than focused groups like the Coalbiters perusing Icelandic and similar texts (or even Tolkien's fictionalised circle, the Notion Club, where some members are partly and loosely based on particular Inklings). Indeed, Christopher Tolkien points out how it would have gone against his father's purpose to specifically portray Inklings members. He writes,

> In 'The Ramblings of Ramer' he wished to allow his own ideas the scope, in the form of a discussion and argument, that they would never have had in fact, in an actual meeting of the Inklings. The professional knowledge and intellectual interests of the members of the Notion Club are such as to make this symposium possible.[12]

It is worth noting that Christopher Tolkien was a member of the Inklings after the Second World War.

A renaissance of Christian faith within a group of friends, together with a broader, more informal membership, created the conditions for the Inklings

---

10. Letter to Donald Swann, quoted in J.R.R. Tolkien, *The Treason of Isengard*, ed., Christopher Tolkien, Unwin Hyman, London, 1989, p. 85, and William L. White in op. cit. [2], Letter 298, pp. 387–88.

11. Letter to Charles Williams, 11 March 1936, in C.S. Lewis, *Collected Letters*, vol 2: *Books, Broadcast, and the War 1931–1949*, ed. Walter Hooper, HarperCollins, London, 2004, p. 183.

12. J.R.R. Tolkien, *Sauron Defeated*, ed. Christopher Tolkien, HarperCollins, London, 1992, p. 151.

as such to begin as a distinct club. Lewis clearly wanted his brother Warren to be part of it, for instance. The circle in the 1930s and well into the 1940s remained quite small. Two short lists of members Lewis included in letters, and his brother Warren's stated opinion about 'the Inklings proper', evidently favoured specifically literary gatherings (those at which work in progress was read) for a proper Inklings meeting rather than the informal pub gatherings, even though pub meetings were greatly enjoyed in general. Tolkien evidently found pub gatherings noisy, though typical of his complexity, there are accounts of him participating in the rowdiness with zest.

## ORIGINS OF THE INKLINGS IN LEWIS'S 'CIRCLE OF FRIENDS'

It is worth looking at members of one of Lewis's circle of friends which had the type of interests that characterised the Inklings, even if loosely. It is from this circle that the early members of the Inklings originated. This is necessarily a brief look. One friend in particular requires a closer focus, as he was a key causal factor in the club's formation – this is Tolkien. Some in the circle were already friends of Tolkien's, and some were introduced to him by Lewis.

Lewis tells us about the friends he made in his autobiography and part memoir, *Surprised by Joy*:

> The first lifelong friend I made at Oxford was A.K. Hamilton Jenkin, since known for his books on Cornwall. He continued (what Arthur [Greeves] had begun) my education as a seeing, listening, smelling, receptive creature.... Jenkin seemed to be able to enjoy everything; even ugliness.... My next was Owen Barfield. There is a sense in which Arthur and Barfield are the types of every man's First Friend and Second Friend. The First is the *alter ego*, the man who first reveals to you that you are not alone in the world ... But the Second Friend is the man who disagrees with you about everything.... It is as if he spoke your language but mispronounced it.[13]

Lewis goes on to introduce A.C. Harwood, who, like Barfield, horrified Lewis by becoming an anthroposophist, a follower of the mystic Rudolf Steiner. He also describes his meeting and friendship with Nevill Coghill, and then Hugo Dyson, and later Tolkien. Of these friends, Jenkin, Barfield, Harwood and Dyson moved away from Oxford before the forming of the Inklings, but Dyson and Barfield, though living in London and Reading respectively, attended meetings

---

13. C.S. Lewis, *Surprised by Joy*, Geoffrey Bles, London, 1955, pp. 188–89.

## COLIN DURIEZ

when they could. In 1945, Dyson returned to Oxford to become a Fellow and Tutor at Tolkien's College, Merton (Tolkien moved there, also in 1945, from Pembroke College).

## TOLKIEN AND THE EARLY YEARS

Tolkien and C.S. Lewis first met in 1926 at an English department meeting quite soon after starting to teach in the Oxford English School. Tolkien was Rawlinson and Bosworth Professor of Anglo-Saxon and Lewis was a Fellow and Tutor in English at Magdalen College, having previously taught philosophy at the university for a year. Through C.S. Lewis, Tolkien discovered a friendship that would have important similarities with the one he had previously enjoyed with Christopher Wiseman of the T.C.B.S. Though not yet a supernaturalist and Christian like the Methodist Wiseman, Lewis was from a north of Ireland Protestant tradition that contrasted with Tolkien's Roman Catholicism. Lewis had been brought up in a Protestant area on the fringe of Belfast called Strandtown, with his father a strong Unionist. Though Lewis's upbringing took place before Partition and the secession of the south in 1922, political feelings were strong and the rhetoric fiery. Lewis and Wiseman were also alike in being committed to realism; in Lewis's case, philosophical realism and in Wiseman's, scientific. Thus, for each, the grounds for truth were based on evidence. Though Tolkien held to the truth of Christianity in this sense, he also held to the authority of the Roman Catholic Church, and its extra-biblical decrees such as the Assumption of the Mary (to give a twentieth-century example, with the Papal decree of the infallibility of the doctrine on All Saints Day, 1950). With both Lewis and Wiseman, Tolkien had a deep and abiding friendship that was fundamental, and which nevertheless had its ups and downs, as is common in such relationships. In one case, Wiseman eventually felt neglected by Tolkien; in the other, Tolkien by Lewis.

The idea that Tolkien was going to create, almost single-handedly, a global adult readership for fairy story and fantasy, and for myth on a heroic scale, would have been beyond even his imagination. Yet Tolkien had a vision, born in his association with his early T.C.B.S. friends, which carried him gradually forward. He was soon to recognise a remarkably similar vision in C.S. Lewis, and to varying extents, some friends they had in common, or introduced to each other, such as Owen Barfield, whom Tolkien got to know through Lewis.

Late in 1929, Tolkien gave a large portion of a poem from his private mythology to his friend Lewis to read, who commented on it in depth. This told the story of Beren and Lúthien. While in the process of reading it, Lewis wrote to Tolkien:

ORIGINS OF THE INKLINGS

I can quite honestly say that it is ages since I have had an evening of such delight: and the personal interest of reading a friend's work had very little to do with it. I should have enjoyed it just as well as if I'd picked it up in a bookshop, by an unknown author. The two things that come out clearly are the sense of reality in the background and the mythical value: the essence of a myth being that it should have no taint of allegory to the maker and yet should suggest incipient allegories to the reader.[14]

What Lewis says of that early poetry from 'The Silmarillion' is also strikingly true of Tolkien's later work, *The Lord of the Rings*, with its presence of myth, and its background of definite places and history. Tolkien somehow creates a sense of reality in his imagined world.

Sharing his mythology with Lewis was an important step for Tolkien in finding an adult readership (then nearly non-existent) for fairy tales. Fairies for Tolkien were the noble Elves of Middle-earth, such as the beautiful Lúthien, and her parents, King Thingol and Queen Melian, rather than tiny beings with fluttering wings. Tolkien took another tentative step by presenting a paper called 'A Secret Vice' to an Oxford society in 1931. This paper is a particular interest because of a number of references to his life. Tolkien speaks of the pleasure of inventing languages, and believes that this technical linguistic 'hobby' is natural in childhood. It can survive to adulthood: he gives examples of his own invention, including Elvish languages.

Tolkien had already intrigued Lewis by alluding to his linguistic and writing 'hobbies'. When Tolkien invited him to come along to the Coalbiters, Lewis gladly accepted. This was a reading club Tolkien had initiated at Oxford in the spring of 1926. Its purpose was to explore Icelandic literature such as the *Poetic Edda*. The name referred to those who crowd so close to the fire in winter that they seem to 'bite the coal'. Tolkien was in his element with such stories that evoked a vast, northern world, with wide, pale skies, dragons, courage against the darkness, and vulnerable gods. There were in the group some seeds of the future Inklings that was, to an extent, to become for Tolkien a replacement for the grievous loss of the T.C.B.S. Some members of the Coalbiters were future Inklings – Lewis, Nevill Coghill, and Tolkien himself. In major ways, however, it did not resemble the Inklings at all, particularly in being completely made up of dons, professors, and similar, and only meeting two or three times a term for a very specific purpose: to become more familiar with Old Icelandic, a close

---

14. Letter to J.R.R. Tolkien, 7 December 1929, quoted in J.R.R. Tolkien, *The Lays of Beleriand*, ed. Christopher Tolkien, George Allen & Unwin, London, 1985, p. 150–51.

relation of Old English.

As a result of the Coalbiter gatherings, Tolkien and Lewis were soon meeting and sometimes talking far into the night. It eventually became a regular habit for Tolkien to drop by Magdalen College around mid-morning on Mondays (a day when Lewis had no students). The two friends usually crossed the High Street and went to the Eastgate Hotel or to a nearby public house for a drink. Sometimes they met at Tolkien's home in Northmoor Road. Amongst other things, they plotted in establishing a coherent undergraduate syllabus for the English School at Oxford. 'Perhaps one of the most significant of [Lewis's] contributions to the study of English literature at Oxford,' wrote Dame Helen Gardner after his death,

> was the part he played with his friend Professor J.R.R. Tolkien in establishing a syllabus for the Final Honour School which embodied his belief in the value of medieval (especially Old English) literature, his conviction that a proper study of modern literature required the linguistic training that the study of earlier literature gave, and his sense of the continuity of English literature and the syllabus, which remained in force for over twenty years, was in many ways an admirable one.[15]

Tolkien's reformed syllabus was accepted, in fact, by 1931, bringing together language and literature.

These frequent conversations were to prove of utmost importance both for the two men's writings, and for Lewis's eventual conversion to the Christian faith. The Ulsterman Lewis remarked in *Surprised By Joy*: 'Friendship with [J.R.R. Tolkien] marked the breakdown of two old prejudices. At my first coming into the world I had been (implicitly) warned never to trust a Papist, and at my first coming into the English Faculty (explicitly) never to trust a philologist. Tolkien was both.'[16] (Lewis often referred to Catholics as 'Papists', a mark of his Ulster heritage, a label Tolkien did not find easy.) It is clear that, from the beginning, Lewis recognised Tolkien's remarkable literary gifts. On Tolkien's side also there was much for which to be grateful.

Tolkien long after, recalled conversation with Lewis at this period: 'C.S. Lewis was one of the only three persons who have so far read all or a considerable part of my 'mythology' of the First and Second Ages.'[17] He also remembered reading aloud to Lewis *The Silmarillion* so far as he had then written it. Lewis described

---

15. Helen Gardner, 'Clive Staples Lewis (1898–1963)', *Proceedings of the British Academy* 51 (1965), 417–28, pp. 422–23.
16. Op. cit. [13], pp. 204–205.
17. Op. cit. [2], Letter 276, p. 361.

ORIGINS OF THE INKLINGS

his reaction to reading a draft of *The Hobbit* in another of his frequent letters to Arthur Greeves:

> Reading his fairy tale has been uncanny – it is so exactly like what we wd. both have longed to write (or read) in 1916: so that one feels he is not making it up but merely describing the same world into which all three of us have the entry.[18]

Lewis had already written to Greeves in the rosiest terms of his friendship with Tolkien, comparing it favourably with their own – like them, Lewis said, Tolkien had grown up on William Morris and George MacDonald. In a letter a few weeks later he mentions Tolkien sharing their love of ' romance' literature, and in the same sense: 'He agreed that for what we meant by romance there must be at least the hint of another world – one must hear the horns of elfland.'[19]

Indeed, Tolkien was an intensely private man, though selectively clubbable. He deeply valued and needed friendship, and he had already found in Lewis a person worthy of the inner core of the old T.C.B.S. Tolkien was responsible at the beginning of the thirties for a dramatic change in the thinking and whole world outlook of his friend, a change that was to lead to the creation of the Inklings, the club of literary friends of central importance to both of them.

Lewis had already moved beyond a bare materialism when he and Tolkien became friends following their initial introduction in 1926 at the English School meeting. After many winding paths, Lewis became a theist, a believer in at least a mind behind the universe. This happened sometime around the end of the twenties. By this time he and Tolkien had discussed many fundamental issues. For Lewis, once a convinced atheist, accepting theism was a huge step. It was not long before he was reading the New Testament (in Greek). On the night of 19-20 September 1931, as they made their way down Addison's Walk, in the grounds of Magdalen College, Lewis had a long conversation with Tolkien, and Hugo Dyson, which shook him to the roots. Like Tolkien, Dyson was a devout Christian. Tolkien recorded that long night conversation, and many previous exchanges with Lewis, in his poem *Mythopoeia* (the 'making of myth'), which he composed perhaps a few months, or well over a year later, the first of at least seven versions. He also noted in his diary:

> Friendship with Lewis compensates for much, and besides giving constant pleasure and comfort has done me much good from the

---

18. Letter to Arthur Greeves, 4 February 1933, op. cit. [11], p. 96.
19. Letter to Arthur Greeves, 25 March 1933, op. cit. [11], p. 103.

contact with a man at once honest, brave, intellectual – a scholar, a poet, and a philosopher – and a lover, at least after a long pilgrimage, of Our Lord.[20]

Undoubtedly Hugo Dyson gave emotional weight to Tolkien's more measured argument that momentous night. Tolkien had argued for the Christian Gospels on the basis of the universal love of story. What convinced Lewis was that the Christian Gospels have all the imaginative pull of pagan myths, with the unique feature of actually describing real happenings in history. There is no separation of tangible events and abstract truth. Lewis later wrote a powerful essay on the harmony of story and fact in the Gospels, specifically remembering that life-changing conversation with Tolkien and Dyson:

> This is the marriage of heaven and earth, perfect Myth and Perfect Fact: claiming not only our love and obedience, but also our wonder and delight, addressed to the savage, the child, and the poet in each one of us no less than to the moralist, the scholar, and the philosopher.[21]

It struck him that the claims and stories of Christ demanded an imaginative as much as a reasoned response from him.

Tolkien in turn expounded his view more fully in his essay *On Fairy Stories*. A form of this was earlier given as the Andrew Lang Lecture in 1939 at St. Andrews University, Scotland. In later published forms of the essay he developed his idea that the very events of the Gospel narratives are actual historical events being shaped by God, the master story-maker, having a structure of the sudden turn from catastrophe to the most satisfying of all happy endings – a structure shared with the best human stories. He famously called this kind of happy ending a 'eucatastrophe' (a 'good catastrophe'). The Gospels, in their divine source, penetrate the seamless 'web' of human storytelling, clarifying and perfecting the insights that God in his grace has allowed to the human imagination. In the Gospels, Tolkien concluded, 'art has been verified'. Among this art, which pointed to the master story of the Gospels, were the northern myths that Tolkien had loved from his boyhood, a love and fascination he shared with Lewis.

---

20. Quoted in Humphrey Carpenter, *J.R.R. Tolkien: A Biography*, George Allen & Unwin, London, 1977, p. 148.
21. C.S. Lewis, *God in the Dock: Essays on Theology and Ethics*, Eerdmans, Grand Rapids, Michigan, 1970, p. 67.

## TOLKIEN AND THE CHRISTIAN ELEMENT IN THE INKLINGS

As a direct result of Tolkien's argument about myth entering real history, Lewis began to see a new dimension to his varied group of friends, which was to have a dramatic impact on the very history of English Literature, and of theology as well. Groups in Oxford that he had belonged to, some of them with Tolkien, were made up of dons and other academics. He now came to value the fact that many of his academic friends, usually friends shared with Tolkien, were professing Christians, albeit of different persuasions – the distinction of Roman Catholic and Protestant being a central one, epitomised in his 'Papist' friend, Tolkien, of course. But then there was Owen Barfield, who claimed Christian belief, but it was modified by the mystical teaching of Rudolf Steiner, and called Anthroposophy. Furthermore, Barfield was no longer in the academic world, but a family solicitor in the City of London. What he was, however, like many of Lewis's friends, revolved around books and poetry – he too was a writer. He could turn his hand to poetry, fiction, and also ground-breaking academic books, like the already published *History in English Words* and *Poetic Diction*. What made up Lewis's friends was therefore quite wide: they were Christians, they tended to write, and they belonged to more than one profession – significantly, they were not all teaching at Oxford, and even those who were taught a variety of subjects. They were not all English language or literature specialists. Amongst his friends, Lewis also counted his brother, Warren, fresh from the British Army, and recently returned to faith, and who was now part of his home on the fringes of Headington, a suburb of Oxford. Through Lewis, Tolkien got to know his brother and to value his friendship, and often got to share a drink with Warren in one of the plethora of Oxford pubs.

It was this group of friends, less distinct than the academic clusters Tolkien and Lewis frequented, that was the core of what became the Inklings. In an important sense, Tolkien brought the Inklings into existence by persuading Lewis that he needed to commit himself to Christian faith, making this the integration point of his life.

## CONCLUSION

The informal club started during the autumn term of 1933, I believe, some months after the ending of the undergraduate club called the Inklings. For the next sixteen years, on through 1949, the literary friends continued to meet, sometimes in later years in Tolkien's spacious rooms at Merton College after his move from Pembroke College, but more often in Lewis's rooms at Magdalen College, usually on Thursday evenings. By wartime, and possibly even before,

Tolkien and others had also begun to gather before lunch on Tuesdays, usually in a snug located in a back room at The Eagle and Child, a public house on St. Giles known to the friends as 'The Bird and Baby'.

The formation of the Inklings in the autumn term of 1933 (if that indeed was when it started) coincided with the natural ending of the Coalbiters, which had by now fulfilled its very specific purpose. Three of the Coalbiters, Tolkien, Lewis, and Nevill Coghill, were now among the new Inklings. C.L. Wrenn, who helped Tolkien with the teaching of Anglo-Saxon, having joined the university in 1930, was invited to come along, soon after the formation of the Inklings. Other early members included Lewis's brother, Warren, the Reverend Adam Fox and Hugo Dyson.

We can only speculate about the subjects of conversations, since there is little documentation of the early days. We do know, however, that chapters of *The Hobbit* were read to the group as it was being finalised for possible publication. We can perhaps glimpse some of the ideas discussed and even celebrated by the Inklings, because Tolkien gave two lectures in the thirties that may have fed into the group, one in London to the British Academy and the other at St. Andrews University for the annual Andrew Lang lecture. Perhaps the concerns of the Inklings encouraged him to say what he did in these lectures, for in 1936 and 1939 they put forward a number of brilliant and innovative insights. It could be said that the lectures changed the way many people thought about myth, fairy story, and poetry, and even about the relationship of imagination to thought and to language. One of the brilliant but cryptic insights he expressed was: 'To ask what is the origins of stories ... is to ask what is the origin of language and of the mind.'[22]

These opportunities to air in public his deepest thoughts about fantasy and fairy tale were an important encouragement to Tolkien – he faced many more years of labour on *LotR*, the 'new Hobbit', as his Inklings friends called it. In giving those lectures, I believe, he was building upon the exchanges and the sharing that was taking place among the Inklings: but in his unique way, of course. Through his influence upon C.S. Lewis, he had been one of the important causes of the existence of the Inklings. What he helped to bring into being in turn proved to be a help and encouragement to him in both his scholarship and fiction. The Inklings helped to sustain the vision that powered all his work.

---

22. J.R.R. Tolkien, 'On Fairy-Stories', in C.S. Lewis, ed., *Essays Presented to Charles Williams*, Oxford University Press, London, 1947, 38–89, p. 47.

# WAR AND ITS EFFECTS

# 'Robert Quilter Gilson, T.C.B.S.:
## A brief life in letters'

# John Garth

*One of the relatively unknown sources of Tolkien's inspiration is his schoolfriend Rob Gilson, a member of the T.C.B.S. or 'Tea Club and Barrovian Society' they founded at King Edward's School, Birmingham. While researching Tolkien and the Great War (London: HarperCollins, 2003), I tracked down his relatives and learned they still had letters from Rob to the love of his short life, Estelle King, and to his stepmother Marianne, nicknamed Donna. Rob wrote so often that his letters become almost a diary. This paper presents a selection.[1]*

RobertQuilter Gilson was born in 1893 and became friends with Tolkien at King Edward's School in Birmingham, where his father was headmaster. The T.C.B.S., the prankish club he and Tolkien founded in 1911, had about 10 members and continued to meet in Cambridge when Rob went to Trinity College to study Classics.

Letters from a 1912 Highland holiday with family friends including the American consul Wilson King and his Quaker family hint at a bond with the consul's daughter:

> Estelle is certainly above the average interesting. It seems so very rare that any-one is really to be found ready to discuss a serious subject seriously. (13 August 1912)

In October 1912 Rob was installed in Trinity College. He regularly mentions tea, talk and tennis with Wiseman and their T.C.B.S. friends Wilfrid Hugh Payton, Ralph Payton, Sidney Barrowclough and T.K. Barnsley, or 'Tea-Cake'. Without Rob's warm, sociable nature, the T.C.B.S. might have petered out. The rather aloof and undependable Tolkien was on the sidelines in Oxford.

June 1913 found Rob at camp with the Cambridge University Officer Training Corps or OTC, describing 'a long and exhausting day' of extended military drill.

---

1. A longer version of this paper appeared in *Tolkien Studies* 8 (2011); I thank West Virginia University Press for courteously allowing me to give this abridgement here. Above all, I thank Julia Margretts and family for their support and for permission to quote from Rob's letters.

I haven't read quite one book of *Paradise Lost* but it is splendidly suitable...

Tomorrow we start out for a 36 hours' campaign – repelling an invasion by Oxford... I expect they will give us a fairly lazy Wednesday after it – a trenching competition I know, and probably little else... I was chosen yesterday to represent the company at shooting.... Also I was called out to drill the Company yesterday, and rumour says that I am in danger of receiving a stripe – which I don't at all want. (22 June 1913)

It is all tragically innocent. War was only a year ahead. In February 1914 Rob visited Oxford with Tea-Cake and Wiseman:

We had such a splendid week-end: 'Full marks', as Tea Cake would say, for everything but weather ... I saw lots of Scopes and Tolkien and G.B. Smith, all of whom seem very contented with life ... T.K. and I dined in Hall at Corpus on Sunday, and afterwards Scopes took me to a meeting at which GBS read a paper on 'The Faust Legend', and I joined in the subsequent discussion, much to my own enjoyment, if to no-one else's. (17 February 1914)

That Easter, Rob went to stay with the Wisemans, who had moved to London, and gives a lively glimpse of the friendship with Chris which is by now a keystone of the T.C.B.S.:

We spent three hilarious days missing trains, going to bed at appalling hours, and getting up near lunch time, and generally leading the erratic life to which his family seems quite accustomed.

They went to see *A Midsummer Night's Dream* at the theatre twice – Rob says it is the second best play he has ever seen, with its 'Russian ballet gestures', Post-Impressionism, orientalism and Elizabethan folk dances.

But of course the real thing is the fairies. Quite to my surprise they did not cause me a moment's doubt.... It was a real stroke of inspiration to make them golden from head to toe.... It had exactly the effect of making them look shadowy and incorporeal. The traditional spangly fairies of *Midsummer Night's Dream* dodge behind horrid cardboard bushes when the mortals appear. But these stood absolutely still, and one never doubted for a moment that they were invisible.... When Titania was left asleep on the bank ... I felt that if ever I did meet a fairy she would look just like that. (26 April 1914)

Tolkien was probably almost a year away from devising the fairies of his mythology, and at first they shared some of the miniature prettiness that Rob, here, is already condemning.

In May 1914 Rob was crushed by exams, then delighted they were over: 'It is a heavenly feeling' (31 May 1914). By now he hopes to drop Classics for architecture, and to have his own practice by 1921. A dearth of letters that summer means we do not know his reaction to the rapidly unfolding international crisis from 28 June or Britain's entry into the war on 4 August. As he told Estelle in October,

I have so often meant to write.... One goes through such constant ups and downs of feeling that it seems rather hopeless to try and say anything genuine to anyone whom one does not see every day.... I either bury myself in something and manage not to think of the war or I just resign myself to the horror of it all. (4 October 1914)

Many of his friends have already enlisted in the military. When Rob writes home from the Wisemans' – as another of Europe's great cities comes under German bombardment – the sense of disaster and uncertainty is plain:

I nearly started inquiries for a flat. Only I am more likely to need a tent first. Isn't it dreadful about Antwerp – and extraordinary? I certainly thought the Germans had their hands full already. London looks very strange and solemn at night. (7 October 1914)

In November Smith visited Cambridge from Oxford. 'Tolkien was to come too, but hasn't,' Rob told his stepmother. No one knows why he couldn't come, least of all G.B. Smith, who was with him on Friday night:

But Smith has actually come, and we are having a great week-end.... It is a real pleasure to sit and hear him talk when he is in good form. He is really a bit of a genius, and has a gift for rapping out preposterous paradoxes that always delight me with their neatness – and often with their absurdity.

And I always value his judgment though I often disagree with it, and am pleased to find that he is immensely enthusiastic about my rooms, and has never seen ones that he preferred – even in Oxford. I had a breakfast party this morning and they looked their best. A sunny morning with shadows across the Bowling Green and just enough mist to make the background of trees a perfect thing – blue and orange. The leaves are nearly all gone from the avenue, but many of the trees are still gorgeous in their colouring. (1 November 1914)

Rob drilled with the OTC but was depressed after a lecture from a major:

The burden of his remarks is the enormous number of chances of making a mistake and how fatal the consequences must be, and after listening to him I always feel as if I should never have the courage to give an order. What a fearful responsibility it is to be entrusted with so many men's lives! (9 November 1914)

On 28th November, Rob won a commission as a junior officer in the new local battalion: the 11th Suffolks, known as the Cambridgeshires. After a week he wrote:

I won't pretend I have enjoyed it, but it has been much better than I expected and has gone much more quickly. I don't like all the officers but they are a good lot on the whole.... Major Morton, my Company Commander, is a quite delightful man and does his very best to make things easy.... I got my uniform on Friday and am now properly a 2nd Lieutenant for all to see. I feel very proud to be wearing it and more glad than I can say to feel able to look anyone in the face with the certainty that I am doing my duty.

The unit's huts were not yet finished and for the moment Rob remained in his rooms at Trinity. T.K. Barnsley and Ralph Payton visit, but Rob reflected that it is 'a little bitter to be reminded so often of the happy days' before the war. That letter came days after the ejection by Tolkien and Wiseman of Tea-Cake, Ralph and others from the T.C.B.S. in a bid to save the club from frivolity and turpitude.[2] The only other two left were Rob Gilson and G.B. Smith. In the same letter, Rob wrote:

G.B. Smith told me a few days ago that he was applying for a

---

2. John Garth, *Tolkien and the Great War*, HarperCollins, London, 2003, pp. 54–56.

commission and rumour says that he has now got one in the Oxford and Bucks [Light Infantry]. I must write and cheer him for I am sure he feels much more a fish out of water than I do.… I hope to see him and also John Ronald Tolkien next weekend. (6 December 1914)

They gathered at Wiseman's family home in a meeting they dubbed 'the Council of London'. Rob wrote nothing to his stepmother about the proceedings, but as we know it was here that Tolkien realised he wanted to be a writer. At least Rob has left us a description of the house:

It is of one of the commonest suburban types – not brand new and pretty-pretty but frankly hideous outside with quite good rooms inside and a garden just big enough for a tennis court. Mrs Wiseman hasn't bad taste and the Drawing-Room is quite a pretty room. It is largely blocked up by a grand piano, but this is much less heavy-looking than usual, – they had the legs specially designed – and is altogether the least offensive piano I have ever seen. (26 April 1914)

Soon we meet another fellowship: the officers who were to share Rob's life in the 11th Suffolks, and his servant Bradnam. Rob describes a gloomy return to duty 'cheered by one bright spot – a large posy of cottage flowers for my room.… My servant brought them from his home: a sign of affection which gives me great pleasure' (15 June 1915).

By February 1915 the war had acquired an air of near-permanence:

I cannot help thinking sometimes of February in Cambridge two years ago, when I watched eagerly for every sign of spring, and knew that spring meant Italy. It has quite a new and terrible meaning this year.… If anyone with a gift of prophecy were to tell me that the war would last ten years, I shouldn't feel the least surprise. (13 February 1915)

Soon Rob was sketching trench-sections and writing instructions for trench-digging.[3] Military exercises seem surprisingly imaginative: during one, the troops have to capture 'a Witch-Doctor … performing incantations' in a church (4 March 1915). In early April 1915 Rob admits he feels 'a fraud'. 'Wrestling

---

3. Gilson's trench-digging drill was incorporated in W.A. Brockington, *Elements of Military Education*, Longmans, Green and Co., London, 1916.

with my dear, stupid, agricultural platoon ... attempting to teach the art of war to Cambridge rustics', he told Estelle, can be dull or funny, but never heroic (9 April 1915).

A few days later, Rob finally revealed his feelings for Estelle at a house party in London. She was shocked and upset, and her father wrote to tell Rob he must wait until he has a good income. Rob's next letter to Estelle says they should not meet. 'It is one of the hardest decisions I have ever had to make,' he tells Donna (10 June 1915).

Just before midsummer 1915 the Cambridgeshires moved from Cambridge to a new training area in the Yorkshire Dales, where they were under canvas with tens of thousands of other soldiers. Duties consumed every waking hour and during a musketry course he fell ill and developed flu. At a military hospital he was neglected by remote doctors and patronised by the local do-gooder, 'a ridiculous old lady':

> I am rubbed up the wrong way by such very self-satisfied and advertising charity. She talked to us about herself for about half an hour yesterday: about her beautiful car that has been absolutely reserved for wounded soldiers ever since the war started; and the hundreds of soldiers that she has taken for rides and given tea and presents to; and all the letters she has had from them. All this, with a few references to the thanks she has had for doing it from General this and that and Sir Rupert so and so, and what Lord Fiddledee said to her about it when last he came to stay with them. (6 September 1915)

In the middle of his hospital stay, Rob wrote his first letter to Tolkien in many months. 'I confess that I have often felt that the TCBS seemed very remote. That way lies despair,' he said. 'At times like this when I am alive to it, it is so obvious that the TCBS is one of the deepest things in my life.' Rob was furious with himself for failing to respond to the poetry that Tolkien has been circulating among the friends, 'Because I do feel that it is one of the best things the TCBS can possibly do at present. Some day I want to submit a book of designs in like manner.'[4] He arranged an impromptu gathering of the four near where Tolkien was now training with the Lancashire Fusiliers. This 'Council of Lichfield' was the last time all four met together.

Rob rejoined the Cambridgeshires on Salisbury Plain a few miles from Smith's unit.

---

4. R.Q. Gilson to J.R.R. Tolkien, 13 September 1915, quoted in op. cit. [2], pp. 100–101.

On Saturday I went to Salisbury with GB Smith ... On Sunday afternoon we met at Westbury ... where we had tea and supper. Best of all the place is almost without soldiers. The rain stopped just as we got there and the evening was beautiful. We walked up on to the top of the bastions of the Plain, and sat down with a wonderful view all around us – greys and dull blues and greens, with wet trees down in the valley all blurred and misty. I drew a little picture of a copse.... He read Herrick to me while I drew, and we got miles away from the war. (5 October 1915)

Rob dines with the officers of Smith's battalion – literary Oxford men – and in a letter home describes plans for a further T.C.B.S. gathering:

Yesterday GB Smith and I went together to Bath, chose and engaged lodgings for our Council next week ... and dined together.... To-day he came to Warminster and had dinner and tea and supper in our mess... He showed me the latest poems he has written. I agree with John Ronald that he seems to have gone off a bit since the war. I am afraid it has damped more inspiration than it has stimulated.

It has been a really pleasant week-end and we have immersed ourselves in an eighteenth century atmosphere – Bath does it of its own accord – and conducted most of our conversation in Johnsonian and Gibbonian periods. GB Smith composes excellent Gibbon.... I very quickly catch his enthusiasm for that extraordinary century. (17 October 1915)

The T.C.B.S. Council of Bath never happened, and instead Rob Gilson, Smith and Wiseman met in London, without the elusive Tolkien.[5]

In mid-November, Rob learned that Estelle wanted to see him before his unit left for active service. Rob wrote her a friendly letter, reserving all passionate feeling for descriptions of Salisbury Plain. But at the end of the month, while he was on leave, she suddenly returned his love. Back at camp he wrote to her as 'My own dearest Estelle' (30 November 1915). He was eager to tell her about his circle:

Ronald Tolkien – of the TCBS – has just sent me a new poem of his own which I like immensely. I must let you see some of his poetry

---

5. Op. cit. [2], pp. 104–106.

some day soon. (2 December 1915)

This was 'Kortirion among the Trees', the magnificent nature poem Tolkien had written a couple of weeks earlier.[6] In December Rob's battalion was suddenly under orders for Egypt. 'Three weeks ago I believe this news would have made me utterly miserable,' he tells Estelle on 12 December 1915; but now he was buoyed up by love. It was also a great relief not to have to face the trenches of northern France, where Smith was now hunkered. Rob and Estelle met with a chaperone one weekend, and the next they managed to get some time alone. Rob wrote that Sunday night:

> While I can still feel your dear kisses on my lips and forehead, I must tell you how thankful I am from the bottom of my heart that you and accident combined to break my resolution not to come and see you ... I still feel my arm around you and my head on your breast.... I feel tonight as if I understood everything that has been sung and written of Love. (19 December 1915)

Just before Christmas the Cambridgeshires and affiliated battalions were inspected by the Divisional commander,

> on a bare down on the very top of the plain, just beside the old Ditch which is an ancient road… and just beside one of the prehistoric barrows. Fifteen thousand men marshalled in one array is a very impressive sight. (22 December 1915)

At the platoon Christmas dinner, Major Morton

> said some awfully nice things about [the Platoon] and some very nice things about me. And then the platoon gave me a most frantic cheering. I feel that I know now what I have always hoped and never been sure of – that the men like me. (26 December 1915)

In the midst of this happy letter, Rob was interrupted. His postscript is grim: 'In the last hour the world has turn to a dismal grey,' he tells Estelle. They had been told they were heading to France after all. 'Back again to the nightmare of those wet cold trenches. It seems almost unbearable.' Rob tells Estelle he has written to all the T.C.B.S. with the news, also sending a copy of Tolkien's great

---

6. J.R.R. Tolkien, *The Book of Lost Tales I*, ed., Christopher Tolkien, George Allen & Unwin, London, 1983, pp. 32–36.

poem, 'Kortirion', to Wiseman and another to Smith.

On New Year's Day 1916 Rob wrote to Estelle – who had decided to volunteer as a nurse in Holland:

> What a wonderful year! I expected nothing but wretchedness and I have found——! I wish I were a poet and then I might be able to express myself.
>
> How I hope and pray that it may be a happy new year for both of us, and that at the end of it we shall have learnt better and better to understand all that this year's happiness means in our two lives.

On the day Estelle took ship for Holland, 8th January, Rob's battalion also departed:

> I felt glad this morning that I had no-one to see me off. The pleasure of such occasions really isn't worth the pain....
>
> I feel as if I were utterly unprepared, which after 14 months' training is absurd....
>
> I wish I could describe or draw for you the lovely sunrise we watched this morning from the train – like one of the Bellinis in the National Gallery, with Salisbury Plain standing up against the sky, bounded by a lovely velvety black line.... It is a long time since I have felt the sheer beauty of things so strongly. It really seems for the moment more like a holiday.

The battalion arrived in the flatlands of northern France a few miles from the Belgian border. Now he had to censor his own letters. He told his stepmother:

> Everything which I am allowed to tell you seems ridiculously hackneyed. It is all part of the theatrical atmosphere – the actual performance after endless rehearsals....
>
> A short crossing – and I wasn't ill – a night at the base in huts and tents – a long railway journey and now our first billets a good many miles at the back of the front. The guns were just audible yesterday, and there is no other sign of war, except the British tommies everywhere and the gravity of the French people.... You could never wonder, as

one does in England, whether they really understand that there is a war. Poor things, I don't suppose they can forget it. (10 January 1916)

He told Estelle:

It is very strange to look out from these windows across miles of flat peaceful country and say to oneself that one a few miles out of sight there are strange and terrible things going on that all Europe is watching. It is so unlike everything that one has ever thought of as real....

At night time the sky to the East is constantly lighted up by flashes. There are big and small ones, lasting for different lengths of time and appearing at all kinds of different points in the sky – some along the horizon and some high up in the air... It is a weird and fascinating sight....

The nearer we get to the war, the more cheerful our men become. How I hope it will last. I am still a good deal afraid of being frightened but less than I was. (12 January 1916)

On 2 February 1916 wrote home from his first trenches:

As yet no shell has come over – and that of course is the terrifying ordeal. Otherwise it is a sort of combination of [the shooting ranges at] Bisley and a firework display. These are much improved trenches and quite elaborate. The amount of human labour expended on them seems incredible – and all for the purpose of getting out of the way of each other's devilish inventions for destroying human life....
The weather is beastly beyond words. Any amount of snow and a resulting slush ... In several places you cannot get round the trench without going through 6 inches of water on top of the floorboards....
In spite of the firing it needs an effort of the imagination to realize that the Germans are only quite a few yards away. We live our life and they live theirs, and we have set up between us the most absolute barrier that can be constructed between men.

Out of the trenches Rob felt a huge weight lifted. 'It has been one of those golden days that foretell spring,' he told Estelle. He has picked oxlip for her [it was still pressed, brown and fragile, between the pages when I went through these letters.] 'Of course we'll go to Italy together some day. Many times.... It is one of the most precious of all my dreams, and I love to know that you dream it too' (19 February 1916).

On 10 March 1916, Rob wrote to Estelle from a new set of trenches with the news that Tolkien was about to marry:

> He is an orphan and has always had something of a wanderer's life. He became engaged on his 21st birthday two years ago, and I believe it was a life long romance. Perhaps the very best of all his poems describes the way in which they had grown up together....[7]

> He has always been desperately poor and I am delighted to hear that he is able to get married now. He has possibly inherited some money.... We are very bad at writing to one another and the news reached me through G. B. Smith. It is a splendid thing for him to reach this anchorage.

Rob's letter to Donna suggests frustration at Tolkien's failure to tell him directly: 'The imminence of the date is a complete surprise to me, as all his movements nearly always are.' By contrast, trench life had remarkably little that was unexpected:

> I have never set out on anything new before for which I have been so completely prepared. Perhaps I least pictured the number of rockets at night. They are going up from both sides the whole night long, and there are many kinds and sizes. Yet with all the lights, it is the easiest thing in the world for patrols in No Man's Land to escape detection. At first when one goes out it feels as if nothing could save one from being seen. But when a light goes up you lie down and stay still and the chances are 20 to one against your being discovered. No doubt the enemy find it just the same. (9 March 1916)

He told Estelle:

> I feel that if I survive this war the only classification of weather that

---

7. This may refer to 'You and Me and the Cottage of Lost Play' with its dream-imagery of Tolkien and Edith Bratt playing together "in old nursery days" (*see* op. cit. pp. 28–30). In reality they did not meet until 1908, when they were 16 and 19 years old respectively. Another possibility is 'As Two Fair Trees' (see Humphrey Carpenter, *J.R.R. Tolkien: A Biography*, George Allen & Unwin, London, 1977, p. 74).

will ever matter to me will be into dry and muddy. I could almost cry sometimes at the universal mud and the utter impossibility of escaping from it or keeping it from one's possessions....
The helpless feeling of being shelled in the trenches is rather horrid. One can only wait and hope that one won't land in the trench, and happily it is only a very small proportion which do. (11 March 1916)

But fine spring weather increased the numbers of casualties from artillery fire, and an officer was shot through the head by a sniper. By the end of March Rob was feeling the tedium and tension. But there were comforts:

G.B. Smith writes me such amusing letters – he has been attached for some time to the Army Service Corps on some special job well back from the line, and, he says he has had time to recover his perspective and see the humorous side of things. I can't imagine that he ever lost it. He makes me feel a dull dog and you, I know, accuse me of taking things too seriously. I wonder if I do. (7 April 1916)

Battalion life for Rob was not devoid of good companionship and talk with fellow officers, and he continued to find interactions with the pragmatic Bradnam amusing:

My servant's aesthetic opinions about this country disagree with mine.... I was walking with him some time ago through the much shelled village ... when he suddenly remarked, 'This must have been a rare pretty place before the war. All the houses look so new.' (3 April 1916)

In April the battalion was pulled back from the flatlands to be trained for a tougher sector. Far from sight of the enemy, he told Donna:

It was with glee that I transferred my Gas Helmet to my packed up luggage, and here I take quite a wicked delight in flashing my electric torch broadcast when I go outside at night. We can sit down to dinner in the evening and hear not the faintest echo of that hateful popopop-pop of machine guns. (8 April 1916)

Rob was disciplined for revealing too much military information in a letter to Estelle. But time off on Easter Sunday was idyllic:

I lay on my back and gazed up at the deep blue sky and white filmy clouds and thought of you and England. I think we have all learned to live in the moment, and only go outside it in dream of happy days that were and that shall come again. (23 April 1916)

In May the battalion went by rail to the Somme region, part of a massive troop build-up for of the 'Big Push' now planned.

It is lovely country – gentle hills and rich green valleys lined with poplars.… I fancy G.B. Smith is not far from here. I wish I could find him. (8 May 1916)

The soldiers carry gas helmets at all times again, and the big guns are plainly audible. Aeroplanes and observation balloons are overhead. Rob grows introspective:

I can't help feeling angered at our short-lived memories. It seems half a life-time since we were last in the trenches, and we now grumble at conditions which would have appeared luxury. I hope we shall not so soon forget this life if we survive it. It ought to cast a rosy glow over everything hereafter.…

Our time up till now has been little more than a picnic and our hardships hardly greater than any we experienced in England. (11 May 1916)

On 16th May the officers toured their new trenches:

As most of these trenches are a full eight or ten feet deep there is almost none of the old bother of keeping heads down. In the other part of the line we acquired a kind of trench stoop ... Here practically no rifles are fired either by us or the Germans, which seems at first almost uncanny.... There is considerably more shelling, or more continuous, and trench mortars and rifle grenades are frequent…

Around the trenches, the wood 'smelt deliciously fresh in the early hours of this morning and I heard the nightingales. It seems so wonderful that shells and bullets shouldn't have banished them...'

From now on his battalion was in and out of these trenches, using a ruined chateau as an HQ. He told Estelle from a dugout: 'The real strain is the strain of waiting. Always waiting with the knowledge that waiting cannot end the war, and nothing stirring to take our minds away from petty worries' (20 May 1916). He confessed to a growing callousness about casualties:

> Either that, or one's nerves give way. I often think that it is Germany's greatest crime of all that she has blunted the sensitiveness of the whole civilized world. Just think of our right and proper horror at the Titanic disaster. – and now! (20 June 1916)

On 6th June, he had no idea that Tolkien was en route across the English Channel, also heading for the Somme. Rob wrote to his stepmother: 'I am simply longing to get home for a day or two to get a little perspective.... I want to talk and talk' (7 June 1916). But he warned: 'There is always the chance of all leave, and even, so it is said, of all *letters*, being stopped....'

Hopes of seeing Estelle also evaporated, and military censors stopped one of Rob's letters to her:

> The worst of it is that my letters must now be censored by an officer in the regiment.... I am afraid I cannot help betraying my consciousness of this censorship and you will find a difference in my letters. (13 June 1916)

On 25th June, he omitted to mention the massive week-long barrage that had just been launched to obliterate the German defences. And his feelings were sublimated:

> I wish you could see a deserted garden that I passed the other day – all overgrown with long grass and weeds. It was a riot of bright colours. Larkspur and canterbury bells and cornflowers and poppies of every shade and kind growing in a tangled mass. One of the few really lovely things that the devastation of war produces. There are many grand and awe-inspiring sights. Guns firing at night are beautiful – if they were not so terrible. They have the grandeur of thunderstorms.
>
> But how one clutches at the glimpses of peaceful scenes … It was that restful feeling that I most looked forward to in the thought of leave. Alas! there seems no prospect of it now.
> I have had letters from all of the TCBS lately, which have much cheered me. There are so many things, apart from mere news, which

one longs to discuss. How I crave for a talk with you.

On 27th June he wrote to Donna of the weather, and a company bath in the river, and added, 'No time for more – ever yr loving RQ.'

There are no more letters. On the night of 30th June the Cambridgeshires moved into position. On 1st July, the barrage stopped and a massive mine was exploded under the German trenches opposite. At 7.30am Rob led his men over the top. The German guns, which had not been destroyed after all, opened up. Major Morton was hit, and Rob took charge of his company, briefly, before being killed by a shellburst.[8] The Gilsons learned of his death a week later. Smith and Tolkien, each less than six miles from him on the fatal day, did not hear for two weeks. Some years later, Estelle found her way to the Somme, and wrote to Donna:

> The little cemetery – I am glad to say Bécourt is a very small one – is a little field in the folds of a green hill by the road side. Just rows of little wooden crosses. They are going to put up marble stones.... There will then be 18 inches for flowers and the grave will be covered with grass. I am asking to have a rose tree put because I think it may last and there is a young Englishman here who has said he will see to it. I think it will not make it conspicuous.... It is just what I like. So quiet in a little less desolate part of this poor torn country.[9]

---

8. According to most reports; see op cit [2], pp. 155–56, 340.
9. Dated 25 May [1923 at the latest].

# 'Tolkien: the War Years'

## Robert S. Blackham

*This paper covers Tolkien's life between 1914 and 1918 and explores the places where he lived, worked and served during the war years. Starting in Oxford at Exeter College at the start of the war the paper covers his move to Bedford for his early army training then to the camps on Cannock Chase, Staffordshire. Following his marriage in 1916 he served in the Battle of the Somme, where he became ill with trench fever and returned to England. The final war years included repeated bouts of illness. The paper ends with his return to Oxford at the end of the war. It is based on my recent book Tolkien and the Peril of War.*

### INTRODUCTION

J.R.R. Tolkien, like many of his generation, was to play his part in The Great War 1914-18. He did not enlist at the start of the war in 1914, like his brother Hilary, but returned to Exeter College in Oxford to complete his studies though he joined the Officers' Training Corps in Oxford and drilled in the University Parks. After taking his final examinations in the summer of 1915 he joined the army and on the 9th July Tolkien's commission as a temporary second lieutenant in the infantry was issued by The War Office, to take effect from the 15th of July. This was announced in *The Times* on the 17th July. On the 19th July he was off to Bedford to start his officer training in De Pary's Avenue where he was being taught how to drill a platoon and having lectures in military custom and practise. He grew a moustache as this was required for officers at the time.

With a group of fellow officers he bought a motor bicycle, which would enable him to travel to Warwick to see Edith, his future wife, when he got a weekend pass, a round trip of about a hundred miles. He finished his training in August and was posted to Whittington Heath Barracks in Staffordshire to join his battalion. He was serving with the 13th Battalion of the Lancashire Fusiliers which had been raised in Hull in December 1914.

### KIT

TCBS colleague Geoffrey Smith wrote to Ronald in June 1915 to advise him on the kit he needed to purchase for his army service. Smith also recommended the Birmingham Household Supply Association at 150-58 Corporation Street in Birmingham city centre for other, more household, items that Tolkien might require for his kit. Smith was rather uncertain where Tolkien should go to buy his boots. But he was very clear where Tolkien should go to buy his wristwatch and this was Henry Greaves in New Street, Birmingham city centre. Before the war wristwatches had been worn by ladies and men would have had pocket-watches but it took time to get your watch out of your pocket and seconds counted in this war because this war was run on time.

## ARMY TRAINING CAMPS ON CANNOCK CHASE

At the start of the war in 1914 there were barracks in Britain for around 175,000 men but by December 1914 over a million men had enlisted and housing them had become a major problem. Plans were put into action to build hutted camps to house the troops and by the summer of 1915 there were places for 850,000 troops within hutted camps. This was a major undertaking carried out at great speed as the camps not only had huts but roads, railway lines, water supplies, sewerage systems and even power stations.

The two camps in the area of Cannock Chase, were Brocton Camp: a part of this camp was built on Anson's Bank a short distance from the main camp but still part of Brocton Camp, and Rugeley Camp that also included the Penkridge Bank portion separated from the main camp by Sherbrook Valley. When the two camps were completed they could house 40,000 men between them with Brocton being the bigger of the two camps. They were to become small towns for the period of the war with hospitals, banks, post offices, YMCAs, branches of W.H. Smith and Son, cinemas and canteen grocery depots which were all staffed by local people.

In mid-October Tolkien and his battalion, 13th Lancashire Fusiliers, moved to the camp at Rugeley on Cannock Chase in Staffordshire. In December they moved across Cannock Chase to Brocton Camp and Tolkien was getting involved with the skills and craft of becoming a signalling officer. Camp life was not to Tolkien's liking. He was billeted in an officers' hut in the Penkridge Bank section of Rugeley Camp but at least the officers' huts had several stoves in them to heat the hut. In December the 13th Lancashire Fusiliers moved across Cannock Chase to Brocton Camp and Tolkien was getting involved with the skills and craft of becoming a signalling officer. Whether he got into signalling as a way to stay alive in the trenches – at the time an officer leading a platoon on the Western Front had a life expectancy of six weeks – or whether his natural interest in languages and codes meant that he felt he could contribute something to his brigade's well-being is hard to determine.

Many years later when Tolkien was writing the chapter 'A Journey in the Dark', in *The Fellowship of the Ring*, did his training as a signals officer inspire the passage in which Pippin drops a stone down a well and a short while later tapping sounds are heard that sound like a signal?

## MARRIAGE

Tolkien married his sweetheart, Edith Bratt, at St Mary Immaculate Church in Warwick on the 22nd of March 1916, the couple then honeymooned in Clevedon in North Somerset. Tolkien then returned to Brocton Camp on Cannock Chase and Edith moved into lodgings close to the camp. In early June the couple visited Birmingham and stayed in the Plough and Harrow Hotel close to the Oratory in Edgbaston before Tolkien embarked for France on the 4th of June 1916.

## FRANCE 1916

Tolkien was posted to one of the camps in the vast complex of camps at Étaples in Northern France. These camps had a very poor reputation with the troops and were the location of the first British army mutiny in September 1917. Wilfred Owen wrote to his mother about the camp in December 1917 'last year I lay awake in a windy tent in the middle of a vast, dreadful encampment. It seemed neither France nor England but a kind of paddock where beasts are kept a few days before the shambles'. And a little further on 'I thought of the very strange look on all faces in the camp; an incomprehensible look, which a man will never see in England, though wars should be in England; nor can it be seen in any battle. But only in Étaples.'[1]

Tolkien left Étaples on the 27th of June to join his new unit the 11th Lancashire Fusiliers travelling through Amiens which was the centre for railway traffic in Northern France for the allies in the First World War. He joined his unit at Rubempre some 14 km north east of Amiens and on the 1st July, the first day of The Battle of the Somme, they were billeted at Warloy-Baillon behind the frontline. They were not to take part in the attack on the first day of The Battle of the Somme but would have witnessed the final bombardment on the German front lines and the massive mines exploding under the German strong points, just before 7.30, before the first wave of troops went over the top. Tolkien's description of the destruction of Mordor towards the end of *The Lord of the Rings* could well have drawn on the sights and sounds he saw that day when the

---

1. Letter to Susan Owen, 31 December 1917, in Wilfred Owen, *Collected Letters*, ed. H. Owen and J. Bell, London. 1967, p. 521.

mines exploded under the German frontlines.

> And even as he spoke the earth rocked beneath their feet. Then rising swiftly up, far above the Tower of the Black Gate, high above the mountains, a vast soaring darkness sprang into the sky, flickering with fire. The earth groaned and quaked (*RotK*, 'The Field of Cormallen').[2]

The first day of the Battle of the Somme had been the greatest disaster in the history of the British Army with 19,240 dead, 35,493 wounded, 2,152 missing and 585 taken prisoner. This was to be a greater tragedy on a different level as many of the battalions were 'Pals' battalions comprised of men who had enlisted from a single town or city. Many officers were not wearing their officer uniform but were dressed as privates to reduce the chance of being shot by German snipers; this was the case with Tolkien's friend Rob Gilson who was in the third wave going over the top some two and a half minutes after the first wave. Gilson was killed attacking up Sausage Valley towards La-Boisselle by a shell-burst a few minutes later and is buried in Becourt Cemetery.

In mid July Tolkien first saw action at the Somme in the attack on the village of Ovillers and after two days of fierce fighting the German troops in the village surrendered. On the 21st of July Tolkien was appointed battalion signal officer, he was now in charge of a large group of men who ranged from runners to telephone operators and in a mobile war they had to set up communications as and when the battalion moved around the battlefield. During this period of fighting Tolkien would have seen the dead bodies of troops killed on the first day of the Battle of the Somme, by this time bloated by the summer heat. Many men had been killed trying to cross the barbed wire entanglements in front of the German lines, could this be the origins of the spider Shelob's webs in *The Two Towers*?

> "Cobwebs!" [Sam] said. "Is that all? Cobwebs! But what a spider! Have at 'em, down with 'em!"In a fury he hewed at them with his sword, but the thread that he struck did not break. It gave a little and then sprang back like a plucked bowstring, turning the blade and tossing up both sword and arm. Three times Sam struck with all his force and at last one single cord of all the countless cords snapped and twisted. (*TT*, 'Shelob's Lair')[3]

---

2. J.R.R. Tolkien, *The Return of the King*, George Allen & Unwin, London, 1955, p. 928.
3. J.R.R. Tolkien, *The Two Towers*, George Allen & Unwin, London, 1954, p. 706.

Tolkien would have also seen piles of bodies in front of the German lines, recalling Beregond's defiant: "Not though the walls be taken by a reckless foe that will build a hill of carrion before them" (*RotK*, 'Minas Tirith').[4]

On Monday the 24th of July Tolkien and the Fusiliers moved back up the line into the frontline trenches at Beaumont-Hamel and Auchonvillers. They stayed there till the 29th July. On the 7th August Tolkien and the Fusiliers moved back into the frontline in trenches opposite Beaumont-Hamlel by the village of Colincamps. Over the next couple of days they were working on repairing the trench system, sometimes under fire from the Germans. On the 15th August Tolkien and the Fusiliers were on the move again, they marched to Acheux-en-Amienois where they once again were undertaking training, they moved to the frontline trenches at Thiepval on the 20th August. But Tolkien was not with them as he had been sent on a course for Battalion Signalling Officers from the 16th to 23rd August. By the 24th August Tolkien had re-joined the 11th Lancashire Fusiliers in the trenches in the wood near to Thiepval. The British attack on the Somme by this time had become focused on the village of Thiepval and the defensive position known as the Schwaben Redoubt. The Fusiliers were not directly involved in the fighting at this time but were constructing new trenches, sometimes under German shellfire; they were relieved on the 26th August and marched back to Bouzincourt.

Tolkien and the Fusiliers returned to the frontline in trenches north of Ovillers by the Leipzig Salient in the early hours of the morning of the 28th August, once again they were working to repair and reinforce the trench system but were hampered by the trenches being flooded, due to downpours of rain, and shelling. Now for a large part of September Tolkien and the 11th Fusiliers were behind the frontline at various locations undertaking drilling, training (practice makes perfect), parading, being inspected and honing their battle skills.

On the 25th of September Tolkien and the 11th Fusiliers set off to return to the frontline, they reached Bouzincourt on the 27th September where they bivouacked overnight. That evening they moved up to the frontline and into trenches by Thiepval Wood. The new battle for Thiepval Ridge started on the 26th September and by the time Tolkien and the 11th Fusiliers were in the frontline. The village of Thiepval and a number of German trenches had been captured. The new wonder-weapon, the tank, had been used in the capture of Thiepval Village although it had first been used earlier in the month in the battle of Flers-Courcelette. Tolkien slept in a German dugout in Thiepval on the night of the 27th September. On the 30th September Tolkien and the 11th Fusiliers were relieved from frontline duty and on the 6th October marched through

---

4. Op. cit. [2], p. 749.

the hinterland beyond Thiepval to the recently captured German positions at Mouquet Farm, sometimes called 'Mucky Farm' by the British troops.

Later in the month they were in the Zollern and Hessian Trenches, then the Hessian Trench and on the 13th October they moved into the trenches at the Zollern Redoubt where they were shelled with tear-gas. They were to spend the next three days in the Zollern and Hessian Trenches, once again they were working on the trench system and Tolkien was involved with improving the communication systems. On the 18th October the Fusiliers were issued with their battle orders and spent the day preparing for the battle to come. They set off for the frontline at 10.30 pm and reached the Hessian Trench in the early hours of the following morning. Due to heavy rain the attack on the German trenches was called off for two days. The attack on the Hessian Trench on the 21st October was a great success with over 700 German prisoners captured and many more lying dead in the Regina Trench. The 11th Fusiliers had 15 men killed, 26 reported missing and 117 wounded.

## TRENCH FEVER

Tolkien and the Fusiliers were taken out of the frontline on Sunday the 22nd October. As they moved back shells exploded around them and on their way to Ovillers they encountered a number of the new wonder-weapons, tanks, grinding their way slowly up to the frontline. They moved into a tented camp outside Albert and took part in a number of parades and inspections and then moved to a hutted camp before going on a route march to Beauval where they were billeted. Tolkien had been at around fifty different locations since he had arrived in France in June. Now relatively safe behind the frontline he was starting to feel unwell and on the 27th October he reported sick to the medical officer with a high temperature, Tolkien was coming down with trench fever.

Trench fever was once described as 'a disease of squalor' and was caused by body lice (*pediculus corporis*) sometimes called 'chats'. The lice infected the soldiers by feeding on their blood after the lice had become infected with trench fever by feeding on infected soldiers. The disease is caused by a bacterium called *Bartonella Quintana* (older names were *Rochalimea Quintana* and *Rickettsia Quintana*) which lived in the stomach wall of the louse. Another route for infection was lousy troops scratching their skin that had infected louse excreta on it: the excreta could remain infectious for several weeks. The lice would live in the seams and folds in the soldiers' uniforms and the best way to destroy the lice was by washing the uniforms in very hot water and taking hot baths but this was not practical in the trenches. However, the troops had their own method to try to remove the lice from their clothing, this was known as 'chatting up' and is where the verb 'to chat' comes from as the troops would undertake this in groups and make it a social event. The method used to remove the lice was to hand-pick them off the clothing or to run the flame of a candle up and down the seams or folds of the clothing, but this was only a short term cure as more lice would be back after a short time.

Lice could move from soldier to soldier in the sometimes closely packed trenches and could only survive for a few days away from human contact. Tolkien came across this during one night which he spent in a German dug-out when he and his colleagues bedded down and masses of hungry lice attacked them. The lice had lost their German hosts who had been killed, captured or withdrawn from the dug-out. Naphthalene in the form of a powder or paste was used to stop inundations of lice; this was made from Naphthalene, Creosote and Iodoform, known as 'NCI'. Tolkien was given some ointment when he was in the German dug-out but claimed that it encouraged the lice.

Trench fever took between eight to thirty days to incubate in its victims and with the disease's onset, which came on suddenly, the patient suffered severe headaches, muscle pains in the trunk and legs, shin pains, shivering attacks and in some cases a pink rash that only lasted a short time. These symptoms were sometimes confused with the symptoms of influenza. Commonly the fever only lasted for five days, hence the name 'five day fever', but in some cases it recurred again and again and victims were often unfit for duty for up to three months. Trench fever in most cases was not fatal but often men suffered from attacks of depression after recovering from the illness. Around 800,000 cases of trench fever were recorded during the war. Strangely trench fever almost completely disappeared after the Armistice in November 1918, and this disease was to be upstaged by a greater epidemic later in the war, influenza.

The best treatment at the time for trench fever was hospitalisation, so on the 28th October Tolkien was admitted to an officers' hospital at Gezaincourt and on the next day he was taken by ambulance train to Le Touquet on the French coast. These were specially equipped trains with medical staff and around forty bunks per carriage. In Le Touquet Tolkien was admitted to the Duchess of Westminster Hospital for Officers which was in a converted casino on the seafront. His fever raged for a further nine days and would not die down so Tolkien was taken, again by train, to Le Havre and put onto the hospital ship HMHS Asturias bound for Southampton on the south coast of England.

HMHS Asturias was built in 1907 for the Royal Mail Steam Co and plied her trade between Southampton and Buenos Aires and when the war started in 1914 she was requisition by the Admiralty and converted into a hospital ship. She operated between France and Britain bringing back wounded, she had accommodation for 896 patients but on one trip she carried 2,400 wounded and sick patients from the Western Front due to heavy casualties at the front. She was torpedoed by a German U-boat off the south coast of England on March the 20th 1917 after unloading her cargo of wounded and sick troops, sadly 35 of her crew and medical staff were killed. She survived the attack and became a floating ammunition store in Plymouth; after the war she was rebuilt and renamed the Arcadian.

HMHS Asturias would have offloaded her cargo of sick and wounded soldiers at Southampton Docks; Tolkien would have been put onto a hospital train bound for his old home town of Birmingham. He would have arrived at Selly Oak railway station in Birmingham, most likely at night and been transferred to a two wheeled ambulance trailer that was towed by a civilian car. The trailers were designed by a local man, a Mr. E. Tailby, and it must be said that they were pretty claustrophobic inside but the journey was only a short one through Selly Oak to the First Southern Military Hospital. This was in the University of Birmingham which had opened in 1909 and had been designed to be turned into a military hospital in times of war. By 1916 it had 1,570 beds but many of the schools and grand houses close to other railway stations in the area had become annexes of the hospital to cope with the ever increasing flood of casualties from the war.

In early December Tolkien took the train back to Great Haywood from Birmingham, at the time the railways would have been packed with troops moving about and congested with wartime goods traffic. While Ronald had been away Edith had plotted his locations in France from the coded information in his letters and marked them on her map of France on the wall of her lodgings. It could be said that by doing this she was playing with fire as in the wrong hands this could be called spying.

Edith decided to stay in Gypsy Green and not to follow Ronald when he was posted to Hull. Since their marriage in 1916 Edith and her cousin Jennie had moved around England more than twenty times following Ronald on his odyssey of camps and hospitals. Edith was still weak from giving birth to their first child, John, and had her hands full caring for him. Maybe the place name, Gypsy Green, where she was living was the straw that broke the camel's back and focused her mind on staying put in one place for a while.

During Tolkien's stay in hospital in July and August he had become a shadow of his former self having lost a large amount of weight. On the 26th of July he was issued with orders to re-join his battalion in France, the orders were rapidly rescinded as he was still in hospital and his battalion had been wiped out close to the River Aisne in France in May 1918. In September Tolkien moved from the east coast of England to the west coast to the Savoy Convalescent Hospital in the seaside resort of Blackpool. In the October of 1918 Tolkien was discharged from the hospital in Blackpool, he was now considered unfit for military service and for a time was on leave. By the end of the month he had returned to Oxford.

# 'Sauron Revealed'

# LeiLani Hinds

*Lord Sauron, the Necromancer, is arguably one of the central figures, if not the central figure, of The Lord of the Rings. But who is Sauron? Since the publication of LotR, Tolkien scholars have shown him to be an abstraction for evil in the fight between good and evil, a Satan-like fallen angel setting himself up against Eru, and a metaphor for the blindness of arrogance. While these are all valid interpretations of this powerful character, there is evidence in the text of LotR and other external sources that Tolkien also had a real-life person in mind when he created Sauron. This paper will discuss Sauron, offer evidence for a 'role model' for Sauron, and identify the person who contributed to the development of the character.*

To start with, I want to make it clear that I do not believe Tolkien's inspiration was either a one-to-one allegorical relationship, a pointed topical reference, or a replacement for the abstraction for evil, the Lucifer-like fallen angel, or the blindness of arrogance. Rather I see this as additional enrichment to those interpretations coming from deep in Professor Tolkien's creative subconscious, buried there as many other aspects of *LotR* have been shown to be. Professor Tolkien himself says in his Foreword to *LotR* at the beginning of *The Fellowship of the Ring*:

> [The Lord of the Rings] is neither allegorical nor topical.... The crucial chapter "The Shadow of the Past", ... one of the oldest parts of the tale ... was written long before the foreshadow of 1939 had become a threat of inevitable disaster, and from that point the story would have developed along essentially the same lines, if that disaster had been averted. (*FotR*, 'Foreword', 1)[1]

Thus, Tolkien denies that *LotR* drew inspiration from World War. However, he continues by saying,

> An author cannot of course remain wholly unaffected by his

---

1. J.R.R. Tolkien, *The Fellowship of the Ring*, Harper Collins, London, 1993.

experience, but the ways in which a story-germ uses the soil of experience are extremely complex , and attempts to define the process are at best guesses from evidence that is inadequate and ambiguous. One has indeed personally to come under the shadow of war to feel fully its oppression; but as the years go by it seems now often forgotten that to be caught in youth by1914 was no less hideous an experience than to be involved in 1939 and the following years. By 1918 all but one of my close friends was dead (*FotR*, 'Foreword', 11–12).

Thus, Tolkien admits that his experiences in World War I did influence him, although not in one-to-one parallels.

Other sources also provide additional evidence that Tolkien drew from his experiences in World War I. The website 'The Heritage of the Great War' reports that Priscilla Tolkien stated that she thought that Frodo and Sam's passage of the Dead Marshes was inspired by her father's wartime experiences. John Garth in 'As under a green sea: visions of war in the Dead Marshes', a lecture given at the Tolkien Society Conference in 2005, has clarified for us the parallels between Tolkien's experiences in World War I and episodes that occur in *LotR*, most notably the Dead Marshes and his memories of the dead soldiers at the Battle of the Somme; the brambles and deep holes Sam and Frodo fall into as subconscious memories of the barbed wires and deep pits in No-Man's Land made by the bombs at the Battle of the Somme; and the Ringwraith steeds screeching as they dive bomb Minas Tirith as memories of Messerschmitt airplanes attacking from the sky and terrifying soldiers on the ground during World War I.[2]

In the meeting of Tolkien and G.B. Smith, his TCBS friend, who were discussing poetry and life in Boggart Hole Clough, as described by Garth in his book, *Tolkien and the Great War: The Threshold of Middle-earth*, we can almost see Merry and Pippin at the Gates of Isengard. Garth describes their meeting like this:

> between their chores in this garrisoned Picardy village smelling of death, the two Oxford TCBSites spent as much time together as they could. Waiting for news of Rob Gilson, they talked about the war, strolled in an unspoilt field of poppies, or took shelter, on Friday, from the heavy rain that fell all day; and in true TCBSian fashion

---

2. John Garth, 'As Under a Green Sea: The Heritage of the Great War in the Dead Marshes', in Sarah Wells, ed., *The Ring Goes Ever On: Proceedings of the Tolkien 2005 Conference*, vol. 1, The Tolkien Society, Coventry, 2008, 9–21.

they discussed poetry and the future.[3]

Thus, there is a significant amount of evidence that Professor Tolkien's experiences at the Battle of the Somme influenced him and that he mythologised them in *LotR*. It would seem reasonable, then, that the character of Sauron might also reflect something that the Professor experienced at this hideous battle in World War I. Although much of Sauron's character seems to fit the behaviour of traditional evil characters, darkness, cruelty to his enemies, a single-minded pursuit of his goals, a quest for power, some of his characteristics seem to me be more individualistic and less traditional in nature.

So what are the characteristics of Sauron that I believe were less traditional in nature? There are four of them: Sauron's conniving to ingratiate himself with powerful people, such as the Elves and the Kings of Númenor in order to achieve a position of power; his fatal mistakes that lead to a catastrophe and thousands of deaths; his poor leadership; and, finally, his heartlessness toward his own troops as well as his enemies. To begin with, Sauron connived to ingratiate himself with the Elves and Men of Númenor. In *The Silmarillion* Tolkien describes Sauron as cunning and shrewd as he manipulates his way into the inner circles of the kings of Númenor in his quest for power:

> Yet such was the cunning of his mind and mouth, and the strength of his hidden will, that ere three years had passed he had become closest to the secret counsels of the King; for flattery sweet as honey was ever on his tongue, and knowledge he had of many things yet unrevealed to Men. And seeing the favour that he had of their lord all the councillors began to fawn upon him. (*TSil*, 'Akallabêth', 335)[4]

Having wormed his way into Al-Pharazon's confidence, Sauron then made a fatal mistake in his advice to the King. *The Silmarillion* recounts that Sauron lied to the King in secret (*TSil*, 'Akallabêth', 335), deceiving him as to his strength (*TSil*, 'Akallabêth', 339). So he managed to persuade the King, who was afraid of his approaching death, to send a fleet of Númenórean ships to Valinor so that men, according to Sauron, by coming ashore to the Undying Lands, could become immortal like the Elves (*TSil*, 'Akallabêth', 340). *The Silmarillion* recounts how this bad advice led to the downfall of Númenor, the deaths of thousands of Númenóreans, and the changing of Middle-earth, which dismayed even Sauron as it went far beyond any destruction he had planned (*TSil*, 'Akallabêth', 347).

---

3. John Garth, *Tolkien and the Great War*, Houghton Mifflin, Boston, 2003, p. 161.
4. J.R.R. Tolkien, *The Silmarillion*, ed. Christopher Tolkien, Ballantine Books, New York 1979.

# 72                           LEILANI HINDS

This utter disaster was survived by only a few loyal Númenóreans, who went on to found the two kingdoms of Arnor and Gondor (*TSil*, 'Akallabêth', 346).

Sauron also exhibits poor leadership in *LotR*. He does not keep his troops well-informed about the concerns he has, so they do not respond as strongly as they might if they knew that certain 'problems' were more important than others. In John Garth's *Tolkien and the Great War*, the title of Chapter 9, 'Something has gone crack', which comments on the problems of the battlefield in World War One, is an echo of Tolkien in *The Two Towers* when two Orcs take Frodo after the battle with Shelob. Sam overhears the Orcs, Shagrat and Gorbag, discussing Frodo:

> "... we've struck a bit of luck at last: got something Lugburz wants."
> "What's the danger in a thing like that?"
> "Don't know till we've had a look."
> "Oho! So they haven't told you what to expect? They don't tell us all they know, do they? .... But they can make mistakes, even the Top Ones can."
> "Sh, Gorbag!" ... "They may, but they've got eyes and ears everywhere ... But there's no doubt about it, they're troubled about something.... Something nearly slipped."

Later they continue their discussion about the war: 'It's going well, they say.' ' "They would", grunted Gorbag.' (*TT*, 'The Choices of Master Samwise', 436).[5] Here Sauron's orc troops, the 'grunts on the ground', as it were, recognise that the Top Ones have made some mistakes, that the leaders do not keep their troops fully informed about what is going on, and that the leaders are not always truthful about the progress of the war. Perhaps if Sauron had better informed his troops about the importance of strangers trying to enter Mordor, Shagrat and Gorbag might have been more careful with Frodo, sent him off to Lugbúrz right away, and the outcome of the war would have been quite different.

Later, of course, in *The Return of the King* Sauron finally recognises his fatal error in focusing on the battles at Helm's Deep and Minas Tirith when Frodo claims the Ring as his own at the Cracks of Doom. All of the battles and skirmishes have been mere distractions from the real source of trouble for him: Frodo and Sam's quiet journey into the heart of Mordor:

> as Frodo put on the Ring and claimed it for his own, even in

---

5. J.R.R. Tolkien, *The Two Towers*, Harper Collins, London, 1993.

SAURON REVEALED

Sammath Naur the very heart of his realm, the Power in Barad-dûr was shaken.... The Dark Lord was suddenly aware of him ... and the magnitude of his own folly was revealed to him in a blinding flash, and all the devices of his enemies were at last laid bare. (*RotK*, 'Mount Doom', 269)[6]

Finally, Sauron treats his own troops with cruelty. Of course, we would expect a leader to treat the enemy troops with cruelty, but not his own troops. In *RotK*, Sauron is shown as making use of Shelob as a guard for the 'back door' to Mordor. In effect, he feeds his orc troops to Shelob as a kind of 'spider fodder'.

he knew where she lurked. It pleased him that she should dwell there hungry but unabated in malice ... And Orcs, they were useful slaves, but he had then in plenty. If now and again Shelob caught them to stay her appetite, she was welcome.... And sometimes ... Sauron would send her prisoners that he had no better uses for ... and report made to him of the play she made. (*TT*, 'Shelob's Lair' 419)

Granted that the Orcs are not on the side of good; they are evil. No one here would want them to succeed in their endeavours. However, they are Sauron's troops, the soldiers he relies on to carry out his war, to fight his battles, to conquer his enemies. Therefore, he should treat them with respect and honour. What kind of leader treats his own troops with cruelty and disdain and does not use their knowledge to help him in his battle strategies?

To find out the answer to this question, Professor Tolkien gives us numerous models of good leadership in his books. We learn what good leadership is from observing the heroes of Middle-earth, among them Elrond, Gandalf, Aragorn, Frodo, and Théoden. They serve as 'anti-parallels' to Sauron in that we learn in what ways Sauron is a poor leader from the ways the leaders on the side of good act. They provide what I call anti-parallels of bad leadership: In *The Fellowship of the Ring*, at the Council of Elrond, we see democracy in action in a kind of college committee meeting where the stories of all the parties are listened to, and their knowledge contributes to success. All of the information is used to arrive at an understanding of the problem and to choose a solution that has a chance of success, the destruction of the Ring at Mount Doom. As Elrond says,

... it seems to me now clear which is the road that we must take....

---

6. J.R.R. Tolkien, *The Return of the King*, Harper Collins, London, 1993.

Now at this last we must take a hard road, a road unforeseen. There lies our hope, if hope it be. To walk into peril to Mordor. (*FotR*, 'The Council of Elrond', 349)

From Gandalf we learn that Sauron cannot conceive that anyone would want to get rid of the ring since he would never want to. In other words, Sauron judges what others would do by what he would do – a rather limited perspective:

let folly be our cloak.... the only measure that he knows is desire, desire for power, and so he judges all hearts. Into his heart the thought will not enter that any will refuse it, that having the Ring we may seek to destroy it. If we seek this, we shall put him out of reckoning.' (*FotR*, 'The Council of Elrond', 352)

Later at the Bridge of Khazad-dûm when the Fellowship discovers that a Balrog has awakened, Gandalf knows that it is beyond the strength of the mere mortals of the Fellowship, and we learn from Gandalf's example that the good leader does not require others to attempt tasks that are beyond their ability. Instead, the good leader sacrifices himself for others rather than requiring others to sacrifice themselves for him. By his own sacrifice Gandalf teaches this lesson to Aragorn, Frodo, and Boromir, all of whom later use this lesson to choose their own paths.

In Lothlórien we learn from Galadriel that, she can understand Sauron, but he cannot understand her, at least not yet. (*FotR*, 'The Mirror of Galadriel', 473) Thus, again we see that the good leader has a broader, clearer understanding of the world than the evil leader does. At the end of the Fellowship Frodo decides to leave alone rather than expose his young friends to the dangers of Mordor and he does not want to corrupt the rest of the Company by continued exposure to the Ring: 'the Ring must leave them before it does more harm. I will go alone. Some I cannot trust, and those I can trust are too dear to me.... I will go alone.' (*FotR*, 'The Breaking of the Fellowship', 522) So we learn that the good leader does not needlessly expose the weak and inexperienced to grave danger. After attacking Frodo in a grab for the Ring, when he repents of his failure, Boromir also protects the inexperienced when he takes on the role of protecting Merry and Pippin at the cost of his own life. Thus, the strong are to protect the weak, not exploit and destroy them as Sauron does.

In *TT* and in *RotK*, Théoden demonstrates good leadership when he goes to war even though he could be forgiven for not doing so because of his age and health, and he does so even though he recognises he may go to war but may not come back. In *TT* when Gandalf suggests he lead his people to Dunharrow,

Théoden replies thus: 'I myself will go to war, to fall in the front of battle, if it must be' (*TT*, 'The King of the Golden Hall', 151). Later, in *RotK* when Denethor sends the red arrow to Rohan to request help in the battle against Sauron, against the advice of Éomer to first go to Edoras and then return to Dunharrow, Théoden replies: 'If the war is lost, what good will be my hiding in the hills? And if it is won, what grief will it be, even if I fall, spending my last strength?' (*RotK*, 'The Muster of Rohan', 73) Once at Minas Tirith, he shows heroic leadership as he leads the charge to attack the amassed troops of Sauron:

> Suddenly the king cried to Snowmane and the horse sprang away. Behind him his banner blew in the wind ... but he outpaced it. After him thundered the knights of his house, but he was ever before them'. (*RotK*, 'The Ride of the Rohirrim', 132–133).

Thus, the good leader does not excuse himself from danger while putting others in it. He leads his troops to war, unlike Sauron who stays in Barad-dûr directing his troops to do his will.

Moreover, the good leader shows mercy and compassion to others, both to their supporters and even to their enemies. In *The Hobbit*, when Bilbo tries to flee the cave after considering killing Gollum, he shows mercy to Gollum, who wants to kill him:

> He must stab the foul thing ... kill it. It meant to kill him. No, not a fair fight. He was invisible now. Gollum had no sword.... And he was miserable, alone, lost. A sudden understanding, a pity mixed with horror, welled up in Bilbo's heart' (*TH*, 'Riddles in the Dark', 82).[7]

When he rescues the Dwarves from their cells in the Elven-king's cave, Bilbo also takes pity on the guard whose keys he steals 'and kindheartedly put the keys back on his belt', saying 'that will save him some of the trouble he is in for. He wasn't a bad fellow, and quite decent to the prisoners (*TH*, 'Barrels out of Bond', 166). Later, in a conversation with Frodo in *FotR* Gandalf reiterates the importance of pity and mercy when he says that it is because of Bilbo's mercy to Gollum that Frodo may be protected: 'My heart tells me that he has some part to play yet, for good or for ill, before the end, and when that comes, the pity of Bilbo may rule the fate of many, yours not least' (*FotR* 'The Shadow of the Past', 89).

As yet another example, in *RotK* Ghân-buri-Ghân, the 'primitive' Wose, is

---

7. J.R.R. Tolkien, *The Hobbit*, Houghton Mifflin, Boston, 1984.

able to forgive the Rohirrim for hunting down his people and allies himself with Théoden and Rohan to help in the fight against Sauron (*RotK* 'The Ride of the Rohirrim', 125–126). So the good leader is able to forgive past animosities, recognise the true threat to survival, Sauron, and unite with others in the battle against evil. Towards the end of *RotK*, Aragorn provides a powerful model of profound mercy to those who are overwhelmed by horror when he leads the troops to the Gates of Mordor, and, on the way, when the farm boys of Rohan are terrorised by the bleak, terrifying surrounds of Mordor, he shows them mercy and gives them a task within their abilities; taking Cair Andros:

> So desolate were those places and so deep the horror that lay on them that some of the host were unmanned, and they could neither walk nor ride further north. Aragorn looked at them, and there was pity in his eyes rather than wrath; for these were young men from Rohan, from Westfold far away, or husbandmen from Lossarnach, and to them Mordor had been from childhood a name of evil, and yet unreal, a legend that had no part in their simple life; and now they walked like men in a hideous dream made true, and they understood not this war nor why fate should lead them to such a pass. "Go!" said Aragorn. "But keep what honour you may, and do not run!"' (*RotK* 'The Black Gate Opens', 194–95)

Thus, the good leader does not demand that his troops take on tasks beyond their strength; nor does he punish them for their lack of strength. Instead, he shows them compassion and gives them tasks they are capable of. Later, in the chapter 'The Steward and the King', Aragorn treats those who fought against Gondor with mercy when he becomes king:

> the King pardoned the Easterlings that had given themselves up, sent them away free, and he made peace with the peoples of Harad; and the slaves of Mordor he released and gave to them all the lands about Lake Nûrnen to be their own. (*RotK*, 'The Steward and the King', 299)

So to summarise, clues in Tolkien's life and *LotR* indicate the following: Tolkien used his World War I experiences at the Battle of the Somme as an inspiration for his books. Sauron insinuated himself into the good graces of the kings of Númenor and connived to achieve power. Thinking he knew everything because of his arrogance, Sauron made critical mistakes which led to the downfall of Numenor and later his own downfall in the War of the Ring.

Sauron exhibited the opposite of good leadership, by ignoring their knowledge. Finally, Sauron was heartless and cruel to his own troops and was willing to sacrifice others in his quest for power. So the question is, was there any real-life person Tolkien encountered at the Battle of the Somme who insinuated himself with authority figures to achieve power and then because of his arrogance, made strategic blunders which led to sacrificing others; who exhibited poor leadership; and who was cruel to his own troops? My answer is I think so. So who is my candidate? It is a controversial figure I am sure every British person is familiar with and the vast majority of Europeans know as well: General Douglas Haig, the Commander-in-Chief of the British Expeditionary Forces at the Battle of the Somme. There are numerous striking parallels between Sauron and General Haig. To give some background, before Haig, the Commander of the BEF since the start of the war was General John French, who differed remarkably from Haig. John Keegan, in *The First World War*, states that General French, who was noted for his humanity, felt so deeply the suffering and loss of the soldiers under his command that he was quite overwhelmed by the thousands of deaths in the early part of this first mechanised war.[8] At this time Haig was the general in charge of the BEF 's First Army, which was under French's BEF, in some ways like Sauron, who was the lieutenant of Melkor/Morgoth, and Keegan says Haig 'was sinuous in his relationships with the great, particularly at court'.[9]

According to Adam Hochschild in *To End All Wars: A Story of Loyalty and Friendship 1914-1918*, to further his ambitions, years before General Haig had taken as his bride a kind of junior Lady-in-Waiting to Queen Alexandra he barely knew. Haig proposed to her two days after he met her and they were married about a month later.[10] To be precise, Dorothy Maud Vivian was the daughter of the third Lord Vivian. Her actual post was as a Maid of Honour to Queen Alexandra. Maids of Honour were chosen because of their social status, served the Queen in Drawing Room ceremonies, played music to entertain the Queen, and had many opportunities to meet and marry very desirable men.[11] This is what happened to Dorothy Maud Vivian and Douglas Haig. Their wedding took place at Buckingham Palace, in a private chapel in July 1905, the first such wedding of a commoner at Buckingham Palace, and because of his connection with Dorothy,

---

8. John Keegan, *The First World War*, Knopf, New York, 1998, p. 288.

9. Op. cit.

10. Adam Hochshild, *To End All Wars: A Story of Loyalty and Friendship 1914-1918*, Houghton Mifflin, Boston, 2001, p. 42.

11. 'Queen Alexandra's Maids of Honour', *Star 9161*, 15 February 1908, Paperspast National Library of New Zealand <http://paperspast.natlib.govt.nz/cgi-bin/paperspast?a=d&d=TS19080215.2.21&e=-------10--1----0--> [accessed 10 April 2013].

Haig was introduced to Edward VII.[12] Years later, Haig was honoured by being asked to carry on a private correspondence with George V, Edward VII's son, after the Western Front settled down in 1915 following the initial onslaught.[13] This rather reminds one of Sauron's meetings with Al-Pharazôn behind closed doors.

Keegan states that as 1914 turned into 1915, those in command of the BEF had come to realise that French was not cut out for leadership of the troops because he did not play politics. He might have been replaced at some later time, but it was Douglas Haig, who was ultimately responsible for his departure, according to Keegan. How it came about was this: Haig saw King George V in France in late October 1915 and was quoted as telling the King at that time that General French was 'a source of great weakness to the army, and no one had any confidence in him any more'. He then followed this up with a statement that 'he was ready to do his duty in any capacity', thus offering himself up as the new Commander-in-Chief by mid-December, with the concurrence of the King, the Secretary of State for War, and the Prime Minister, Haig was appointed to the position.[14]

Like Sauron, Haig's arrogance led to major miscalculations at the Battle of the Somme. The situation before Haig took over as Commander-in-Chief was that during the peaceful interlude after 1914, on the British side of No-Man's Land, no construction had taken place whereas on the German side there had been extensive digging of trenches as well as the installation of cables for phones and communication, of machine guns, and of barbed wire.[15] In his planning of strategy and tactics, Haig made assumptions based on his own limited knowledge and in his arrogance assumed that the way the British planned their tactics would also be how the Germans planned their tactics. His first, and possibly most serious, miscalculation, since it set up a devastating series of tragic events that later transpired, was Haig's assumption that since the British trenches were eight feet deep, therefore, the German trenches would also be eight feet deep. This led him to the next part of his battle plan, the tactic of bombarding the German trenches for about a week, with the goal of destroying the trenches and killing most of the German soldiers in them, thus removing serious threats to the British soldiers. His plan was to use both heavy artillery fire and planes dropping bombs from the air.[16] As part of this step in his battle plan, Haig assumed that the bombardment would also destroy the heavy barbed wire strung across No-Man's land, thus

---

12. Op. cit. [10].
13. Op. cit. [10], pp. 286–87.
14. Op. cit. [8].
15. Op. cit. [8], p. 289.
16. Op. cit. [8], p. 290.

removing another barrier for the British troops. Another part of Haig's plan was to use a 'creeping barrage' in front of the British troops advancing across No-Man's Land, thus obscuring them from any scattered German troops who might remain alive after the bombardment ended. Finally, Haig's last serious pre-battle miscalculation was that since virtually all of the Germans would be dead because of his battle plan, it would be perfectly safe for the British troops to cross No-Man's Land standing up straight, marching in a line as one sees in eighteenth-century paintings of historic battles rather than using the more modern method of advancing across No Man's Land hunched over in a 'fire and movement' stance to present a smaller target, which would offer at least some protection to the British troops. They would then cross in to German-held territory and take possession of it.[17]

So how well did Haig's plan work? Not very well at all. First of all, his assumption that the German trenches would be eight feet deep was wrong. The German trenches were thirty feet deep and were virtually untouched by the bombardment; moreover, most of the Germans in them were still alive at the end of the week of bombing.[18] Therefore, when the British troops started crossing No-Man's Land, they met a terrible onslaught of gunfire from the German soldiers, and on the first day of the Battle of the Somme, July 1st 1916, the very day when Tolkien arrived at the Battle of the Somme,[19] there were 60,000 casualties, about 20,000 dead and the rest wounded.[20] This was the greatest loss of life in British military history, and the loss of life continued for six months for a grand total of 600,000 lives lost, according to some calculations; according to others, about a million lives on both sides, Keegan notes.[21] This is comparable to the thousands of Orc lives lost at the Battle of the Black Gates when the Ring went into the fire, Barad-dûr was destroyed, and Sauron was defeated.

Haig's assumption that the bombing would destroy the barbed wire was also wrong. It was left intact.[22] Indeed, *History's Worst Decisions* reports a soldier's comments that: 'How did our planners imagine that Tommies, having survived all other hazards – and there were plenty in crossing No Man's Land – would get through the German wire? Had they studied the black density of it through their powerful binoculars? Who told them that artillery fire would pound such wire to pieces, making it possible to get through? Any Tommy could have told them that shell fire lifts wire up and drops its down, often in a worse tangle

---

17. Op. cit. [8], p. 291.
18. Op. cit. [8], p. 292.
19. Op. cit. [3], p. 152.
20. Op. cit. [8], p. 295.
21. Op. cit. [8], pp. 298–99.
22. Op. cit. [8], p. 292.

than before'.[23] Perhaps, if Haig had treated his troops with respect, he would have heard this information ahead of the battle, and there would have been less loss of life. However, the bombing did create huge holes in the landscape, and when they started marching across No-Man's Land, the soldiers would trip and fall into these gaping over-sized 'pot holes', becoming sitting ducks for the Germans on the other side.[24] Haig's plan to use a 'creeping barrage' in front of the advancing British troops also went wrong when the timing for the barrage was mis-calculated, and instead of the barrage landing in front of the British troops to obscure them, it landed behind the troops, silhouetting the troops in front and further serving them up as targets for the Germans.[25]

Of course, all of these mistakes were further worsened by Haig's decision to have his troops advance across No-Man's Land in upright stances. If the soldiers had made somewhat lower profiles, there might have been fewer casualties on that terrible day and the two following days when Haig, thinking everything was going well on the battlefield, continued with the same plan. Indeed, on July 3rd he even went so far as to say:

> The first day of the offensive is very satisfactory. The success is not a thunderbolt, as has happened earlier in similar operations, but it is important above all because it is rich in promises. It is no longer a question here of attempts to pierce as with a knife. It is rather a slow, continuous, and methodical push, sparing in lives.[26]

In this comment, in some ways Haig was even more myopic than Sauron. At least Sauron, when he finally realised that Frodo was at the Crack of Doom and that he was in grave danger of losing the Ring, immediately understood the true situation and did everything he could to turn it around in his favour:

> From all his policies and webs of fear and treachery, from all his stratagems and wars his mind shook free.... The whole mind and purpose of the Power that wielded them was now bent with overwhelming force upon the Mountain. At his summons ... in a last desperate race there flew, faster than the winds, the Nazgul, the Ringwraiths, and with a storm of wings they hurtled southwards to Mount Doom. (*RotK*, 'Mount Doom', 269)

---

23. Stephen Weir, *History's Worst Decisions and the People Who Made Them*, New Holland, London, 2009, p. 124.
24. Op. cit., pp. 124–25.
25. Op. cit. [8], p. 292.
26. Haig quoted in op. cit. [23], pp. 121–22.

So Haig made several grave errors in his strategy. How well did he do in his relations with his troops? Like Sauron, and in contrast to Aragorn, Haig lacked compassion and humanity for his own troops. Most people expect the enemy leaders to have no compassion for the troops on the other side, but most expect leaders to show some compassion and respect for their own troops. However, once installed in his new position as Commander-in-Chief, Keegan noted that Haig showed absolutely no humanity toward his troops:

> Haig, in whose public manner and private diaries no concern for human suffering was or is discernible, compensated for his aloofness with nothing whatsoever of the common touch. He seemed to move through the horrors of the First World War as if guided by some inner sense, speaking of a higher purpose and a personal destiny.

Moreover, Keegan states that Haig seemed to have thought that God had chosen him to carry out a divine plan for the world and that the men under his command also believed this and 'were inspired thereby to bear the dangers and sufferings which were their part of the war he was directing'.[27]

Haig in his disdain for his own troops rivalled Sauron in his cruelty to his own troops. Keegan notes that at the Battle of the Somme, when the German troops realised that the British soldiers could not cause any harm to their side because of the massacre that was happening, they lowered their guns and permitted the British soldiers to carry their wounded and dead away behind their lines,[28] thus showing more humanity to their enemies than Haig did to his own troops, the farm boys and factory workers whom he ordered to run over the tops of the trenches into almost certain death. Haig's inhumanity to his own troops was further demonstrated by his response to those soldiers who were overwhelmed by the horrors of World War I.

Many of these troops were in units called 'Pals' and 'Chums', which were formed when British Army recruiters would go into English villages and recruit whole villages of young men to go to war together.[29] In those days birth certificates were not always required, so young boys of fifteen or sixteen could sign up and go off to war with their brothers, uncles, and friends. When I first started researching World War I, especially the Battle of the Somme, I had assumed that at that time the military commanders did not understand that this first mechanised war had afflicted many of the soldiers with early versions of Post Traumatic Stress Disorder, or as it was then known, Shell Shock. Therefore,

---

27. Op. cit. [8], p. 289.
28. Op. cit. [8], p. 296.
29. Op. cit. [3], pp. 147–50.

the leaders could be excused some of the horrors they inflicted on their young soldiers because of their ignorance, including threatening them with death if they ran from the artillery fire or refused to leave the trenches to run into almost certain death. However, the website *Shot at Dawn: Lest We Forget WWI Crimes and Haig: an Overdue Tribute to All Those Executed for Cowardice in World War I* disabused me of that notion. The website states that Haig had known since 1915 that his troops, especially the younger ones who had lied about their ages to be accepted into the military and serve their country, were affected by Shell Shock.[30] This affliction was first written about by Dr. Charles Myers of the British Psychological Society in 1915, according to the website, BBC History *British History in Depth Shot at Dawn: Cowards, Traitors, or Victims?*, and Myers estimated that eight percent of the soldiers were afflicted by Shell Shock, including most of the youngest soldiers.[31] Haig was familiar with Myers' research, but rather than reacting with a minimum of compassion and mercy to his troops, like Aragorn did when the farm boys of Rohan were overwhelmed by the horrors of Mordor, he responded with even more harshness: he increased both the intensity of the artillery fire and the executions of soldiers in order to make examples of those who were 'cowards and deserters'. Moreover, *Shot at Dawn: Lest We Forget WWI Crimes and Haig: an Overdue Tribute to All Those Executed for Cowardice* reports that in a final atrocity, Haig personally signed orders of execution for all of these traumatised young men.[32]

In the British Army it was customary to give soldiers two weeks to prepare their defence before a court-martial. However, most of the young men condemned as cowards at the Battle of the Somme were given summary courts-martial on the field of battle on the same day as their deeds, and at dawn the next day were dragged out on to the field, tied to stakes, and summarily executed by firing squad (*Shot at Dawn: Lest We Forget*). In a final horror, their friends and family members in their own 'Pals and Chums' units were their executioners, not only traumatising the young 'cowards' but also further traumatising their friends and family members who were charged with executing their friends and family members (*Shot at Dawn: Lest We Forget*).[33] There were three hundred and six young men whose orders of execution General Haig signed and who were shot

---

30. 'Shot At Dawn; Lest We Forget: WWI Crimes and Haig: an Overdue Tribute to All Those Executed for Cowardice in World War I', *HubPages* <http://hubpages.com/education/Shot-at-Dawn-Lest-We-Forget-An-Overdue-Tribute-To-All-Those-Shot-For-Cowardice-During-World-War-1> [accessed 11 April 2015].

31. Peter Taylor-Whiffen, 'Shot at Dawn: Cowards, Traitors, or Victims?', *BBC History* <http://www.bbc.co.uk/history/british/britain_wwone/shot_at_dawn_01.shtml> [accessed 9 April 2013].

32. Op. cit. [30].

33. Op. cit. [30].

at dawn for cowardice and desertion, and the controversy over their executions had resonance as recently as 2006 as reported in the article in the *The Telegraph*, 'Pardoned: the 306 soldiers shot at dawn for cowardice', when an effort was made in Parliament to pardon those soldiers executed for cowardice. A few years before, at the 80th anniversary of the end of World War I, *The Express* wrote an opinion piece stating that the statue of Haig in Whitehall in London should be removed since it was not 'appropriate' that he should be a symbol of the thousands who died under his command in World War I.[34]

To conclude, I would say that Sauron, in addition to being an abstraction for evil, a Lucifer-like fallen angel, and a metaphor for the blindness of evil, also embodies some of the characteristics of General Douglas Haig, who connived with authorities to reach his position, who led the Battle of the Somme to such terrible consequences due to his poor leadership, and who displayed no humanity to his own troops. As a final note, Professor Tolkien actually met Haig on the battlefield of the Somme. On October 25th Tolkien was beginning to feel ill, but he delayed going to the medical tent because Haig was scheduled to inspect his battalion, the Lancashire Fusiliers, the next day, and Tolkien wanted to see him. So, on the 26th Haig inspected the troops, and on the 27th Tolkien went to the medical tent.[35] By then, Tolkien had contracted a full-blown trench fever according to Sir Martin Gilbert recounting 'What Tolkien Taught Me About the Battle of the Somme' on the website *The Cutting Edge*.[36]Tolkien ended up spending time in a field hospital in France and ultimately was sent home to England to recover.[37]

John Garth in *Tolkien and the Great War* and Nic van Holstein and Rob Ruggenberg note that even in England, it seemed every time Tolkien appeared almost recovered from trench fever and be fit to be sent back to the battlefield, he would have to stay in the hospital, which ultimately saved his life. I see a hint of a psychosomatic bent to these relapses in that even the stress of thinking about going back to war seemed to make Tolkien take sick. Ironically, having caused so much tragedy for so many thousands of people, Haig may have accidentally done one good thing. As Tolkien would say, 'Even Gollum may have something yet to do' (*RotK*, 'Mount Doom', 271): Tolkien's delay in going to the medical tent until after he had seen Haig at the troop inspection, may have allowed the

---

34. 'Opinion', *The Express*, Friday 6 November 1998, <http://www.aftermathww1.co.uk/statue. asp. [accessed 12 April 2013].

35. Op. cit. [3], p. 200.

36. Martin Gilbert, 'What Tolkien Taught Me About the Battle of the Somme', *The Cutting Edge* <www.thecuttingedgenews.com/index.php?article=716> [accessed 15 Apr 2013].

37. Nic van Holstein and Rob Ruggenberg, 'Frodo and the Marshes of the Great War', *The Heritage of the Great War* <www.greatwar.nl/tolkien/tolkiene.html> [accessed 10 May 2013].

84

trench fever to 'take hold', so Tolkien took so sick that he was sent home to England, living through the war and giving the him the germ of an idea for a powerful figure of evil that lived on in his creative sub-conscious until twenty years later.

When he returned to Birmingham for a school reunion and 'the ghosts of his friends from St. Edward's School rose from the streets of Birmingham',[38] his memories of World War I came flooding back, and worries about his own children's service in World War II overtook his thoughts and resulted in the completion of the chapters of *RotK* where Frodo and Sam journey across Mordor, observing the terrible destruction of war in the landscape, overhearing the conversations of Orcs discussing their leaders and the progress of the war, and experiencing for themselves the results of Sauron's fatal inability to see the world from the perspective of others.

---

38. Op. cit. [2], p. 10.

# 'Clean Earth to Till: A Tolkienian Vision of War'

## Anna E. Thayer (née Slack)

*Unlike some fantasy writers, Tolkien was not a man unlessoned in either war or the pity of it. He knew both from first-hand experience and that experience, matched by his faith and love of ancient literature, proved a potent combination when it came to the penning of his works. This paper traces how Tolkien's most famous work envisions war. Particular consideration is given to two distinct types of war – temporal war and a more Ephesians-like spiritual war – and how, in the setting of Middle-earth, particular tenets of literature and faith crucially underpin both. Finally, the paper examines the ends of war – peace and healing – and how, in Tolkien's vision, war and its suffering is made heroic in song and reconciled in clean earth.*

### INTRODUCTION

It is no secret that a subject as expansive as war is always hard to pin down. Tolstoy was able to write on it at considerable length, and many philosophers and war historians have always done so. This paper is a preliminary investigation into how war is envisioned in one sample of Tolkien's canon of works: accordingly, it cannot and does not pretend to offer a thorough and conclusive investigation into every facet of that vision. Rather, it is an exploration into some aspects of it that seem significant. This exploration will focus on *The Lord of the Rings*, examining the causes, motives, waging and ends of war in the context of the literary and spiritual underpinnings of Tolkien's work. The first question we must ask is what, so far as literary tradition is concerned, are the *causus belli*?

Causus Belli

> Was this the face that launched a thousand ships
> And burnt the topless towers of Ilium?[1]

Many genres of literature intersect over the question of war, handling it differently depending upon the time and function of their writing. One thing

---

1. Christopher Marlowe, *Doctor Faustus*, Methuen Educational Ltd, London, 1987, scene xviii, lines 99–100.

is certain: in one form or another, conflict is expected. It drives story-telling. Conflict arises on a sliding scale. It ranges from the microcosmic, focused entirely on inter-personal relations at the level of the individual, and goes through dozens of variations to reach, as is so often the case with the grander end of literature, the macrocosmic, where the focus is on the disputes between nations or worlds. In this latter case of macrocosmic conflict, war and violence by definition almost inevitably play a part in the proceedings. But how do we come to be embroiled in a macrocosmic conflict? This question has troubled philosophers for many years. We can perhaps summarise a very complex process by saying that wars are entered into either to avenge or defend against a perceived or actual wrong, or for gain. The two circumstances can have a considerable measure of overlap.

In the literary genre of fantasy, and especially that sub-genre called heroic fantasy, we will typically encounter a plot where the macrocosmic 'wrong' facing the heroes is that of unlawful dominion. The villain of the piece is either actively seeking or has already obtained a particular gain. Whether he is seizing an inheritance, object of power or entire realm, the heroes' task is either to stop the villain from achieving his ends or to overthrow him and restore the usurped order. It is the description of the heroes' efforts that make up the story that we read.

It is clear that on a basic level *LotR* uses this kind of plot; all the protagonists' efforts are towards keeping Sauron from seizing unlawful control of Middle-earth. We can see similar traits in other works of modern fantasy: in Narnia, the Pevensys are called upon more than once to drive out usurpers, Prydain's Taran defends against Arawn's increasing power and Earthsea's archmage Ged confronts Cob as he seeks immortality at the cost of the archipelago. Widening our scope a little, Luke Skywalker and his space-faring kindred face exactly the same problems. What unites the heroes of these heroic genres is that they all face villains seeking to destroy or control something that is not theirs to seek. Evil tries to corrupt, pervert and destroy while good tries to redeem, restore and be just.

A villain with his sights set on unlawful dominion is prone to dealing out destruction and violence and doing whatever it takes to obtain his end. Consequentially the stakes in these kinds of stories are often unimaginably high. Failure is measured in suffering and death, and not only for the heroes. This ripple effect means that the heroes' actions take on global or even universal significance. When the final battle-lines are drawn we end up with a rendering of good on one side and evil on the other. Thanks to the macrocosmic nature of this conflict, these lines are not usually metaphorical either – light and dark quite literally go to war.

## WAR IN HEAVEN

The war of good versus evil forms a very particular thread in western story-telling traditions. If we trace it back just three hundred years we find it featuring heavily in Milton's *Paradise Lost*. The concept we encounter is that of war in heaven, good and evil clashing on the grandest scale imaginable. Of course, the meeting of such forces is not unique to the Christian tradition – but its crucially defining element with that tradition is that good is ultimately and unquestioningly victorious. This is a kind of prevailing wind that quietly breathes life into the genre of heroic fantasy: good triumphs. When it does, virtues other than strength and swords – like hope, charity and courage – often seem to count the most, and the most unlikely and lowly pieces – farmboys, children and peasants – are played against the powers of darkness in the endgame. The biblical parallels are clear: weakness becomes strength, the humble are raised up and the wicked are brought low.

Yet Christianity is not the only tradition wielding power over the fantasy genre. Under our umbrella of the war of good against evil we find a cornucopia of other traditions informing our narratives. They are predominantly pre-Christian and especially, in Tolkien's case, northern. With them come easily-recognisable heroic staples: feats of arms, desperate last stands, battles against impossible odds and deeds done for honour, glory, reputation and song. Over time, these ideas bled into the later, more Christianised notions of mediaeval romances, whose sword-wielding knights were, in their imitation of Christ, also called to moral and spiritual virtue that would have grave consequences in the temporal world.[2] This is the melting pot from which heroic fantasy emerges. The tropes and stances of warfare, whether rooted in sagas and heroic epic or in later Christian ideas of moral and spiritual courage, is a vital ingredient and defining element of the genre.

So, we have the conflict of good and evil and the various virtues and vices of the pagan and Christian traditions. By any culture's definition, righteous or just action is laudable and heroic. Violence and war must be faced with physical skill and spiritual strength. Sometimes, as in the case of Spenser's knight Guyon throwing down the 'bowres of blisse' in *The Faerie Queene*, physical deeds are morally and spiritually motivated. The rule seems simple: fight the good fight, and all will be well.

But life in a work of modern heroic fantasy is more complicated than this. For writers of Tolkien's generation, and in many cases those writing after him

---

2. In terms of the relations between virtue and physical action, *Sir Gawain and the Green Knight* is a highly articulated case in point.

even up to our own day, we also have to add to this mix the issues thrown up by a world disenchanted with morality, heroism and above all with war. Fantasy lives still in the literary shadow of the Great War and many writers, especially in Tolkien's time, swallowed that era's aversion to war and its relentless questioning of whether bloodshed and sacrifice can ever be justified, or achieve the good, whatever that might be. In other words, can war ever be good, whether it is thought of as a 'just war' or not?

Tolkien's works are born in these complex literary circumstances, just as Tolkien's writing is itself born in times of war and nurtured by 'the desire to express [his] feelings about good, evil, fair [and] foul'.[3] Perhaps because of the press of disillusionment in his contemporaries and his own encounters with violence, Tolkien found himself driven to talk about good, evil and war. The emerging fantasy genre, a product of the classics and sagas and Christian thought, was his chosen vehicle. Tolkien powerfully reconnected heroic fantasy to its literary and warfaring roots, creating a vision of war that stood against the status quo of his time. He does this by re-establishing war's morality in terms of its temporal and spiritual ends. Tolkien builds up a picture of a just war, but never denies the very human complexity of being in the line of battle.

## SPECTRUMS OF RESPONSE

In *LotR* Tolkien presents us with the vast canvas of a world at war where each culture and character responds differently to the threat posed by the Dark Lord. In fact, just as some critics have called Tolkien's most famous work a travelogue we might also call it an opinion poll, one whose results show attitudes to war that would be at home among cultures far earlier than ours, as well as our own. Everyone that we meet on the road to Mordor has a slightly different take on the war that will end the Third Age. There are those who help and those who hinder, those who are passionate and those who are indifferent, those who stridently face the situation with all their courage and those who will not look it in the eye. Tolkien presents us with a spectrum of responses – some of them canonically heroic, some of them decidedly post-modern, and all of them very human. Most characters can be read as a confluence of the literary and historical tradition they represent and that tradition's stance on virtue and on war. Tolkien uses these points of confluence as a way of exploring and re-envisioning a just war.

An excellent example of this kind of exploratory confluence is in the Rohirrim and, more specifically, in Théoden. Rohan is a culture that seems at once Anglo-

---

3. Humphrey Carpenter, ed., *The Letters of J. R. R. Tolkien*, with the assistance of Christopher Tolkien, HarperCollins, London, 1995, Letter 66, p. 78.

A TOLKIENIAN VISION OF WAR 89

Saxon, Norse and Classical: it has a sense of northern spirit in its literary links to the tale of *Beowulf* and in its emphasis on deeds and song. This same emphasis also links the Rohirrim to the heroes of ancient Greece, whose deeds sought glory, *kleos*, while in nomenclature Théoden's people are clearly linked to the Anglo-Saxons. Tolkien presents us with a people whose concerns seem to be centred on war:

> Where now the horse and the rider? Where is the horn that was blowing?
> Where is the helm and the hauberk, and the bright hair flowing?
> Where is the hand on the harpstring, and the red fire glowing? (*LotR*, 'The King of the Golden Hall', 497)[4]

This elegiac verse by 'a forgotten poet' is clearly indebted to the Anglo-Saxon alliterative tradition. It shows us that song-making for the Rohirrim, as for many historical peoples, is commemorative, and demonstrates that a driving purpose for these songs is to remember war, and those lost in it. The song for the horse and the rider connects war ('the helm and the hauberk'), beauty ('the bright hair flowing'), song ('the hand on the harpstring') and the singing of songs by the fire ('the red fire glowing') together. By doing so, Tolkien suggests that song and war encompass every aspect of the Rohirrim's existence, from the cradle to the grave. Peter Jackson took up this idea in his film version: in the extended edition of *The Two Towers* we see Éowyn singing a funerary dirge for Théodred:

> Bealocwealm hafað fréone frecan forth onsended giedd sculon singan gléomenn sorgiende on Meduselde.

> [An evil death has set forth the noble warrior / A song shall sing sorrowing minstrels in Meduseld.] [5]

The fact that the death was evil and the warrior noble compounds our sense that the warrior's participation in war was a just one. At the same time, the minstrel's lament guarantees that this noble warrior will be remembered.

When Théoden is contemplating the final defence of the Hornburg Tolkien again sketches for us how outstanding deeds of martial heroism – and remembering them in song – is of crucial concern to the Rohirrim:

> When dawn comes, I will bid men sound Helm's horn, and I will ride

---

4. J.R.R. Tolkien, *The Lord of the Rings*, HarperCollins, London, 1995.
5. Quote and translation from <http://www.warofthering.net/forum/vbulletin225/upload/showthread.php?t=5852> [accessed 1 August 2012].

forth. Will you ride with me then, son of Arathorn? Maybe we shall cleave a road, or make such an end as will be worth a song – if any be left to sing of us hereafter. (*LotR*, 'Helm's Deep', 527)

Théoden uses the vocabulary of epic: Aragorn is the epithetical 'son of Arathorn', the killing is presented in terms of cleaving – a vivid verb suggesting mass bloodshed – and the deed is to be worth a song. Théoden's connecting of song, memory and noble deeds done in war is a rendering of an ethos familiar to us from both Classical and Northern sources – a cursory glance through the pages of *Beowulf* or Homer's *Iliad* would furnish us with many examples for comparison. These ideas add up to show us that, for the Rohirrim, the battlefield is a place where virtue is proven by noble, violent deeds and songs are written to perpetuate that nobility.

With epic language and gestures left, right and centre, we seem to be dealing with a culture that exclusively values martial and physical prowess. However, Tolkien adds another layer of depth to the Rohirrim when King Théoden parts with Wormtongue:

"Give him a horse and let him go at once, wherever he chooses," said Gandalf. "By his choice you shall judge him."
"Do you hear this, Wormtongue?" said Théoden. "This is your choice: to ride with me to war, and let us see in battle whether you are true; or to go now, whither you will. But then, if we ever meet again, I shall not be merciful." (*LotR*, 'The King of the Golden Hall', 509)

It is subtle, but in this short quotation we see moral notions of judgement, mercy, and forgiveness underscoring warring acts – and all are crucially tied to the element of choice. Théoden makes it clear that battle is a place where a man can prove true in his fealty, but he also implicitly agrees with Gandalf that Wormtongue's choice is the keenest measure of his truth. It is implied that achievement in battle is only worthy if it is 'true', and that truth can only be judged by a man's choices. The heroism of choice is a much more Christian idea – one that is crucial to Frodo's non-violent protagonism – and Tolkien here suggests that the moral and spiritual capacity to be true and choose rightly must be the precursor to any deed in battle. This concept of what we might call *jus in delectu* – not just in war but just in choice – is crucial to Tolkien's view of the relations between morality, deeds and war.

The aligning of morality with martial skill is a step towards the world of mediaeval romance, and a firm step away from our first impressions of Théoden's hall as a place of song and glory, firmly in the tradition of Hrothgar's own. Despite the best efforts of Augustine, St. Thomas Aquinas, and the company of just war theory, uniting morality and war under one banner can seem contradictory, and doubly so to those enchanted by blind pacifism. Indeed, once Théoden arrives at Isengard, Saruman is quick to try to work the apparent incongruity of the epic stance and moral choice against our heroes:

> "Am I to be called a murderer, because valiant men have fallen in battle? If you go to war, needlessly, for I did not desire it, then men will be slain. But if I am a murderer on that account, then all the House of Eorl is stained with murder; for they have fought many wars, and assailed many who defied them." (*LotR*, 'The Voice of Saruman', 566)

Saruman uses heroic language ('valiant men', 'slain') to cast moral aspersions on Théoden, implying that war and morality are incompatible. Morality affects the semantics of war: if he wishes to be moral Théoden will have to reinterpret all the heroic deeds that the Rohirrim hold so dear as nothing more than murder. In other words, Saruman insists that morality must equate with inaction and pacifism. The Rohirrim are not pacifists and therefore cannot be moral. Saruman's intent is to divorce warfare from its moral and heroic roots.

This conversation with Saruman represents a different kind of conflict for Théoden – this is not a battle against 'flesh and blood' but against the convincing power and authority of Saruman's voice. It is an 'inner war',[6] and it is Théoden's growing moral courage that enables him to withstand the onslaught:

> "We will have peace," he said, *now in a clear voice*, "we will have peace, when you and all your works have perished – and the works of your dark master to whom you would deliver us." (*LotR*, 'The Voice of Saruman' 566, emphasis mine)

Théoden's language here is uncompromising and may even seem extreme, yet it is unquestioningly the right answer. Théoden has become a channel for a steely glimmer of the heroism of moral choice, epitomised throughout *LotR* by Frodo. The biblical – and in every way apocalyptic – resonance of his words takes us back to the idea of a battle of light against dark, one that is conducted both in a temporal and spiritual plane. It also gives us a bold picture of the ultimate goal of war – peace, as defined by the perishing of all the works of evil. That Théoden's

---

6. Op. cit. [3], Letter 71, p. 82.

voice here is 'clear' is a signal to the reader that he is doing rightly and that, in line with Pauline tradition,[7] Tolkien views moral and spiritual capacity as vital and as necessary in war as feats of arms. War is waged in the material and the spiritual worlds, but on both planes it must be waged with *clarity*.

We have seen the Rohirrim move from the ranks of the classical and northern traditions towards the mediaeval allegorical stance of the inner war, where morality and physical courage must have a symbiotic relationship. We have also seen how Tolkien uses this progression to highlight the compatibility of spirituality, morality and arms – a mixture that would have seemed out of place to a generation still reeling from Paschendale and the Somme. Having taken, in Théoden's encounter with Saruman, a step towards the apocalyptic, Tolkien also ideologically here sets the scene for the Rohirrim at the battle of the Pelennor where, driven forward by a moral conviction in the justice of joining battle:

> They sang as they slew, for the joy of battle was on them and the sound of their singing that was fair and terrible came even to the city. (*LotR*, 'The Ride of the Rohirrim', 820)

The admixture of singing that is 'fair and terrible' with battle creates the flavour of an apocalyptic vision: the representation has something in common with passages in the book of Revelations. Tolkien presents a brief and stunning prefiguring of the war in heaven whose eschatological nature heightens our perception of the necessity of the moral strength needed to face evil. It also acknowledges the inherent contradiction at the heart of war – it is both fair and terrible.

Tolkien compounds his argument for the necessity of moral conviction by presenting Denethor as a foil to Théoden. While Théoden has clarity Denethor has become clouded by despair:

> "Pride and despair!" he cried ... "thy hope is but ignorance. Go then and labour in healing! Go forth and fight! Vanity!... The West has failed ... I will have naught: neither life diminished, nor love halved, nor honour abated." (*LotR*, 'The Pyre of Denethor', 835–56)

Denethor's moral sin of despair withdraws him from battle and compels him into taking his own life – an act only previously performed by 'heathen kings, under the domination of the Dark Power'.[8] Tolkien uses Denethor to underline

---

7. See for example, 'Ephesians', *The Holy Bible*, New International Version.

8. It is interesting to note that the word *heathen* is one of the few religiously charged words to remain in the text following Tolkien's careful removal of them. This heightens the notion that

# A TOLKIENIAN VISION OF WAR

the necessity of choosing hope and taking a stand in war, showing his belief that '…it has [been,] is and will be necessary to face [war] in an evil world'.[9] In his letters Tolkien writes of the material, moral and spiritual 'waste' of war – of which Denethor, in his lack of stewardship, moral discernment, and overarching despair, seems emblematic. This same despair pejoratively labels both fighting and healing as 'vanity' – and, paradoxically, Tolkien's use of Denethor here brings healing to the reader's attention as one of the ends of war.

Denethor is not alone in grappling with despair; another character hounded by it is Éowyn:

> [Merry] caught the glint of clear grey eyes; and then he shivered, for it came suddenly to him that it was the face of one without hope who goes seeking death. (*LotR*, 'The Muster of Rohan', 785)

This use of 'clear' is very different to when we saw it used to describe Théoden's moral clarity. Tolkien is not suggesting that Éowyn's desire to seek death is morally correct or glorious. Rather, by juxtaposing the apparent clearness of her eyes with their colour, 'grey', he suggests the clouding of her internal, moral clarity by despair. While going to battle may be an outward gesture of nobility and courage the signal to the reader (compounded by Merry's shivering) is that there is no moral virtue behind this gesture. Tolkien shows that despair can look very much like heroism from the outside, but that heroism without internal moral decisiveness is 'without hope'. I have little doubt that Tolkien had seen its like in fellow soldiers in the trenches.

You may be thinking that this use of the virtues of hope and the vices of despair as a way of defining a character's moral capacity is a clean-cut system inside a work of fantasy: hope = good = just in war, despair = bad = violent in war. But we all know that the real world is more complicated than this. Like Samwise on the road to Mordor, we are afflicted by hope and despair in turns, and have likely all felt how it affects our judgements. Tolkien has often been charged with 'escapism', and perhaps a superficial and simplistic view of Tolkien's dialogue of hope and despair has contributed to that charge. Although he is showing us a moral system Tolkien is not giving us a 'disneyfied' vision of hope and despair. On the contrary, he makes the very human recognition that at the toughest moments in our lives – at the end of all things or at the very brink – 'hope and despair are akin' (*LotR*, 'The Last Debate', 862), when Imrahil asks:

---

despair is a moral sin.
9. Op. cit. [3], Letter 63, p. 75.

"... you would have us retreat to Minas Tirith ... and there sit like children on sand-castles when the tide is flowing?' said Imrahil. "That would be no new counsel," said Gandalf. "Have you not done this and little more in all the days of Denethor? But no! I said this would be prudent. I do not counsel prudence. I said victory could not be achieved by arms. I still hope for victory, but not by arms." (*LotR*, 'The Last Debate', 860)

The dialogue between hope and despair as moral forces for driving temporal warfaring action is made very clear during the last debate. In fact, the Aristotelian sense of the word 'prudent' here alerts us, as readers, to the tricky mid-way between hope and despair that the heroes are attempting to fare. The decision to march out and make a last stand is canonically and classically heroic, while the determination to do so self-sacrificially for Frodo, thus leaving his heroism of choice and pity the hoped-for time to triumph, has definite moral connotations. The march is neither entirely altruistic nor entirely desperate. If we weigh it we find that Aragorn's decision defies canonisation – it is too altruistic to sit in the heroic camp and too desperate to sit in the moral one. In this regards it is the denouement to Tolkien's vision of war. War is not glorified. Tolkien recognises that the real, historic world, unlike the world of sub-creation, cannot simply be divided into canons of northern or moral heroism or into camps of light and dark, good and evil. As Tolkien put it in his letters: 'In real (exterior) life men are on both sides: which means a motley alliance of orcs, beasts, demons, plain naturally honest men, and angels'.[10] While acknowledging this historical grey-scale in the morality of men, Tolkien's portrayal of his heroes suggests that the 'naturally honest men and angels' are those who inform their deeds with moral clarity – and that, if waged with moral clarity, war can be just and good.

## THE END OF ALL THINGS AND THE ENDS OF WAR

At this point we must ask: what are the ends of war? The canvas of a battle of light against dark, and the associated underpinning of both spiritual and temporal war, could lead us to the conclusion that, for Tolkien, the end of war is in apocalypse – if our heroes are driven to act morally and righteously against evil villains then war must lead to the final showdown between good and evil. While this is an understandable conclusion to draw it isn't a whole one. Although, dramatically speaking, the story ends with the destruction of the Ring and the crowning of Aragorn that is not where Tolkien chooses to end his narrative. To those who

---

10. Op. cit. [3], Letter 71, p. 82.

complain of the 'multiple endings' of *LotR* this can seem incomprehensible. Why doesn't Tolkien stop at what seems to be the natural end of his tale – where the fighting finishes?

This refusal to end the story with the end of the fighting points to a much deeper vision of war. For the first traces of our answer we must look back to the despair of Denethor. Tolkien unveils that despair as moral corruption and underscores that message by showing us how even in his despair, Denethor paradoxically thinks of healing. Although the Steward dismisses healing as an unthinking travail he is still aware that it is the compassed goal of those who desire to keep on fighting. And when Éowyn, another victim of despair, comes to understand her heart her new-found clarity shows her that she 'will be a shieldmaiden no longer, nor vie with the great Riders, nor take joy only in the songs of slaying. [She] will be a healer, and love all things that grow and are not barren' (*LotR*, 'The Steward and the King', 943). There are, as Tolkien put it in his letters, those who are needed for 'things other than war'.

As *LotR* winds to its conclusion peace, as defined by healing, sowing and rebirth and the turning of swords into ploughshares, is shown as the end of war – but Tolkien does not hand us peace on a silver platter. It is a process, as the ever practical Samwise Gamgee observes, of 'clear[ing] up the mess' which takes 'a lot of time and work' (*LotR*, 'The Scouring of the Shire', 997). Unlike many writers of the genre, Tolkien invests time and effort into considering the after-effects of war – and he does not sugar-coat it. Sometimes, what seem to us as the best possible legacy of moral choices doesn't quite work out.

After the scouring of the Shire Frodo – who, in being 'wounded by knife, sting, tooth and a long burden' is both temporally and spiritually injured – 'drop[s] quietly out of all the doings of the Shire'. The Shire has been saved, 'but not for [him]' (*LotR*, 'The Grey Havens', 1002). Tolkien acknowledges that an inevitable consequence of war is that not all 'victors [are] able to enjoy victory'.[11] This is something he would not have been able to show had the story ended at Mount Doom. Haunted by darkness and the lingering horror that he did not give up his life to destroy the Ring,[12] Frodo withdraws from his active narrative role, encouraging Sam to take it in his place:

> The title page had many titles on it, crossed out one after another.
> "Why, you have nearly finished it, Mr. Frodo!" Sam exclaimed …
> "I have quite finished, Sam," said Frodo. "The last pages are for you." (*LotR*, 'The Grey Havens', 1004)

---

11. Op. cit. [3], Letter 181, p. 235.

12. In some ways, this could be seen as a Christianised or 'martyrish' version of classical *kleos*.

In his depiction of Frodo's consuming hurt, Tolkien shows us that those who are too deeply tainted by war long after the 'hidden paths' that lead to 'a far green country under a swift sunrise'. The spiritual heroism that sustained Frodo to the Crack of Doom has been exhausted. Frodo is juxtaposed with Sam, who takes an active role in healing the Shire and whom Frodo calls his 'heir'. By presenting Sam as an heir to 'everything [Frodo] had and might have had' (*LotR*, 'The Grey Havens', 1006), Tolkien is also making Sam the heir to Frodo's moral heroism of choice. It is something Sam must use when deciding what to do with his gift from Galadriel:

> "I'm not sure the Lady would like me to keep it all for my own garden, now so many folk have suffered," said Sam.
> "Use all the wits and knowledge you have of your own, Sam," said Frodo, "and then use the gift to help your work and better it ..."
> So Sam planted saplings in all the places where specially beautiful or beloved trees had been destroyed ... and at the end he found that he still had a little of the dust left; so he went to the Three-Farthing Stone, which is as near the centre of the Shire as no matter, and cast it in the air with his blessing. (*LotR*, 'The Grey Havens', 1000)

Initially under Frodo's tutelage and then independently, Sam comes to embody how the moral heroism of choice so necessary in war is to be turned into a force of rejuvenation once violence is ended. Tolkien's description of the following summer seems to compound the spiritual virtue of Sam's choice: 'Not only was there wonderful sunshine and delicious rain, in due times and perfect measure, but there seemed something more: an air of richness and growth, and a gleam of a beauty beyond that of mortal summers that flicker and pass upon this Middle-earth' (*LotR*, 'The Grey Havens' 1000). The heroism that led in times of war to the destruction of the Ring leads, in times of peace, to clean fields and glimpses of something beyond this mortal coil – and perhaps, in the long run, to a new heaven and a new earth.

## THE FIELDS THAT WE KNOW

We have seen how Tolkien's vision is clearly conscious of the temporal and spiritual aspects of war, and the necessity of acting from a clear moral standpoint. This vision of war in the sub-created world enables the division of good from evil, hope from despair and morality from indifference, attributes that contribute to an apocalyptic feel but which serve to highlight the virtue and necessity of moral, spiritual and temporal good. Ultimately, *LotR* recognises war as something to be faced with courage and faith for, as Tolkien writes in his letters: 'evil labours with vast power and perpetual success – in vain: preparing always only the soil for unexpected good to sprout in'.[13] This is a vision that recognises the final haven of humanity from war in a place where there shall be 'no more weeping', and sees that our earth-bound lives are caught in a struggle against evil. Throughout his work and especially his letters, Tolkien acknowledges that in our temporal plane we will always be called upon to go to war, whether literally or metaphorically. Evil will happen, but each of us has a moral and spiritual obligation to stand against it where we find it, and to pursue peace:

> "Other evils there are that may come … yet it is not our part to master all the tides of the world, but to do what is in us for the succour of those years wherein we are set, uprooting the evil in the fields that we know, so that those who live after us may have clean earth to till. What weather they shall have is not ours to rule". (*LotR*, 'The Last Debate', 861)

These fields, cleaned by clear-hearted moral heroism, are the ultimate end of war – and they are to be worked no less courageously in times of peace.

---

13. Op. cit. [3], Letter 64, p. 76.

# 'The Importance of Home in the Middle-earth Legendarium'

## Sara Brown

*Amongst the many definitions of the term, 'home' may be understood as being delineated by the bricks, mortar and roof which one inhabits, a dwelling place for a family or a social unit. Or, more widely, it may be comprehended as an environment offering security and happiness, a valued place regarded as a refuge or place of origin or the place – a country or town – where one was born or has lived for a long period. Either definition invokes a sense of 'belonging'. In The Lord of the Rings it remains at the forefront of the thoughts and desires of the various characters. In this paper, I will explore how home plays a central part in the narrative. Inevitably, home must undergo irrevocable alteration and the characters themselves cannot remain untouched.*

The Second World War had been an all-consuming experience for the people of Britain: large numbers of both men and women were drafted into either the armed forces or the Home Guard, and industry shifted almost entirely to the provision of necessities for war. Jobs previously done almost exclusively by men were taken over by women, many of whom did not wish to revert to their traditional domestic role as the men returned.[1] Post-war austerity measures, imposed to meet the enormous war debt, a national fuel shortage and one of the worst winters on record in 1947 meant that food rationing continued to create hardship until it finally ended on the 4th July 1954.

James Obelkevich notes that 'the one post-war trend that stands out above all the rest is the growing significance of the home'.[2] In post-war British society, attention was increasingly centred on the emergence of the 'nuclear family', living 'in a home of their own and enjoying the benefits of leisurely home life'.[3]

It is unsurprising that home gained such importance at this time. The British people had been through two world wars, lost large numbers of both soldiers and

---

1. Norman Brook, 'Notebook: War Cabinet Minutes 6th July 1945', in The National Archives, CAB/195/3, pp. 2–3.
2. J. Obelkevich, and P. Catterall, *Understanding Postwar British Society*, Routledge, London, 1994, p. 144.
3. G. Crow, 'The Post-war Development of the Modern Domestic Ideal' in G. Allan, and G. Crow, eds, *Home and Family: Creating the Domestic Sphere*, Macmillan, Basingstoke, 1989, p. 20.

civilians and made many sacrifices. The Mass-Observation File Report 1616 of 3rd March 1943 reported that, for returning soldiers, the safety and comfort of home was all the more apparent after their wartime experiences. One returning soldier is reported as saying:

> Leisure, quiet, privacy, courtesy, relative luxury and comfort, forgetfulness of the army and all idiocy and petty oppression, muddle, hurry and noise and squalor and discomfort, anxiety and worry.... I never appreciated home before the war so much as I do now.[4]

Tolkien's own appreciation of what home represents is revealed in some of the opening lines of the Prologue to *LotR*, in which we learn that Hobbits 'love peace and quiet and good tilled earth' (*FotR*, 'Prologue', 1).[5] Here, he contextualises the increasing significance of home in the lives of ordinary British people during this post-war period.

The increase in new legislation, Royal Commissions and government reports concerning family life in the post-war era all point to an increasing belief that 'a happy home and family life is the bulwark of the nation'.[6] The Beveridge Report of 1942, which was a survey of all national schemes of social insurance available at the time, had many of its recommendations implemented following the Labour Party election victory in 1945.[7] The 1945-1949 Royal Commission on Population was set up to examine population decline (although the post-war baby boom allayed fears before the Commission reported) and the 1946-1949 Report into Procedure in Matrimonial Causes investigated growing rates of marriage failure. The National Insurance Act of 1946 established the most far-reaching of Britain's social reforms to date, enshrining in law the entitlement to benefits involving maternity, unemployment, disability, old age and death. In 1948, the newly-formed National Health Service began to ensure access to free medical care for all British citizens. Having begun this programme of social reform, one of the main problems the new Labour government faced was the chronic shortage of housing.

---

4. C. Langhamer, 'The Meanings of Home in Post-war Britain', *Journal of Contemporary History* 40 (2005), 341–62, p. 343.

5. J.R.R. Tolkien, *The Lord of the Rings*, HarperCollins, London, 1993. All quotations from *LotR* are taken from this edition.

6. Op. cit. [4], p. 343.

7. These included The Family Allowances Act 1945, The National Insurance (Industrial Injuries) Act 1946, The National Insurance Act 1946, The National Health Service Act 1946, The Pensions Increase Act 1947, and The Landlord and Tenant (Rent Control) Act 1949, amongst others, collectively known as the Welfare State.

The 1919 Housing Act had been set up to ensure that Britain could provide homes and, as David Lloyd George promised, 'make Britain a fit country for heroes to live in'.[8] The reality of the situation in the immediate post-war period was that there were simply insufficient houses for those who needed them. The outbreak of the Second World War effectively put a stop to any further house building and, as the war drew to a close, Britain faced its worst housing shortage of the twentieth century. Bomb damage had only worsened the already poor condition of social housing projects that had existed prior to the outbreak of war, necessitating wide-spread clearances of slum areas in various cities.[9] Rebuilding took longer than the clearances, leaving many families struggling to find suitable accommodation and, by the end of 1945, it was estimated that 'there was an immediate need for over a million homes' in England and Wales.[10] The new Labour government of 1945 had housing policy as a central theme in their plans for welfare reform and, for the first time, this relied heavily on local authority involvement rather than reliance on the public sector. For these ambitious plans to succeed, new policies and ways of thinking were required that would forever change the face of Britain.

Confronted with a seemingly enormous task, the Labour government realised that it would need an injection of additional labour power if Britain was to be rebuilt and the scarcity of housing solved. The problem of labour shortage had been exacerbated by the fact that women had been encouraged to leave their wartime occupations in industry to make way for returning soldiers. In 1947, the government began to broadcast radio appeals for women to re-enter the workforce. Plans to repatriate thousands of Polish war refugees were shelved when it became obvious that they were an excellent and immediate source of labour.[11] Workers from Ireland and other parts of Europe were encouraged to come to Britain to help with reconstruction. Over the next twenty-five years, people from the West Indies, India, Pakistan, and later Bangladesh, travelled to work and settle in Britain, bringing with them new foods, customs, languages and cultures that would soon have an impact on British society as a whole.

This 'invasion' of British culture by the foreign and the strange was not universally welcomed. Discrimination in employment was common-place,

---

8. *The Times*, 25 November 1918, reporting the speech at Wolverhampton delivered on 23 November 1918.

9. H.U. Willink, 'Memorandum to the Cabinet 6th October 1945', The National Archives, CAB129/3, p. 1. Willink was Minister for Health.

10. H.U. Willink, 'Conclusions of a Meeting of the Cabinet, Wednesday 18th July 1945', The National Archives CAB/65/53/15, p. 101.

11. C. Homes, *John Bull's Island: Immigration and British Society* 1871-1971, Macmillan, London, 1988, pp. 211–12.

as often only the lowest paid jobs were accessible.[12] The Royal Commission on Population concluded that immigrants could only be welcomed without reservation if 'the migrants were of good human stock and were not prevented by their religion or race from intermarrying with the host population and becoming merged with it'.[13] Assimilation may have been a key objective, but miscegenation clearly was not. Increasing immigration brought with it racial tensions, particularly in working-class communities, culminating in a number of race riots in the inner city areas where these migrants were concentrated. It is in this Britain, rebuilding itself after two disastrous wars, constructing a new understanding of society and the importance of home, and beginning to experience the changes that the mass economic immigration of foreign cultures would soon bring, that Tolkien was writing *LotR*.

The concept of 'home' is at the heart of the Middle-earth *legendarium*. Particularly in *LotR*, the defence and protection of home is one of the main motives for the Fellowship's quest to destroy the Ring of Power. Despite the threatened danger of the Ring, however, Frodo is reluctant to leave his home. In *The Fellowship of the Ring*, Tolkien's paradisiacal description of the Shire leaves the reader in no doubt of its being worthy of such self-sacrifice: 'The Shire had seldom seen so fair a summer, or so rich an autumn: the trees were laden with apples, honey was dripping in the combs, and the corn was tall and full' (*FotR*, 'Three is Company', 66). Tolkien portrays the landscape of the Shire as an agrarian idyll, an ideal rural countryside with its coppices, hedgerows, narrow lanes, 'woods and fields and little rivers' (*FotR*, 'A Long-expected Party', 32). In Frodo's mind, leaving the Shire feels like an exile from all he has ever known and he feels 'very uprooted' (*FotR*, 'The Shadow of the Past', 61). In the early stages of the journey, the tension between his love for the Shire and the acknowledgement of his duty to relinquish it are obvious, as he wonders if he will 'ever look down into that valley again' (*FotR*, 'Three is Company', 70).

At the start of his journey, Frodo is cushioned from his sense of loss in that he encounters other, comforting homes – Crickhollow, the house of Tom Bombadil, the inn at Bree, each of them cosy and welcoming – so that it is not until he stands upon Weathertop that he fully appreciates his loss:

> In that lonely place Frodo for the first time fully realized his homelessness and danger. He wished bitterly that his fortune had left him in the quiet and beloved Shire. He stared down at the hateful Road, leading back westward – to his home. (*FotR*, 'A Knife in the

---

12. Op. cit., p. 79.
13. Op. cit. [11], p. 116.

Dark', 183–184)

Frodo's feelings at being torn from his roots and thrust out into the wild, wide world are obvious. As Matthew T. Dickerson and Jonathan Evans comment, hobbits are:

> a race defined by their identification with the soil ... it is probably more than coincidental that Frodo uses the terminology of growing things rooted in the soil to characterise his sense of belonging in the Shire and his sense of alienation upon having to leave it.[14]

Deliberately, Tolkien lingers in the Shire for four chapters – indeed it is Chapter V before the Hobbits even reach the village of Crickhollow, just over the border into Buckland – and this allows him to draw a detailed picture for the reader of what Frodo is willing to sacrifice for the sake of his home and his people.

Even within this central theme of the *legendarium* things are not always straight-forward, as what is 'home' to one of the peoples of Middle-earth may be a source of fear and mistrust for others. There are a number of examples in *LotR* of such unease and suspicion: for instance, Fangorn Forest, which many avoid, including Celeborn who counsels the Fellowship to avoid 'becoming entangled' there (*FotR*, 'Farewell to Lórien', 364). Tolkien's description of the Forest seems to confirm these feelings of trepidation, yet it is here that the Ents, whose assistance is much needed in the attack on Isengard, are encountered. Boromir believes Lothlórien to be a 'perilous land', from whence 'few come out who once go in; and of that few none have escaped unscathed' (*FotR*, 'Lothlórien', 329). The Rohirrim fear both Lothlórien and Galadriel, referring to her as 'The Sorceress of the Golden Wood' (*TT*, 'Helm's Deep', 512). Éomer is at first suspicious of Aragorn, Legolas and Gimli because they have come from Lothlórien and therefore 'also are net-weavers and sorcerers, maybe' (*TT*, 'The Riders of Rohan', 422). Farmer Maggot's very name, which conjures Kristevan images of decay, revulsion and abjection, as well as Frodo's discomfort at childhood memories of fearing him and his dogs, may make a suspicious reader wonder at just how trustworthy this hobbit is. Despite the many links between them and the similarities in their culture, the people of Bree and the rest of the Shire each regard the other as strange and somehow different. 'The Shire-hobbits referred to those of Bree ... as Outsiders, and took very little interest in

---

14. Matthew T. Dickerson and Jonathan Evans, *Ents, Elves, and Eriador: The Environmental Vision of J. R. R. Tolkien*, University Press of Kentucky, 2011, p. 90.

them', whereas the Bree-folk reserve the term 'Outsider' for travellers from the Shire (*FotR*, 'At the Sign of the Prancing Pony', 147). Aside from this difference between the two hobbit communities, which appears to stem merely from long years of separation, it is apparent that a lack of understanding lies at the root of such fear and mistrust. This is an issue of some consequence, as Tolkien makes it plain throughout the narrative that unity of purpose between the various cultures is vital if Sauron is to be defeated.

Home is of primary importance; the principal motivation for the quest to destroy the Ring is its defence and protection. Frodo states at the very beginning of *FotR* that 'as long as the Shire lies behind, safe and comfortable, I shall find wandering more bearable: I shall know that somewhere there is a firm foothold, even if my feet cannot stand there again' (*FotR*, 'The Shadow of the Past', 61). To Gandalf, as a steward, all of Middle-earth is home; he therefore has a duty at least to attempt to preserve all of it and to do so will require bringing together its various peoples. The Council of Elrond in *FotR* is a meeting of many different cultures and, despite a similarity of purpose, each member of the Fellowship brings something different to the quest. Each initially has the desire only to defend his own home; bringing them together reminds them that all are members of a wider community and their responsibility is therefore greater than just to their own part of Middle-earth, or even their own people. Each member of the Fellowship has his own idea of where his duty lies in the quest; this becomes apparent when they reach Amon Hen, where the choice must be made as to whether they should 'turn west with Boromir and go to the wars of Gondor; or turn east to the Fear and Shadow' (*FotR*, 'The Breaking of the Fellowship', 387).

In *LotR*, almost all the places encountered by the members of the Fellowship are under constant threat, in a state of change, or newly under threat. As Simon Malpas argues:

> If Bilbo's adventures lead him through a series of comparatively stable homelands ... the journey undertaken by Frodo and his companions is through a world whose peoples exist in states of continual conflict, migration and vagrancy, which even the destruction of the Ring only problematically renders secure.[15]

The village of Bree, encountered in *FotR*, seems at first to be a traditional, welcoming place in which Hobbits and Men live side-by-side in harmony. It soon becomes apparent that this is not the case, as the Bree-folk's way of life is

---

15. Simon Malpas, 'Home', in R. Eaglestone, ed., *Reading The Lord of the Rings: New Writings on Tolkien's Classic*, Continuum, London, 2005, 85–89, pp. 85–86.

now at risk from 'the big folk' arriving from the South (*FotR*, 'At the Sign of the Prancing Pony', 152).

By the time of *LotR*, Rivendell and Lothlórien are also homes in a state of imminent change. Tolkien shows the reader that these may be temporary places of respite but they are no longer the Elven strongholds they had once been. Similarly, Minas Tirith was once a vital and impenetrable fortress of the civilisation of the Men of the West, the blood of Númenor. Now it is weakened by the broken line of kings and vulnerable to attack. Throughout the course of *LotR*, Minas Tirith stands in very real danger of being overrun by Sauron's forces, a threat which becomes all too real in *RotK*. The safety of Rohan is threatened by Sauron, particularly after the weakening of Théoden through the influence of Saruman and Wormtongue. In addition, Saruman encourages the fierce Dunlendings to attack Rohan, to reclaim the land taken from them generations before. Moria, once the Dwarven kingdom of Khazad-Dûm, is discovered to have been overrun by Orcs and is unlikely ever to be occupied by the Dwarves as it once was. This period is a time of great change as well as great danger, and this has an inevitable effect on the Peoples of Middle-earth. In an unmistakable parallel with both twentieth- and twenty-first-century problems, *LotR* 'struggles to make sense of the possibility of community during a period where industrialisation, war and rapid transformations of technology threaten to destabilise traditional notions of being in common'.[16]

In *LotR*, it is evident that home itself is not always 'safe', nor a haven of stability. Dangers previously unseen, unnoticed, or at least overlooked, may lie within and threaten its people. In Rohan, its king has been weakened by the machinations of Saruman, whose stronghold lies on its borders. Gríma Wormtongue has slowly achieved control over Théoden and, in so doing, helps Saruman to gain power over Rohan. This control fundamentally debilitates Rohan and greatly endangers its entire population. Similarly, in Gondor, Denethor is weakened by his struggle with Sauron through the palantír and is losing control. This has a similar effect on Gondor as Théoden's debilitation has on Rohan. Denethor's over-confidence in believing that he had mastery over the palantír and could pit his own mental strength against that of Sauron, his arrogance in refusing Gandalf's counsel and his eventual slide into madness would have signalled disaster for Minas Tirith, and subsequently for the rest of Gondor, had it not been for the actions of Gandalf, Aragorn and their allies. Once a mighty power, formidable in its opposition to Sauron, Gondor was already lacking its former strength before Denethor's failure; his weakness jeopardises the safety of Gondor and its people.

Of course, the Shire itself is also in danger, and this is increasingly apparent

---

16. Op. cit., p. 86.

long before the events of the Scouring of the Shire. Sam's visions in the Mirror of Galadriel, in which he sees the felling of the trees in the Shire and Bagshot Row dug up, are only the first indication that something terrible may occur at home before the Fellowship can complete its quest (*FotR*, 'The Mirror of Galadriel', 353). Here lies the key difference between *The Hobbit* and *LotR*, and Tolkien's message is clear: not only is change inevitable and inescapable, 'home' can never be truly regained. As John C. Hunter asserts, 'the life of the Shire is represented as a fantasy that cannot last. The novel's depiction of the old life in the Shire makes it tempting to mourn its passing, but it was only ever a delusion'.[17] Despite his longing for home, Frodo cannot go 'there and back again' as both he and the Shire are damaged. After the Scouring, the Shire may be rebuilt but there has been death and destruction at the heart of what was home. Frodo himself is so badly affected that the Shire can never again be home for him; as he tells Sam in the final chapter of *RotK*, 'I tried to save the Shire, and it has been saved, but not for me' (*RotK*, 'The Grey Havens', 1007). Change is inevitable and, despite victory over Sauron and the Ring, unavoidable.

From the beginning, Tolkien reveals that the Shire is not the stable, unchanging place that the Hobbits, in particular, had assumed. Frodo, especially, learns that home is not something to which one can always return. Home is a concept that is constantly being realised as a result of experience, change and adaptation to the flux of history. One of the messages of *LotR* is that there must be an acceptance of the possibility that home may be fundamentally changed, as a result of actions which are, paradoxically, necessary if home is to be protected. As Verlyn Flieger observes, 'Tolkien's philosophical and religious outlook was that change is necessary, although his psychological and emotional yearning was for much of his world that had vanished or was vanishing'.[18] The Shire does not escape change; it may appear to be a haven of stability but, below the surface, there lurk a few individuals who threaten its safety. There are those, even amongst the Hobbits, who are more than willing to be part of Sharkey's plans. Lotho Sackville-Baggins is drawn in by his greed and desire for Bag End; Ted Sandyman is an enthusiastic proponent of the changes in the Shire and his mill becomes a symbol of the destruction caused by the industrialisation of Hobbiton and its environs. In the Shire, the 'Big Folk' have been gradually arriving in greater numbers on the borders of the Shire for some time and, as is made plain in The Prancing Pony in Bree, not all of them are good people.

The very act of being part of the quest, and therefore going out into the wider

---

17. John C. Hunter, 'The Evidence of Things Not seen: Critical Mythology and *The Lord of the Rings'*, *Journal of Modern Literature* 29 (2006), 129–47, p. 141.
18. Verlyn Flieger, *Splintered Light: Logos and Language in Tolkien's World*, Kent State University Press, Kent OH, 2002, p. 154.

world, brings Hobbits to the attention of those who had previously either been unaware of their existence, or who had discounted and overlooked them as being irrelevant in the great events of that world. The addition of their race to Treebeard's list brings to an end the relative anonymity the Hobbits had previously enjoyed. The Shire's borders are opened and seclusion is ended. The end of the novel is not 'the result of a return 'back again' to a secure and unchanging community;' nothing is as it was but, in fact, some change is possibly for the better as there is now more trust and unity between the different Peoples of Middle-earth. Rohan strengthens its ties with Gondor and the city of Minas Tirith emerges from its cold, grey, barren state, slowly coming to life again.

From the outset, then, the reader understands that 'change is inevitable, growth is necessary, much that is fair and wonderful will disappear and pass away'.[19] Even what had once seemed the most stable of cultures, the Shire, is now inexorably caught up in the history of all the struggles of Middle-earth. On the other hand, there is a sense of optimism at the end of *LotR*. The Shire is scoured, homes are rebuilt and trees re-grown and Bag End, once a quiet, bachelor home, will fill with children and be bursting with new life.

The destruction of the Ring and the defeat of Sauron cannot be achieved without a willingness to put 'home' at risk. In doing so, many of the characters come to the realisation that 'home' can never be the same again; success lies in encountering and allying with foreign cultures, a process which cannot leave the characters untouched. The parallels with our own world are undeniable and the applicability of Tolkien's arguments to the problems and concerns of the twenty-first century is obvious. Home is not merely a place, nor is it solely the bricks and mortar that form our shelter; for Tolkien, 'home' is defined as being a reflection of our own experiences, subject to change and adaptation as individual identities are transformed through interaction with other cultures, and encounters with geographical and psychological borders.

---

19. Wayne G. Hammond, 'All the Comforts: The Image of Home in *The Hobbit* and *The Lord of the Rings'*, *Mythlore* 51 (1987), 29–33, p. 32.

# PHILOSOPHY AND ETHICS

# 'Tolkien versus the history of philosophy'

## Franco Manni

*This paper is not concerned with themes and ideas but deals with Tolkien's attitude towards philosophers: picking up and using some of their ideas, but always obliterating the sources. He idealised himself as a plain, down-to-earth, thorough 'philologist' as opposed to vague, nebolous, eccentric and narcisistic 'philosophers', and he fostered the ideology that Philology was without debts and connections to Philosophy.*

### ANCIENT AND MEDIEVAL PHILOSOPHERS

In his works published during his lifetime (with one exception) Tolkien never referred to philosophers by name,[1] neither classical figures such as Plato, Aristotle, Augustine, Aquinas, Descartes, Kant, Hegel, or Marx, nor his contemporaries such as Freud, Bergson, Croce, Wittgenstein, or Ryle. Plato's name appears once in the posthumous works *The Notion Club Papers* in the context of the myth of Atlantis, which is connected with that of Númenor. Although he does not cite Kant, he does make use of the Kantian neologism 'noumenon.'[2] The ideas of *perennis philosophia* (a syncretic compound of ancient and medieval traditions) are also frequently employed, but without reference to sources. Tom Shippey thinks that Tolkien did not mention philosophers like Plato, Boethius and others in spite of his knowledge of them because of his anticlassicist bias, and because he wanted to promote native English literature but could not find English philosophers before Chaucer's times.[3]

A clear example may be found in note 8 of the self-commentary Tolkien made on *Athrabeth Finrod ah Andreth* (*The Debate of Finrod and Andreth*). The note discusses 'desire' and distinguishes three kinds: 'natural' desire which are shared by all members of a species: 'personal' desire, 'the feeling of the lack of something, the force of which primarily concerns oneself, and which may have

---

1. J.R.R. Tolkien, *Sauron Defeated*, ed. Christopher Tolkien, HarperCollins, London, 1993, p. 249. There is a passing reference to the little-known German philosopher Theodore Haecker in Humphrey Carpenter, ed., *The Letters of J.R.R. Tolkien*, with the assistance of Christopher Tolkien, George Allen & Unwin, London, 1981, Letter 338, p. 419), but the context suggests that Tolkien was referring to a literary essay, not a philosophical one.
2. Op. cit., Letter 131, p. 151.
3. Personal correspondence, 21 August 2009.

little or no reference to the general fitness of things', and 'illusionary' desire which obstructs the understanding that things are not as they should be and leads to the delusion that they are as one would wish them to be.[4] This distinction is the same as that made by Aquinas in *Summa Theologiae*,[5] a work which Tolkien owned,[6] and which was also present on Lewis's bookshelf during the Inklings' evening meetings.[7]

A further undeclared Thomistic point can be seen in the difference between the two kinds of Hope: 'Admir' and 'Estel'. In the Andreth reflects about the nature of Hope: 'What is hope?' she asks. 'An expectation of good, which though uncertain has some foundation in what is known? Then we have none.' 'That is one thing that Men call 'hope',' says Finrod. 'Amdir we call it, "looking up". But there is another which is founded deeper. Estel we call it, that is, "trust". It is not defeated by the ways of the world, for it does not come from experience, but from our nature and first being' (*Morgoth's Ring*, 'Athrabeth', 320). In the *Summa Theologiae* Aquinas distinguishes 'spes' as a pre-moral 'passio' (feeling) which belongs even to drunk people and brute animals and whose content is '*bonum futurum arduum possibile adipisci*',[8] from 'spes' as a theological virtue, of which he writes: '*spes non innititur principaliter gratiae iam habitae, sed divinae omnipotentiae et misericordiae, per quam etiam qui gratiam non habet eam consequi potest*'.[9]

But Bradley J. Birzer thinks that the most significant Thomistic element in Tolkien's work is the character of Aragorn. He represents the ideal of the Thomistic king (*De regimine principum*) where Aquinas argued that the only truly good king is one who acts as Christ, sacrificing himself for the good of the community (for Christ the Church, for the Christian king the *respublica*).[10]

Concerning Thomistic themes we should remember that through the philosophical tradition – even in the Christian one – the so-called 'eternity' is quite different from 'endless time': Time concerns Change, while instead Eternity concerns Immutability, *tota simul existens*, and therefore, if immortality

---

4. J.R.R. Tolkien, *Morgoth's Ring*, ed. Christopher Tolkien, HarperCollins, London, 1994, p. 343. All quotations from *Morgoth's Ring* are taken from this edition.
5. Aquinas distinguishes three kinds of 'pleasure.' Thomas Aquinas, *Summa Theologiae*, trans. Marcus Lefébure, Eyre and Spottiswood, London, 1975, pars prima secundae partis, quaestio 34, art. 2.
6. Claudio Testi has purchased Tolkien's copy and received a positive *expertise* by Carl Hostetter.
7. Humphrey Carpenter, *The Inklings*, George Allen & Unwin, London, 1978, chapter 3.
8. Op. cit. [5], quaestio 40, art. 1,3,6.
9. Op. cit. [5], pars secunda secundae partis, quaestio 18, art., 4, ad secundum et ad tertium.
10. 'Aquinas', in Michael Drout, ed., *Tolkien Encyclopedia: Scholarship and Chritical Assessment,* Routledge, New York and London, 2007, 21–22, p. 21.

is meant as 'eternal life, it is *not* a life lasting for an endless time.[11] Rightly Renée Vink observes: 'Just like true immortality has often been confused with serial longevity, there is a related concept that has often been confused with never-ending time. I am referring to eternity. Though Tolkien does not use the word, I would venture to say that "eternity" is the state of existence where what he calls true immortality has its proper place. Death may not be the enemy, but Time surely is.'[12]

Further references to ancient and medieval philosophers (Plato, Augustine, Boethius) have been pointed out by Tolkien scholars:

PLATO: on 27 February 1913 Tolkien had the First Public Examination for the Honour School of Latin and Greek Literature; on Plato, his choice of two of the *Gorgias, Protagoras* and *Phaedo*.[13] Gergely Nagy parallels Plato and Tolkien in using 'myths' to tell philosophical truths; in using the metaphor of Light – Plato with the Sun as the Idea of Good in the *Republic* (508b-509a), Tolkien in the beginning of *The Silmarillion*, in the hierarchy of the world (the Demiurge and the Valar.[14] Gregory Bassham notes:

> Tolkien's repeated use of the term "demi-urgic" (e.g., *Morgoth's Ring* 332) to describe the creative/shaping activity of the Valar (borrowed from Plato's *Timaeus*); Númenor as based on Plato's story of Atlantis in *Critias*; the Ring as based on Gyges's ring in *Republic*, Book 2; reincarnation of the elves is likely to have been borrowed from Plato, especially the *Phaedo*.[15]

Personally, I think that the main idea of Plato's *Gorgias*: 'it is better to suffer an injustice than to do it', inspires Tolkien's main idea for the use of the One Ring: it is better to suffer deep pains and face deadly dangers not using the One Ring, than to win the war using it.

Platonic themes are present in Tolkien's writings not intended for publication, such as *Laws and Customs among the Eldar* and *Athrabeth Finrod ah Andreth* and in his various explanatory comments on these fictional writings.[16] Here he

---

11. Op. cit. [5], quaestio 10, art. 1.

12. Reneé Vink, 'Immortality and the Death of Love: Tolkien and Simone de Beauvoir', in Sarah Wells, ed., *The Ring Goes Ever On: Proceedings of the Tolkien 2005 Conference*, vol 2, The Tolkien Society, Coventry, 2008, p. 127.

13. Christina Scull and Wayne G. Hammond, *J.R.R. Tolkien Companion and Guide*, vol.1: Chronology, HarperCollins, London, 2006, p. 37.

14. Gergely Nagy, 'Plato', in op. cit. [10], p. 513.

15. Personal correspondence, 15 June 2009.

16. Op. cit. [4].

discusses traditional anthropological and theological themes of body and soul and God's plan for these; death for him is always the 'severance' of the two 'components', which should remain united. The Elf Finrod says to Wisewoman Andreth: 'do you not think that the separation of soul and body could be experienced as a liberation, as a returning home?' Andreth replies: 'no, we do not think so because this would be to disparage the body and is a thought of Darkness, for in the incarnate it is unnatural' (*Morgoth's Ring*, 'Athrabeth', 317). As Ralph C. Wood writes, this is a 'radical non-Platonic turn'.[17] And Claudio Testi writes: 'Approximately one could say that it seems to be an Aristotelian element in a Platonic context.'[18] Damien Casey thinks that theologically Tolkien is aware that the heart of Christianity is the incarnation, notwithstanding the atrophy of this heritage in the Platonic tradition.[19] This 'non-Platonic turn', Wood acutely explains, is also an implicit – but interesting and well-founded – explanation of the motivations behind Platonic dualism: it would seem that Men, or rather their 'souls', possess the memory of 'another world' from which they have become estranged and to which they seek to return as the Platonic soul which tends towards its original Hyperuranic homeland, but Andreth denies this, for her soul and body are each essential to the other, and thus their 'severance' is a calamity caused by Melkor. So the 'nostalgia' that the Elves have noticed in Men is *not* the desire for a world different to this one, but rather an effort to return to the harmony and unity between body and spirit which were lost by Men in the rebellion against Ilùvatar, and remain lost in corrupt Arda. Plato,

---

17. Ralph C. Wood, *The Gospel According to Tolkien: Visions of the Kingdom in Middle-earth*, John Knox Press, Westminster, 2003, p. 159. Anne Mathie comments: 'The body and the world of matter are not something to be escaped or transcended as such. To separate the body from the spirit, the dweller from the house, is considered to be a terrible thing.' See Anne Mathie, 'Tolkien and the Gift of Mortality', *First Things*, <http://www.firstthings.com/article/2003/11/tolkien-and-the-gift-of-mortality> [accessed 30 November 2003].

18. See Claudio A. Testi, 'Logic and Theology in Tolkien's Thanatology', in Roberto Arduini and Claudio A. Testi, eds, *The Broken Scythe: Death and Immortality in the Works of Tolkien*, Walking Tree Publishers, Zurich and Jena, 2012, 175–91, p. 176.

19. Damien Casey 'The Gift of Ilùvatar', *The Australian Journal of Theology* 2 (2004) <http://dlibrary.acu.edu.au/staffhome/dacasey/tolkien.htm> [accessed 1June 2009]. Shippey observes: 'the theology of 'body and soul' took some time to develop, but it was a favourite theme for Anglo-Saxon poets and homilists.... The point is that by Aquinas's time the theology is clear: one should NOT say that the body is evil and the soul is good.... I'm sure Tolkien knew the theology of this and was careful to give full value to the Incarnation, perhaps the more so because he had read works like the two Anglo-Saxon "Soul and Body" poems.' (Personal correspondence, 27 June 2009). Among the books formerly owned by Tolkien and now in the English Faculty Library in Oxford, the *Old English Homilies* include 'Hic Dicendum est de Quadragesima' which includes the idea that 'the body loves what the soul hates'. (R. Morris, ed., *Old English Homilies*, N. Trübner and Co., London, 1868, pp. 11–25).

that is, confuses the moral and theological problem with the anthropological and metaphysical, indicating 'another world' for the 'soul' when he should have indicated moral conversion for Men.[20]

Although the original Jewish/Christian message is both non-Platonic and in some respects anti-Platonic, it has for many centuries been spread widely by means of Platonic categories. Tolkien is, however, a Christian of the twentieth century, a century in which theology and Christian spirituality have strongly criticised the fundamental category of Platonism, so-called 'dualism' (a category which had already been philosophically opposed, in different ways, by both Hegelianism and nineteenth century Marxist and positivist materialism), and he follows the debate which for him was contemporary, observing explicitly, for example, that his friend Lewis was not philosophically a dualist, but had a 'dualist' imagination.[21] And this was because, notes Christopher Garbowski, 'a general philosophical movement' had influenced Tolkien: in this the value accorded to psychosomatic phenomena had made obsolete a material conception of the separate 'soul', thus permitting a return to biblical monism.[22]

AUGUSTINE: John Willim Houghton writes there are two issues relating to this philosopher in Tolkien's work: 1) creation (including the nature of evil), and 2) free will and predestination. As regards 1): against Manicheanism Augustine states that God created the universe good and evil is fundamentally nothing; in *De Genesi ad litteram* Augustine thinks that God explained the divine plan to the angels before creating the world. The *Ainulindale* presents a similar process. As for 2) against Pelagianism, Augustine in *De gratia et libero arbitrio* states that a Christian has to pray God this way 'give what you command and command what you will', while Pelagius argues that God commands no more than people are able to will and perform; and in Tolkien's work Frodo is predestined to receive the Ring and for this purpose he is aided by unexpected helpful events and persons.[23]

BOETHIUS: before the end of Trinity Term 1915 at Oxford University Tolkien had to prepare a selection from Alfred's translation of the *De Consolatione Philosophiae*, and Gregory Bassham writes: 'The question of

---

20. Wood, op. Cit. [17], pp. 158–160.
21. Op. cit. [1], Letter 291, p. 371.
22. Christopher Garbowski, *Recovery and Transcendence for the Contemporary Mythmaker*, Maria Curie-Sklodowska University Press, Lublin, 2000, p. 168.
23. 'Augustine of Hippo', in op. cit. [10], p. 43. See also: 'Augustine in the Cottage of the Lost Play, *The Ainulindalë* as Asterisk Cosmogony', in Jane Chance, ed., *Tolkien the Medievalist*, Routledge, New York and London, 2003, pp. 171–82.

# FRANCO MANNI

how much philosophy Tolkien read is probably unanswerable'. However, two philosophical works he almost certainly would have had in his library are (1) Alfred's translation of Boethius's *Consolatio* and (2) Chaucer's translation of the same. In fact, Boethius seems to have influenced Tolkien fairly heavily. His solution to the freewill/divine foreknowledge problem in *Osanwe-kenta* and elsewhere is identical to Boethius's (God is outside time, so strictly there is no foreknowledge). Also, Tolkien's use of the term 'consolation' for one of the three benefits of fantasy-reading (escape, recovery, consolation) likely derives from Boethius. Furthermore, Tolkien's insistence that evil is a *privatio* is likely due mainly to Boethius (though Boethius himself borrowed the idea from Plotinus and Augustine). Some of Tolkien's ideas on 'chance' and 'luck' may also be indebted to Boethius's *Consolatio*. Tolkien certainly had Chaucer's translation of Boethius' *Consolatio* in his personal library. For many years he served as co-editor of the Clarendon *Chaucer*, but eventually had to bow prior to publication.[24] He wanted to produce a new text of Chaucer but was obliged by the Press to use Skeat's edition of Chaucer's *Poetical Works*. That edition includes the whole of Chaucer's translation. As for Alfred's translation: as one of the world's leading Anglo-Saxon scholars, Tolkien surely would have had essentially every surviving Anglo-Saxon text in his personal library.

In my own reading of the *De Consolatione*, I found: 1) the main idea of *Providentia* (Liber III), and more particularly that Chance does not exist (Liber V) – *LotR* is full of not-casual coincidence. 2) Since Evil is *privatio entis* (lack of being), evil persons persisting in their sins become nothing (Liber IV) – like Sauron at the end of *LotR*. 3), Plato's idea in *Gorgias* that good persons are able to fulfil their wishes, while evil ones are not (Liber IV) – in the *LotR* this explains the different goals, deeds, fulfilments and failures of Gandalf and Saruman. 4) Plato's idea in *Gorgias* that evil people who receive and suffer their right punishment at the end are happier than people who keep living unpunished (Liber IV), an idea that we can recognise in several parts of *The Silmarillion* concerning Melkor and Sauron, and in *LotR* concerning Boromir, Saruman and Gollum. 5) The idea that God's omniscience does not determine future facts (Liber V) appears in *The Silmarillion* to be reflected in Iluvatar's foreknowledge of Arda's history.

## MODERN PHILOSOPHERS
## THE AESTHETICS OF COLERIDGE

Edgar Frederick Carritt, lecturer in Philosophy at University College, Oxford,

---

24. Op. cit. [13], p. 121ff.

in his *Theory of Beauty* quotes Joseph Addison former editor of *The Spectator*: 'Imagination: this faculty is pleased with Greatness, Novelty and Beauty.'[25] In the last case it is a 'secret satisfaction,' perhaps subjective in the case of colour, in 'anything that hath such a variety or regularity as may seem the effect of Design in what we call Works of Chance'. Chris Seeman reports the thought of Gareth Knight, Randel Helms, Frank Bergmann, Henry Parks who think that Tolkien took the ideas of 'secondary belief' and of 'fantasy/imagination' from Coleridge, who for his part took them from Neoplatonists like Cudworth, Plotinus and Proclus.[26] In a letter of January 1804 Coleridge writes: 'Imagination is a dim analogue of creation.'[27]

Another interesting path for the investigation of Tolkien's philosophical sources is Arthur Schopenauer's thought on Art and Music. Firstly 'Music music gives us the *Universalia ante rem*', to which we may compare the Music of the Ainur in *The Silmarillion* before the shaping of Arda. Secondly,

> If ceasing to consider the when, why and whither of things we concentrate ourselves on the what; not allowing abstract thought with its concepts to possess our consciousness, but sinking ourselves wholly in perception of the object; then we escape our individuality and will, and continue to exist only as the pure mirror of the object, with which we become identified; so that what is known is no longer the particular thing, but the idea, and the knower is no longer an individual but the pure knowing subject.

Here we may compare Tolkien's idea of art as 'escapism' in *On the Fairy-Stories*. Thirdly, Art is just a 'short hour of recreation' to which we may compare Tolkien's idea of art as restorative. Fourthly 'Imagination is useful in enlarging and improving the sphere of perception, but may be used for the selfish pleasure of castle-building.'[28] In fact, Tolkien distinguishes at least two meanings of imagination, one good and one bad.

---

25. Edgar Frederick Carritt, *Theory of Beauty,* MacMillan, New York, 1914, p. 98.

26. Chris Seeman, 'Tolkien's Revision of the Romantic Tradition', in Patricia Reynolds and Glen Goodnight, eds, *Proceedings of the J.R.R Tolkien Centenary Conference*, The Tolkien Society and The Mythopoeic Press, Milton Keynes and Altadena, 1995, 73–83, p. 74.

27. S.T. Coleridge, *Letters of Samuel Taylor Coleridge*, vol. 2, ed. Ernest Hartley Coleridge, Houghton Mifflin, Boston and New York, 1895, p. 450. See also S.T. Coleridge, 'Biographia Literaria', chapter XIII, in H. J. Jackson, ed., *Samuel Taylor Coleridge*, Oxford University Press, Oxford, 1985, p. 313.

28. Schopenauer quoted in op. cit. [25].

# FRANCO MANNI

## CONNECTIONS BETWEEN TOLKIEN AND NINETEENTH-CENTURY PHILOSOPHERS AND PHILOLOGISTS

Two years ago at Modena I presented documentary evidence on eminent philologists of the nineteenth century who were influenced and inspired by philosophers. Philologists such as Grundtvig, Grimm, and Ker greatly influenced Tolkien. The philologist Ulrich von Wilamowitz writes that without the work of the philosophers Vico and Herder research into the origins of languages and the comparative analysis of parallel phenomena in humankind would not have been possible. The Danish philologist Grundtvig claimed to have been influenced by the philosophers Bruno, Schelling and Fichte. Similarly the philologist Johan C. Adelung was influenced by the philosopher Leibniz; the philologist Franz Bopp by the philosophers Friedrich Schlegel and Karl Windischmann; Jacob Grimm by the philosophers Niebhur and Savigny; Karl Lachmann by the philosopher Schleiermacher; August Schleicher by Herbert Spencer; Adolphe Pictet by Victor Cousin; W. P. Ker by Aristotle; and Werner Jager Nietzsche and Dilthey.[29] All the philosophers named, like the philologists, were also known to Tolkien.

## TOLKIEN AND R.G. COLLINGWOOD

Though he made no explicit references, Tolkien probably knew the philosopher Robin G. Collingwood, a former student of Edgar Frederick Carritt.[30] They were in the same places at similar times: both were Fellows at Pembroke College, and the latter was well known in academia and outside for his writings on the

---

29. On my debate with Tom Shippey on this topic see Roberto Arduini and Claudio Testi, eds, *Tolkien e la filosofia*, Marietti 1820, Genova-Milano, 2011, pp. 31–37.

30. See Alex Lewis, 'The Ogre in the Dungeon', *Mallorn* 47, (2009), p. 15. The author suggests that Collingwood provided Tolkien with his 1939 Andrew Lang Lecture *On Fairy Tales*. Dimitra Fimi writes: 'Tolkien certainly knew R. G. Collingwood. In p. 264, n. 1 of Collingwood's and Myres's *Roman Britain* the authors acknowledge Tolkien's help with the philology of the name Sulis. It also seems that Collingwood was the reason why Tolkien was consulted on the name 'Nodens' found in inscriptions at the excavation of Lydney Park.' (Personal correspondence, 05 April 2009). Tolkien's report is reprinted in *Tolkien Studies* 4 (2007), pp. 177–83. Douglas Anderson, referring to his 2004 unpublished lecture, writes: 'Much of the work that I did ... was on the similarity of interests between W.G. Collingwood, his son Robin, and JRRT, as well as what I could piece together of R.G. Collingwood's and J.R.R. Tolkien's friendship. I barely touched on Collingwood's view of history, and there's a lot that could be said there.' (Personal correspondence, 8 April 2009). Claudio Testi notes that in a manuscript (Bodleian Library, A 14/2, folios 28 and 29), Tolkien observes that Collingwood is writing an introduction to the history of Roman Britain. (Personal correspondence, 7 August 2009). Collingwood's recent biography mentions Tolkien three times but is vague on the relations between the two authors. See Fred Inglis, *History Man: The Life of R.G. Collingwood*, Princeton University Press, Princeton, 2009.

philosophy of history and his specific historical research regarding Roman Britain. Collingwood's most important work is *The Idea of History* (1946); its central idea is that of 're-enactment': historical thought (not only on the part of professional historians, but everyone) consists of *re-living* the thoughts of people from the past.[31] This idea of re-living inspired the two 'time travel' novels which Tolkien left unfinished: *The Lost Road* and *The Notion Club Papers*.[32] Verlyn Flieger has discovered that in these Tolkien was directly inspired by a 1927 book, *An Experiment with Time*, by the non-academic philosopher J. W. Dunne.[33] The idea of 'immortality' which it contains, and which Tolkien abandoned in his novels, features people who, in dreamlike or excited mental states, cause the reincarnation of persons or repetition of events from the past, however remote. The possible influence of Collingwood on Tolkien – if it should ever be proved – would have been different to that of Dunne,[34] because he makes reference not to excited or dreamlike states, but to fully conscious and rational, critical thought. For example, Aragorn and Arwen 're-live' the stories of Beren and Luthien inasmuch as they remember them and think about them, but they also judge them, and thus add to them in an original and creative way.

I note that Collingwood's book *Philosophy of Enchantment: Studies in Folktale, Cultural Criticism, and Anthropology*,[35] one section of which is entitled *On the Fairy Tales*, was written during the same period when Tolkien was preparing his lecture On Fairy-Stories. In his book Collingwood deals with topics such as: 1) the geographic and historical diffusion of fairy tales, 2) their relation to 'archetypes', 3) their function for adult people rather than the children. These were all themes which Tolkien also focused on in his lecture.

## TOLKIEN AND THE 'PHILOSOPHERS OF LANGUAGE'

Verlyn Flieger has underlined the correspondences between Tolkien and those philosophers of the Twenties and the Thirties such as Ernst Cassirer, Owen

---

31. R.G. Collingwood, *The Idea of History*, Oxford University Press, Oxford, 1946, pp. 215–16, 287, 300.
32. 'The Lost Road' was published in J.R.R. Tolkien, *The Lost Road and Other Writings*, ed. Christopher Tolkien, Unwin Hyman, London, 1987. 'The Notion Club Papers' was published in J.R.R. Tolkien, *Sauron Defeated*, ed. Christopher Tolkien, HarperCollins, London, 1992.
33 Verlyn Flieger, 'Tolkien's Experiment with Time: The Lost Road, "The Notion Club Papers" and J. W. Dunne', in op. cit. [26], 39–44.
34. Verlyn Flieger suggests that J.W. Dunne's 1927 book *An Experiment with Time* could have influenced Tolkien's *Lost Road* and *The Notion Club Papers*: op. cit. [34].
35. R.G. Collingwood, *Philosophy of Enchantment: Studies in Folktale, Cultural Criticism, and Anthropology*, Clarendon Press, Oxford, 2005.

# FRANCO MANNI

Barfield, Edward Sapir and Benjamin Whorf who thought that the culture and 'mind' of each Nation are embedded in its own natural language, and the speakers of that language see the World through that culture and mind. Although Flieger is aware that there is no positive documentary evidence, so far, of the direct influence of any of those thinkers on Tolkien, with the exception of Barfield.[36]

## TOLKIEN AND TWENTIETH-CENTURY IDEAS OF 'INTERPERSONAL SALVATION' AND 'PHILOSOPHY OF HISTORY'

In *LotR* the plot of the story and the characters' interpersonal relationships continually communicate and demonstrate to us how individual destinies are closely and necessarily interwoven, in life as in death; the relationship between Frodo and Sam and Gollum is a good example of this.[37] This idea of the interpersonal quality of salvation, typical of twentieth-century Christian theology – it is not a coincidence that in the letter quoted above Weisman mentioned the 'Communion of Saints' – which strongly emphasised throughout the twentieth century the biblical and patristic message of 'collective eschatology'.[38] Shippey notes that the entire story of Middle-earth is bound by a condition of interpersonality: it is like a Limbo in which the un-baptised dead await the Day of Judgement (for Tolkien, the events he narrated were set in pre-Christian times) when they will be reunited with their baptised and saved descendants.

But during the course of the twentieth century, outside of the visible churches (perhaps earlier than inside them), the widespread sensitivity of the century for 'interpersonality' was manifested in many fields: in political movements, pedagogy, clinical psychology, historiographical research and philosophy.

Tolkien wrote that every event had at least two aspects: one regarded the history of the individual, the other the history of the world.[39] He was concerned, at least in his fiction, with the 'history of the world'. In the aftermath of the powerful

---

36. Op. cit. [29], pp. 68–70.

37. Alliances and groups are necessities of life, couples survive and those alone die, because individuals are overcome by hubris, 'la solitude conduit avec certitude à la mort'. Vincent Ferré, *Tolkien: sur les rivages de la terre du milieu,* Christian Bourgois Éditeur, Paris, 2001, pp. 197–99. Anne Mathie observes: 'This fertility, this willingness to pass life on to a new generation rather than grasping for "endless life unchanging" is the Hobbits great strength, as it should likewise be mankind's proper strength. It makes them at once humbler than immortals, since they place less confidence in their own individual abilities, and more hopeful, since their own individual defeats are not the end of everything.'(Mathie, op. cit. [17]).

38. For a synthesis of this development see Ruiz de la Peña, *La otra dimensiòn. Escatologìa cristiana*, EAPSA, Madrid, 1981, chapters 5–8 and 11.

39. Op. cit. [1], Letter 181, p. 233. For a longer analysis of this topic, see Franco Manni, 'Eulogy of Finitude', in op. cit. [18], 5–38, pp. 23–32.

historical philosophies of the nineteenth century (Hegelian, Marxist, Positivist), Tolkien found himself living in a period – the first half of the twentieth century – in which the nineteenth-century lesson was repeated and over-abundantly varied: several classical and highly influential philosophies of history such as those of Oswald Spengler,[40] and Arnold Toynbee,[41] together with others, intellectualist and extravagant such as that of Edmund Husserl,[42] or terrible and obscure such as that of Alfred Rosenberg.[43] All somewhat pessimistic, perhaps not surprisingly given what was happening and was about to happen in Europe and the rest of the world.[44] After the Second World War, this surfeit of philosophies of history contracted and disappeared. The appalling drama proved to be a decisive factor in the selection from and development of the nineteenth-century inheritance, which (like many others) was no longer considered and events took a different turn.

Tolkien's 'philosophy of history' is not pessimistic as were those in fashion at the time.[45] In the Age of Men Tolkien does express melancholy for the disappearance of Elvish Beauty, but not moral or other kinds of decadence. When he speaks of the fading of Elvish Beauty (or of the Ents) and the coming of the Age of Men, Tolkien – unlike Spengler, Rosenberg or Husserl – does not give us message of 'decadence', but instead one of 'finiteness'. His refusal to add to the already numerous 'twilights of the West' then in vogue is made explicit, for

---

40. Oswald Spengler, *Der Untergang des Abendlandes* (The Decline of West), Verlag Braumüller, Wien, 1918. See also Oswald Spengler, *The Decline of the West*, ed. Arthur Helps and Helmut Werner, trans. Charles F. Atkinson, Oxford University Press, New York, 1991.

41. Arnold Toynbee, *A Study of History*, 12 vols, Oxford University Press, Oxford, 1934–1961.

42. Edmund Husserl, 'Die Philosophie in der Krisis der europäischen Menschheit' (Philosophy and the Crisis of European Man), a lecture delivered by Husserl in Vienna during May 1935. See Edmund Husserl, *Phenomenology and the Crisis of Philosophy*, ed. and trans. by Quentin Lauer, Harper Torch Books, 1965.

43. Alfred Rosenberg, *Der Mythus des 20 Jahrhunderts* (The Myth of the Twentieth Century), Hoheneichen-Verlag, München, 1934. For an interesting comparison between Rosenberg's philosophy of history and Tolkien's, see Christine Chism, 'Middle-earth, the Middle Ages, and the Aryan nation: myth and history in World War II', in Chance, op. cit. [23], 63–92, pp. 72–75.

44. Michael Drout writes: 'The relationship between Tolkien and philosophers has not been explored as much as it should be (the focus has been almost entirely on Theologians), so your research is important. Unfortunately, I cannot help very much. There have been rumours over the years that a catalogue of Tolkien's personal library would be published, but that has not yet happened. I don't know of any direct evidence, but I would be shocked if he didn't know something about Spengler and Toynbee, but proving it is another story.' (Personal correspondence, 22 March 2009.)

45. Even less pessimistic than that of Christopher Dawson. Tolkien several times quotes Dawson. The relation between the two authors is underlined in Bradley J. Birzer, *J.R.R. Tolkien's Sanctifying Myth: Understanding Middle-earth*, Intercollegiate Studies Institute, Wilmington DE 2002; and by Gregory Bassham (personal correspondence, 15 June 2009).

# FRANCO MANNI

example, in the dialogue between Gimli and Legolas at Minas Tirith.

## THE WORD 'PHILOSOPHY' (ALMOST)
## OMITTED IN PUBLISHED WRITINGS

Tolkien never uses the word 'philosophy' in his fiction and amongst other published works only thrice in the lecture *On Fairy Stories* and thrice in the lecture on *Beowulf*. Thereafter this lexical ostracism – consciously wished for, I think - continues into Tolkien's scholars. In the two massive, erudite and up-to-date Tolkien encyclopedias by Drout and by Scull and Hammond there is no place – in the midst of hundreds of others – for the entry *Philosophy*. With regard to writings not intended for publication, this word appears a few times in his letters, usually as a synonym for 'religion',[46] or with the meaning of generalised 'theory',[47] but also at times in more strict sense, such as when he writes that the word 'Ent' has slightly philosophical overtones, or that he does not believe that there can be philosophers able to deny the possibility of reincarnation,[48] or when he explains the significance of the Ring of Power, or speaks of the moral corruption present in Eddison's novels.[49] Sometimes though, philosophy as rational knowledge is explicitly distinguished from religion, e.g. when he says that the hobbits might have misunderstood Aragorn's miraculous healings because of their lack of philosophical and scientific knowledge, or when he makes it clear that although religion had a minor role among the Faithful of Númenor the same could not be said regarding philosophy and metaphysics, or when he observed that in *LotR* evil and falsity are represented mythically whereas good and truth are represented in a fashion more 'historical and philosophical' than 'religious'.[50] The 'home' of philosophy is, according to him, 'in ancient Greece',[51] and not in Germany, which he considered 'home' of philology,[52] for the reason that 'southern' mythology rests on deeper foundations than that from the north, and so must lead 'either to philosophy or anarchy'.[53] In the aborted *The*

---

46. Op. cit. [1], Letters 26, 49, 153, 156, 183.

47. Op. cit. [1], Letters 15, 49, 52.

48. Op. cit. [1], Letter 153, p. 189 (implicitly showing, it seems to me, that he knew some of them).

49. Op. cit. [1], Letters 157, 211, 199.

50. Op. cit. [1], Letters 155, 84, 156: in the latter, it is interesting to note that 'religion' is equivalent to 'myth' ('story', in Greek) and to tangible 'representativeness'. Tolkien also says this more than once in his work *On Fairy-stories* (but without ever giving explanations).

51. Op. cit. [1], Letter 84.

52. See Tom Shippey, *Goths and Huns in Roots and Branches, Selected Papers on Tolkien*, Walking Tree Press, Zurich and Berne, 2007, pp. 114–36.

53. J.R.R. Tolkien, 'Beowulf: the Monsters and the Critics', in Christopher Tolkien, ed., *The*

*Notion Club Papers* the word appears twice: once in reference to the character Rupert Dolbear (who is also interested in psychoanalysis and often falls asleep during discussions) and once in reference to the character Michael Ramer (a philologist alter-ego of Tolkien), who says that he is *not* a philosopher, but rather an 'experimenter'.[54]

Several Tolkien scholars agree that it is not possible to find traces of Tolkien's philosophical readings. Patrick Curry's opinion is similar (though not identical) to mine: 'I have never heard from anyone that Tolkien ever read any philosophy, I'm afraid; and that is my subjective impression too. If you are looking for a direct connection, I think you will be disappointed. (Of course, his work has deeply philosophical implications, but that's another matter)'.[55] John Garth says: 'I've seen none of these philosophers' names in Tolkien's writings, published or unpublished; I've never seen a philosophical title among lists of his books; and I can't think of any of his papers at the Bodleian which have a philosophical bent. The closest, I suppose, is *On Fairy-stories*'.[56] Similarly Dimitra Fimi: 'I have looked at Tolkien's books in the Bodleian and in the English Faculty at Oxford, but I cannot remember any philosophy books within them (although I was looking for different things so I might have overlooked them)'.[57] And I could see the same myself, when last August I went to consult manuscripts and books in both these libraries.

These non-occurrences of the names of philosophers,[58] or the word 'philosophy', bring to mind Carpenter's reconstruction of a typical Inklings' session.[59] When they are together, the friends talk of many things: the war under way, *LotR*, the philosophy of history, literary criticism, Shakespeare, religion, ethics. But when they refer to thinkers by name, they do so polemically, disparaging contemporary thought.[60] They also make me think of Tom Shippey – an intellectual often identified with his hero Tolkien – who says he knows nothing of philosophy, but also demonstrates a certain (latent) polemical attitude towards

---

*Monsters and the Critics and other Essays*, George Allen & Unwin, London, 1983, 5–48.

54. Tolkien, *Sauron Defeated*, op. cit. [1], pp. 159, 178.

55. Personal correspondence, 21 March 2009.

56. Personal correspondence, 26 March 2009.

57. Personal correspondence, 5 May 2009.

58. Wholly deliberate, I think; for example, in the preparatory versions of the lecture *On the Fairy Stories* Tolkien writes the name of Carl Gustav Jung, while in the definitive version he only quotes the word 'archetype' but omits the name of the psychiatrist. See Verlyn Flieger and Douglas A. Anderson, eds, *Tolkien on Fairy Stories*, HarperCollins, London, 2008, pp. 129, 170, 307.

59. Set in Magdalene College in the evening at a date between autumn 1940 and December 1941. See op. cit. [7].

60. They are against Karl Marx and the theologian Karl Barth.

it, calling philologists 'tough minded' and philosophers 'tender minded'.[61] Perhaps both Tolkien and Shippey were thinking of, on one hand, the abstruse and often essentially empty philosophy of nineteenth-century German idealism and twentieth-century French and German existentialism and, on the other, the differently abstruse and differently empty 'Oxbridge Analytical Philosophy' which was already strong before the Second World War and afterwards dominant in the English-speaking academic world.[62] In Tolkien we find respect (though not *declared* love) for ancient and medieval philosophy, together with scepticism or at least lack of interest regarding modern and contemporary philosophy.

And maybe this happened – as I have hinted – because of social context and interpersonal relations. Shippey ponders: 'philosophy – why does Tolkien not mention it? Unlike Lewis he never took the philosophy part of the Oxford Classics course'. Maybe he felt that he was professionally ill-equipped in an Oxford environment full of philosophers. 'Maybe he felt that that was Lewis's business. Or he could just have decided to keep his thoughts to himself.'[63] Ross Smith writes that even if there are no mentions of Tolkien on analytical philosophy, Tolkien was nevertheless a close friend of C.S. Lewis who opposed it'.[64]

## TOLKIEN AS 'NATIONALIST', PHILOLOGIST AND FRIEND OF THE PHILOSOPHER C.S. LEWIS

In my opinion Tolkien was not significantly influenced by the philosophers of his times: neither those associated with Oxford Idealism: J.A. Smith, E.F. Carritt, F.H. Bradley, H.H. Joachim, B. Bosanquet,[65] nor with the Oxbridge Realists and

---

61. Personal communication with Shippey.

62. See Shippey's critical comment concerning the Anglo-American analytical philosopher G. E. Moore in Tom Shippey, *Tolkien: Author of the Century*, HarperCollins, London, 2000, p. 158, and also this personal experience: 'I intervened in an interview among philosophers at Oxford once, querying a point about language — the thesis was about the distinction in Augustine between "God" and "a god", and I said "but Augustine wrote in Latin, where there is no such distinction. How can you tell?" — and this caused a most violent inter-college and inter-disciplinary dispute. W.H. Auden, Tolkien's friend, wrote a sarcastic verse about Oxford philosophers' (personal correspondence, 14 July 2009).

63. Op. cit.

64. Ross Smith, *Inside Language: Linguistic and Aesthetic Theory in Tolkien*, Walking Tree Press, Zollikofen, 2007, pp. 140–41.

65. Tolkien may have known Croce's *Aesthetics* via Collingwood and Lewis. While criticising Chambers, Tolkien refutes the theory of 'literary genres' much as Croce did in his *Aesthetics*. See Michael Drout, ed., *J.R.R. Tolkien Beowulf and the Critics*, Arizone Center for Medieval and Renaissance Studies, Tempe, 2002, pp. 90, 107, 109. Tolkien had notice as well of the Croce-Collingwood idea of 're-enactment'. In 1925 Collingwood read Croce's *Autobiography*

Logical Positivists: B. Russell, G.M. Moore, L. Wittgenstein, G. Ryle, A.J. Ayer.[66] I agree with Shippey's assessment that Tolkien may well have had an adversarial relationship with the Oxford philosophers of his time (as C.S. Lewis did), and he may also not have wished to engage in any kind of argument with them, since he had not had any training in philosophy (in this case, unlike Lewis). He may have consciously decided to abstain from an argument he knew he could not win.[67]

Shippey reports Lewis's opinion that Tolkien was a man who could not be influenced.[68] But Lewis also said that after a criticism Tolkien would rewrite everything over again, as when he discarded the *Epilogue of the LotR* because it was condemned by others,[69] and this *is* an influence. Shippey says concerning Collingwood: 'Tolkien was often annoyed by people who shared his interests, but did not see them in quite the same way that he did'.[70] But Shippey himself in *Roots and Branches* documents many of Wagner's influences on Tolkien, even though the final and decisive moral interpretation of those ideas was absolutely different. Tolkien simply *erases* the references as he erased the name of Jung from the first draft of the *On Fairy Stories* lecture. We may describe this habit of consciously dropping off the references to names of unwelcome authors as a 'question of personality'.

In what way was this personality? I attempt some answers. Tolkien was a 'nationalist': in personal correspondence Shippey has written that: 'we'll just say that Tolkien's conviction that English tradition had been slighted, marginalised, and largely lost, is no more than the truth.... As for not naming philosophers he did read and know, Boethius, Plato etc.... maybe this is part of his anti-Classical bias. We know that Tolkien read Latin very well and Greek quite well, but he rarely mentions these either, though when you look, the connections are often

---

where he could find that 'Croce filled his unslaked religious longings by a saturation in the great philosophers and an understanding that cannot be acquired by reading their books but only re-enacting their mental drama in one's own person, under the stimulus of actual life'. This, Inglis thinks, is the first sighting of Collingwood's key term: the 're-enactment', see Inglis, op. cit. [30], p. 121.

66. This second group was explicitly disliked by Lewis: '*apud Cantabrigienses communistes rariores sunt et pestipheri philosophi quos logicales positivistos vocamus haud aeque pollent quam apud nostros [Oxonienses]*', (Letter to Don Giovanni Calabria, 5 December 1954, in C.S. Lewis, *Collected Letters*, vol. 3: *Narnia, Cambridge and Joy, 1950–1963*, ed. Walter Hooper, HarperCollins, London, 2006, p. 539.); 'don't imagine that the Logical Positivist menace is over. To me it seems that the apologetic position has never in my life been worse than it is now. At the Socratic the enemy often wipe the floor with us. *Quousque domine?*', (Letter to Dom Bede Griffiths, 22 April 1954, in *Collected Letters*, vol. 3, p. 462).

67. Personal correspondence, 21 August 2009.

68. Op. cit. [29], p. 28.

69. Op. cit. [1], Letter 144.

70. See, for example, op. cit. [1], Letter 26.

quite clear. But Tolkien always felt he was a spokesman for the neglected native tradition – not that England produced any early native philosophers other than King Alfred as King Alfred's Boethius seems to me to be more realistic an interpreter of Boethius.' Tolkien himself writes: 'Grundtvig's emendations [to *Beowulf*] seemed almost like sorcery to those unable to swallow the notion that other languages than Latin and Greek and Hebrew had any shape or rules.'[71] Shippey maintains: 'I will just say that, and of course more English, than Boethius's Boethius.'[72] I would add that King Alfred translated a philosopher who did not belong to the English tradition.

Tolkien was a philologist, but he was a 'Germanistic' philologist, not a Classicist one. He wrote that 'Greek Gods are timeless and do not know or fear death. Such beliefs may hold promise of a profounder thought, so that the Greeks could make philosophy, but the Germanic North created specially the *hero*'.[73] So Tolkien as a '*Germanistik*' scholar could more easily focus on, quote from, and make bibliographical references to heroism rather than philosophy. He was also a Christian philologist who had to defend his point of view in the University Departments, and in literary criticism from the fashionable literati who were both Modernist in their poetics and atheist in their philosophy. His Inkling friend Lewis wrote criticising the criticism by Croce, Carritt and Arnold that: 'culture is the storehouse of the best sub-Christian values'.[74] Tolkien was a Christian philologist when not only the literati, but also most of philosophers of his time, were atheist. His mode of apologetics (different from Lewis's mode) was perhaps to avoid surrendering to the 'enemy' by the tactic of not naming him. If this was not the case, then it is hard to explain why Tolkien mentions Dawson, a popular inter-War Catholic writer, in *On Fairy Stories*, but not Spengler and Toynbee though all of them were philosophers of history, but only the first was a committed Christian.

Tolkien was a philologist who was also a writer of fiction. As a philologist he was not so concerned with philosophical conceptualisations (unlike other more speculative philologists such as Karl Lachmann or Ferdinand De Saussure). He was instead more concerned with inspirations for poetical images. He wrote that 'History, Philology, Archaeology, Folk-lore were the Fairy-godmothers at the Christening: few [critics of *Beowulf*] thought to invite Poetry'.[75] And Lewis wrote that:

---

71. Drout, op. cit. [65], p. 99.
72. Op. cit. [29], p. 28.
73. Drout, op. cit. [65], p. 128.
74. Letter to Warren Lewis, 28 April 1940, in C.S. Lewis, *Collected Letters*, vol. 2: *Books, Broadcasts, and the War 1931–1949*, ed. Walter Hooper, HarperCollins, London, 2004, 401–406.
75. Drout, op. cit. [65], p. 80.

# TOLKIEN VS THE HISTORY OF PHILOSOPHY

Tolkien thinks that is impossible to invent a language without inventing a mythology, and that the philologist Müller was wrong in calling mythology a disease of language, while it would be truer to say that language was a disease of mythology. I do not understand that.[76]

Finally, I present the hypothesis that C.S. Lewis did influence Tolkien during the twenty years of their close friendship. If this is at least partly true it would be worth knowing something about Lewis as a philosopher.[77] In his letters, Lewis makes references to almost all the great names of the history of philosophy from Plato, Augustine and Aquinas, to Descartes, Locke, Hegel, Nietzsche, Kant, and others. But, more specifically, he was a sort of Aristotelian. Throughout his adult life he refers to Aristotle's works. He writes: 'I fear that Plato thought the concrete flesh and grass bad, and have no doubts he was wrong'.[78] He did not consider all paganism pantheistic because of the 'almost miraculous avoidance of the Pantheistic swamp by Plato and (still more) Aristotle'.[79] He declared: 'I appear to be a Thomist because I am often (especially on ethics) following Aristotle where Aquinas is also following Aristotle.' He qualified this when he remarked: 'many people think I'm being Thomistic where I'm really being Aristotelian.'[80]

But Lewis's philosophers were *not* his contemporaries. In his letters there are *many* references to Aquinas, but *no* references to Wittgenstein, Russell or A.J. Ayer; almost nothing referring to Gilbert Ryle, nothing on the *Wienerkreis*, nothing on Dewey. Writing on J.A. Smith's death, he writes that he was an honest man but not a believer, and says nothing on his philosophical thought; the same position was held by Lewis on Carritt, Bradley, Joachim, Collingwood and Bosanquet and the other Oxford and Cambridge philosophers whom he almost does not mention in his letters.

## SOME CONCLUSIONS

Summing up what I have said concerning Tolkien and the History of Philosophy: a) I am quite sure he read (at least to some extent) Plato, Aristotle, Augustine,

---

76. Letter to William Kinter, 24 September, 1951, op. cit. [66], p. 140.

77. Vague analogies only are presented in David Baggett, Gary Habermas and Jerry Walls, eds, *C.S. Lewis as Philosopher: Truth, Goodness, Beauty*, InterVarsity Press Academic, Downers Grove IL, 2008.

78. Letter to Dom Bede Griffiths, 17 January 1940, op. cit. [75], pp. 325–27.

79. Letter to Dom Bede Griffiths, 15 April 1947, op. cit. [75], p. 770.

80. Letter to Corbin Carnell, 13 October 1958 op. cit. [66], p. 980; Letter to Corbin Carnell, 10 December 1958, op. cit. [66], p. 995.

Boethius, Aquinas; b) I present the hypothesis that he read (at least to some extent) Schlegel, Schopenauer, Croce, Collingwood, Freud, Spengler and – though I admit it is improbable – Vico;[81] c) I am sure that the ideas of Romanticist philosophers such as Schlegel, Herder, Schleiermacher, Fichte, Schelling and Hegel and the ideas of Positivist philosophers such as Comte and Spencer come to Tolkien's attention, however indirectly, through the great nineteenth-century philologists who in some cases knew those earlier philosophers well; d) I think that Tolkien had notice – from Lewis and other scholars of his acquaintance – of the ideas of the philosophers of his times: the Idealists, the Logical Positivists, and Existentialists. However, I think that Tolkien was not interested in them in the same way as Lewis and the other Inklings.

So, I was looking for philosophical sources. Shippey has quoted Tolkien's metaphor of the soup: 'He was rejecting the utility of source-study, and as he often did, overstating his case to make a point. I think source-study can be useful, and that philosophers were no doubt among Tolkien's sources. But Tolkien was right in that it is very difficult to analyse soup into its component parts'.[82] I agree with Shippey in saying it is very difficult, but I want to quote Tolkien's other famous statement in *The Monsters* where he writes:

> even the man's own descendants were heard to murmur: "He is such an odd fellow! Imagine his using these old stones just to build a nonsensical tower! Why did not he restore the old house? He had no sense of proportion." But from the top of that tower the man had been able to look out upon the sea.

I think here Tolkien criticises the 'Philological Criticism'[83] which focuses just on sources and is not interested in the creative synthesis of them made by the

---

81. Marek Ozievicz writes that, to his knowledge, that Tolkien did not read Vico because Vico's *New Science* was translated in English only in 1948: Marek Ozievicz, 'From Vico to Tolkien', in S. Caldecott and T. Honegger, eds, *Tolkien's Lord of the Rings: Sources and Inspirations*, Walking Tree Publishers, Zurich and Jena, 2008, 113–36. But the English translation by R.G. Collingwood of Croce's *The Philosophy of G.B. Vico* was published in 1913. In his paper Ozievicz presents several similarities and differences between Vico and Tolkien, but he never mentions that while Vico discussed and was discussed by other philosophers this was not the case with Tolkien.
82. Op. cit. [29], p. 41.
83. While in the two first drafts of the lecture as we can read in Tolkien's *Beowulf* (Drout, op. cit. [66]): 'not the tower, but the "rock garden" and the "beautiful commonplace flowers"), I fancy that Tolkien deals more with 'Literary Criticism' *à la* T.S. Eliot – the use of Ancient Cultural Sources has to be done with the purpose of displaying the author's refined culture, not *just as means* to display the commonplace beautiful flowers – i.e. the perennial Moral Values of *all* Men– *à la* Inklings.

individual work of art, but – in the meanwhile – Tolkien is saying also that without the old stones (with their carvings and inscriptions) the man could not reach those heights.

# 'Tolkien's Boethius, Alfred's Boethius'

# Gerard Hynes

*King Alfred's Boethius is a relatively neglected text among the Old English sources of Tolkien's Legendarium. This paper attempts to highlight the importance of Alfred's influence and argue that Tolkien's thought is not so much Boethian as Alfredian and argues that Tolkien's thought, as expressed in his Legendarium, reflects the Old English text more than its Latin original, revealing Tolkien's indebtedness to the peculiar ethical and philosophic shifts of the Old English Boethius.*

This paper first situates the Old English Boethius in the context of Tolkien's academic work. It then examines Alfred's influence on Tolkien's presentation of the issues of providence, fate and free will in light of his recently published notes on 'Fate and Free Will' in *Tolkien Studies*. The effect on Tolkien of Alfred's innovative reactions to the Boethian text regarding the integration of public and private morality will be examined. This will lead to the question of the nature of evil, where my study will attempt to complement the work of Tom Shippey, one of the few Tolkien scholars to study the Old English Boethius at length.

The interaction of providence, fate and free will has been a contentious and fruitful subject for Tolkien scholarship.[1] The debate about these three topics has received impetus in recent years by the publication of Tolkien's notes on the word 'fate' as it appears in Quenya and Sindarin.[2] In these notes, from 1968 or later, Tolkien considered the implications of the connection between the

---

1. The primary works include: Verlyn Flieger, *Splintered Light: Logos and Language in Tolkien's World*, rev. edn, Kent State University Press, Kent OH, 2002; Verlyn Flieger, 'The Music and the Task: Fate and Free Will in Middle-earth, *Tolkien Studies* 6 (2009), 151–81; Thomas Fornet-Ponse, '"Strange and Free" – On Some Aspects of the Nature of Elves and Men', *Tolkien Studies* 7 (2010), 67–89; Kathleen E. Dubs, 'Providence. Fate and Chance: Boethian Philosophy in *The Lord of the Rings*', in Jane Chance, ed., *Tolkien and the Invention of Myth: A Reader*, University Press of Kentucky, Lexington, 2004, 133–44; Troels Forchhammer, 'Voices of a Music – Models of Free Will in Tolkien's Middle-earth', in Christopher Kreuzer, ed., *Freedom, Fate and Choice in Middle-earth: Proceedings of the 21st Tolkien Society Seminar*, The Tolkien Society, Whitton, 2012, 10–25; 'Free Will and Fate', in Christina Scull and Wayne G. Hammond, eds, *The J.R.R Tolkien Companion and Guide*, vol. 2: *Reader's Guide*, HarperCollins, London, 2006, 324–33.
2. J.R.R. Tolkien, 'Fate and Free Will', ed. Carl F. Hostetter, Tolkien Studies 6 (2009), pp. 183–88

Quenyan words *ambar* 'world' and *umbar* 'fate' through a commentary on their Primitive Eldarin base MBAR. From MBAR, meaning 'settle, establish' and hence 'settlement, home', derive Quenyan *ambar* and Sindarin *amar* meaning 'world', 'the great habitation'. Tolkien insisted that this word's full implications could not be understood without reference to Elven views concerning 'fate' and 'free will'.[3] The connection between the physical world and fate is apparent from Tolkien's gloss on Sindarin *amarth* 'fate'. He wrote that the basic sense of MBAR was 'permanent establishment/order', hence 'fate', that is to say:

> The order and conditions of the physical world (or of Eä in general) as far as established and preordained at Creation, and that part of this ordained order which affected an individual with a will, as being immutable by his personal will.[4]

Here fate is presented primarily as the constraints placed upon the actions of creatures by the physical limitations of the world in which they act. *Umbar* 'fate' was, to the Elves, clearly related to *mbar'ta* 'permanent establishment' as they conceived of fate as primarily a 'physical obstacle to the will'.[5] Tolkien elaborates with the example of a man being 'fated' to meet an enemy at a certain time and place but not 'fated' to speak to him with hatred or to kill him. The meeting of two persons has a complex series of events leading up to it, including the intervention of 'will'. Tolkien comments, however,

> [T]he Eldar held that only those efforts of 'will' were 'free' which were dedicated to a fully *aware purpose*.... His setting-out may have been a free decision, to achieve some object, but his actual course was largely under *physical* direction – and it *might have* led to/or missed a meeting of importance. It was this aspect of "chance" that was included in *umbar*.[6]

We can, in a sense, be both fated and free at the same time. The word 'fate' describes those things which influence our actions but are outside our control – physics, climate, topography, the circumstances of time and place. These circumstances can incline you to will something but your conscious mind has the power and freedom to overrule this. Later, when discussing fate, Tolkien appears

---

3. Op. cit. p. 183.
4. Op. cit. p. 184. Cf. Quenyan *ambarmenie* 'the way of the world', 'the fixed, and by 'creatures' unalterable. conditions in which they lived.' (op. cit., p. 183).
5. Op. cit. p. 185.
6. Op. cit.

to equate it with providence:

> *if* the downfall of Sauron and the destruction of the Ring was part of Fate (or Eru's Plan) then if Bilbo had retained the Ring and refused to surrender it, some other means would have arisen by which Sauron was frustrated.[7]

Here providence makes use of our free decisions to achieve its goal. In both examples fate unavoidably influences us but does not lock the world in a deterministic stasis. Our conscious decisions give shape to our lives, beyond the power of fate.

The problem of reconciling providence and fate with human free will was acutely felt by medieval thinkers. As a medievalist, Tolkien knew, and arguably had to be influenced by the Roman statesman and philosopher Anicius Manlius Severinus Boethius (c.480–525 AD).[8] Holding high office in the afterlife of the Roman Empire (about a generation after the point where historians normally describe it as having fallen), Boethius dedicated his life to transmitting classical knowledge through translations and commentaries. He was accused of conspiring against Theodoric, the Gothic ruler of Italy, and was exiled, imprisoned, and brutally executed. During his exile he wrote the philosophic dialogue *The Consolation of Philosophy*, a work so popular it was repeatedly translated into English: by Alfred the Great, Chaucer, and Elizabeth I.[9] More important, however, than direct exposure to Boethius' Latin text may be Tolkien's familiarity with the Old English version traditionally attributed to King Alfred.[10] Less a translation than a reinterpretation of Boethius this version has its own philosophical agenda,

---

7. Op. cit.

8. The other most important authority is St Augustine of Hippo (AD 354–430), especially Book V of his *De Civitate Dei*. Augustine and Boethius are by and large in agreement on the reconciliation of providence and human free will though Augustine stresses human wills as causes present in divine foreknowledge while Boethius emphasises the relationship between temporality and eternity. See Augustine, *The City of God Against the Pagans*, ed. George William McCracken et al, 7 vols, Heinemann, London, 1957–72. *De Civitate Dei*, V. 9.

9. As C.S. Lewis put it: 'To acquire a taste for it is almost to become naturalised in the Middle Ages.' C.S. Lewis. *The Discarded Image: An Introduction to Medieval and Renaissance Literature*, Cambridge University Press, Cambridge, 2010, p. 75.

10. Excerpts of the Old English Boethius were included among the set texts for Tolkien's final English examinations. See Scull and Hammond, op. cit. [1], p. 332. So far discussion of the possible influence of the Old English Boethius on Tolkien has focused on the question of evil rather than the question of free will. See Tom Shippey, *The Road to Middle-earth*, rev. edn, HarperCollins, London, 2003, pp. 141–42; Tom Shippey, *J.R.R. Tolkien: Author of the Century*, HarperCollins, London, 2002, pp. 131–34; John Wm. Houghton and Neal K. Keesee, 'Tolkien, King Alfred, and Boethius: Platonist Views of Evil in *The Lord of the Rings*', *Tolkien Studies* 2 (2005), 131–59.

134 GERARD HYNES

as will be seen.

To begin with Boethius, he and Tolkien agree on the essentially ordered nature of the universe. Though Tolkien mentioned an aspect of 'chance' within *umbar*, in *The Lord of the Rings* characters repeatedly claim chance does not exist. Elrond says: 'You have come and are here met, in this very nick of time, by chance as it may seem. Yet it is not so. Believe rather that it is so ordered.' (*FotR*, 'The Council of Elrond', 242),[11] while Tom Bombadil says 'Just chance brought me then, if chance you call it.' (*FotR*, 'The Old Forest', 126).[12] *LotR* is perhaps misleadingly definitive in these statements. In *The Hobbit* Gandalf subsumes Bilbo's 'luck' into a hinted-at divine providence but his repeated mentioning of luck to the hobbit and the dwarves demonstrates that the concept forms part of their shared worldview.[13] The providential interpretation is given more weight by Tolkien's wisest characters but it is not the only view presented.

As such, Tolkien is in near, but not complete, alignment with the *Consolation* where Boethius argued that chance, in the sense of completely random events, cannot exist in a providential cosmology:

> Now causes are made to concur and flow together by that order which, proceeding with inevitable connexion, and coming down from its source in providence, disposes all things in their proper places and times.[14]

Tolkien does not use the word 'providence' in any of his works set in Arda, instead using 'fate' or 'doom', but in *LotR* at least depicts Middle-earth as ordered towards a providential goal, in the limited sense of the defeat of Sauron.[15]

---

11. J.R.R. Tolkien, *The Lord of the Rings*, 50th anniversary edn, HarperCollins, London, 2004. All quotations from *LotR* are taken from this edition.

12. Cf. Gandalf's comment on his meeting with Thorin Oakenshield which saved Eriador from Smaug: 'A chance-meeting. as we say in Middle-earth.' (*RotK*. 'Appendix A'), p. 1080.

13. J.R.R. Tolkien, *The Hobbit*, 5th edn, HarperCollins, London, 1995, pp. 8, 24, 31, 133, 155, 160–61, etc. A non-providential interpretation of chance is suggested by Túrin and Nienor's gravestone being named the Stone of the Hapless. Hapless, from Old Norse *happ* 'good luck', implies a belief in luck, both good and bad, on the part of at least *The Silmillion*'s hypothetical translator, if not the human poet Glirhuin himself: J.R.R. Tolkien, *The Silmarillion*, ed. Christopher Tolkien, HarperCollins, London, 1999, p. 275. See also Geir T. Zoëga, *A Concise Dictionary of Old Icelandic*, University of Toronto Press, Toronto, 2004, p. 185.

14. '*Licet igitur definire casum esse inopinatum ex confluentibus causis in his quae ob aliquid geruntur eventum; concurrere vero atque confluere causas facit ordo ille inevitabili conexione procedens. qui de providentiae fonte descendens cuncta suis locis temporibusque disponit.*' Boethius, *The Consolation of Philosophy*, V pr. 1 in Boethius, *The Theological Tractates*, trans. H.F. Stewart et al., *The Consolation of Philosophy*, trans., S.J. Tester, Heinemann, London, 1973.

15. 'Providence' was almost certainly too loaded with Christian significance to be used in

Boethius reconciled the terms 'fate' and 'providence' by explaining fate as the temporal dimension of the eternal order of providence:

> For providence is the divine reason itself, established in the highest ruler of all things, the reason which disposes all things that exist; but fate is a disposition inherent in movable things, through which providence binds all things together, each in its own proper ordering.[16]

They are distinct, but fate subsists in providence.

Boethius's attempted solution hinges on the issue of time and timelessness, arguing that since God is outside of time God never *foresees* but merely *sees*:

> God has an always eternal and present nature, then his knowledge too, surpassing all movement of time, is permanent in the simplicity of his present.... So if you should wish to consider his foreknowledge, by which he discerns all things, you will more rightly judge it to be not foreknowledge as it were of the future but knowledge of a never-passing instant.[17]

As such, God's knowledge of a creature's actions is no more determining than any other observer.[18] Although Tolkien described the issue of free will in just these terms in his essay, it is clear Boethius' solution was not satisfactory. 'But the ultimate problem of Free Will in its relation to the *Foreknowledge* of a Designer ... was of course not resolved by the Eldar.'[19] Or sadly by anyone else, including Tolkien. Though Tolkien was influenced by Boethius on providence and free will, the solution he depicts the scholars of Middle-earth proposing is quite different.

Tolkien has his hypothetical Elvish philosophers describe divine foreknowledge in terms of the relation of an author to their tale. Authors may have general designs for the plot and a clear understanding of their characters but

---

Tolkien's carefully pre-Christian world. Tolkien. like Boethius and unlike Alfred. usually eschewed explicit Christianity.

16. '*Nam providentia est ipsa illa divina ratio in summo omnium principe constituta quae cuncta disponit; fatum vero inhaerens rebus mobilibus dispositio per quam providentia suis quaeque nectit ordinibus.*' See op. cit. [14], IV pr. 6.

17. '*deo semper aeternus ac praesentarius status; scientia quoque eius omnem temporis supergressa motionem in suae manet simplicitate praesentiae infinitaque ... Itaque si praescientiam pensare veils qua cuncta dinoscit. non esse praescientiam quasi futuri sed scientiam numquam defiscientis instantiae rectius aestimabis*'. See op. cit. [14], V pr. 6.

18. Boethius can hardly be blamed for not anticipating Heisenberg.

19. Op. cit. [2], p. 186. Original emphasis.

that is the limit of their 'foreknowledge'.

> Many others have recorded the feeling that one of their actors
> 'comes alive' as it were, and does things that were not foreseen at
> all at the outset and may modify in a small or even a large way the
> process of the tale thereafter. All such unforeseen actions or events
> are, however, taken up to become integral parts of the tale when
> finally concluded. Now when that has been done, then the author's
> 'foreknowledge' is complete, and nothing can happen, be said, or
> done, that he does not know of and will/allow to be. Even so, some
> of the Eldarin philosophers ventured to say, it was with Eru.[20]

This picture of a dynamic and responsive God changing the details, but not the overall aim, of the divine plan in response to creatures' actions, marks a rupture with more than a millennium of Christian theology. Scholastic theology in particular held that God, being perfect, could not change (e.g. in response to creatures).[21] Tolkien's apparent position in his notes – God can foresee that the divine purpose will be fulfilled but leaves it to creatures to decide the particular way it is fulfilled – shows him willing to question even the highest theological authorities and places him in line with radical developments in twentieth century theology (e.g. Nelson Pike in his work *God and Timelessness*).[22] Tolkien, admittedly, surrounds the theory with qualifications; some philosophers *venture* this theory (with a connotation of risk). As radical as this position is, however, it has intriguing precedents in another reader of Boethius: King Alfred.

The Old English version of Boethius' *Consolation* deliberately refashions Boethius' text. For example, Mind, in Old English *Mod*, and Wisdom replace Boethius and Philosophy as the characters of the dialogue.[23] Alfred did, however,

---

20. Op. cit. [2], pp. 186–87.

21. E.g. Aquinas: '*Dicendum quod ex praemissis ostenditur Deum esse omnio immutabilem*' 'Our findings so far prove God to be altogether unchangeable.' Thomas Aquinas, *Summa Theologiae*, ed. Thomas Gilby, Eyre and Spottiswoode, London, 1964–74, Ia. 9.1.

22. Nelson Pike, *God and Timelessness*, Routledge and Kegan Paul, London, 1970, pp. 172–90. Also Keith Ward, *Religion and Creation*, Clarendon Press, Oxford, 1996, pp. 266–84; and Richard Swinburne, *The Coherence of Theism*, rev. edn, Clarendon Press, Oxford, 1995, pp. 177–83, and 217–34.

23. See Malcolm Godden and Susan Irvin, eds, *The Old English Boethius: An Edition of the Old English Version of Boethius' De Consolatione Philosophiae*, 2 vols, Oxford University Press, Oxford, 2009, vol. 1, pp. 50–79, 140–51. See F. Anne Payne, *King Alfred and Boethius: An analysis of the Old English version of the 'Consolation of Philosophy'*, University of Wisconsin Press, Madison WI, 1968, for the classic argument for Alfred's intentional changes. The question of whether Alfred actually was the author of the Old English Boethius is not important to the argument of this paper.

# BOETHIUS

retain Boethius' temporal distinction between providence, *foreðonc*, and fate, *wyrd*. Alfred writes: 'But that which we call God's providence [*foreðonc*] and his far-seeing, that exists for the time it is there in his mind, before it is effected, while it is thought, but after it is effected then we call it fate [*wyrd*].'[24] (I should stress that *wyrd* is a word which should really be left untranslated as it does not have any close equivalent in modern English. It could mean anything from 'fate' to 'circumstances').[25] Alfred departs from Boethius by introducing a distinction between what God ordains *must* happen and what God merely knows *can* happen, but leaves open to change.

> It does not all have to happen without change, but some of it must happen without change, that is, that which is necessary for us and is his will. But some of it is so conditioned that there is no necessity for it, and yet it does no harm if it happens, and there is no harm if it does not happen.[26]

This marks a real loosening of the rigid causality of Boethius' thought and addresses providence in terms more in line with Tolkien's notes.

While he asserted its stable basis in God's providence, Alfred also acknowledged that *wyrd* appears mutable and unreliable. Indeed his choice of words emphasises *wyrd*'s changeability. Alfred usually translated *fortuna* as *wyrd* or *gesæld*, but distinguished between *gesæld* as 'prosperity, good fortune' and *wyrd* as the mutable bestower of both prosperity and adversity.[27] But Alfred also used *wyrd* as the exclusive translation of *fatum* to carry the sense 'fate', a subset of providence. This maintains a clear connection between our changeable experience of fortune and misfortune and the ultimate control and order of divine providence; *wyrd* serves foreðonc, perhaps accounting for the apparent examples

---

24. '*Ac þæt þætte we hata∂ Godes foreðonc and his foresceawung. þæt bi∂ þa hwile þe hit þærmid bi∂ on his mode. ærþam ∂e hit gefremed weor∂e. þa hwile þe hit geþoht bi∂. ac si∂∂an hit fullfremed bi∂. þonne hata∂ we hit wyrd.*' Godden and Irvin, op. cit. [23], vol. 2, ch. 39.

25. 'Fate' is the most common translation of *wyrd*. but by no means an exact fit. See e.g. Stanley, *The Search for Anglo-Saxon Paganism*. D.S. Brewer, Cambridge, 1975, for the highly debated nature of *wyrd*.

26. '*Ne þearf hit no eall gewior∂on unawendenlice; ac sum hit sceall wyrþan unawendenlice. þæt bi∂ þætte ure nydþearf bi∂ and his willa bi∂. Ac hit is sum swa gerad þæt his nis nan neodþearf. and þeah ne dera∂ no þeah hit gewior∂e. ne nan hearm ne bi∂ þeah hit no ne gewir∂e.*' See op. cit. [24], ch. 41.

27. See op. cit. [24], vol.1, p. 77. 'Would you not have paid for that when you had most felicity [*þa þu gesælgost wære*] and thought that fate [*wyrd*] went wholly with your desires?' '*Hu woldest þu nu gebycggan þa þu gesælgost wære and þe þuhte þæt seo wyrd swi∂ost on þinne willan wode?*' Op. cit. [24], vol. 2, ch. 20.

## GERARD HYNES

of 'chance' that can be seen even in a providential cosmology.

Regarding human freedom outside the compulsion of providence, Alfred has Wisdom state: 'He who has reason can judge and distinguish what he ought to desire and what he ought to shun, and every man has the freedom that he knows what he desires and what he does not desire.'[28] If this appears to limit freedom to volition rather than action, Wisdom also says: 'If they then wish to take the middle way [between prosperity and misfortune], then they must themselves moderate the pleasant and carefree *wyrd* for themselves. Then God will moderate the adverse *wyrd* both in this world and in the one to come.'[29] God helps those who help themselves, as it were. Far from being unalterable, a person can change *wyrd* as ill fortune by living with moderation when faced with good fortune. Control of ourselves allows us to change our circumstances.

Anne Payne has described Alfred's changes to the *Consolation* as Alfred replacing a theory of order with a theory of freedom.[30] One subtle but very important change occurs in Alfred's depiction of the events leading up to Boethius' imprisonment. Boethius had stressed his innocence of any plot against Theodoric while Alfred has Boethius explicitly strive to free his country form the Gothic occupiers.[31] Though both writers were concerned with the challenge divine providence poses to human freedom, their different emphases can be seen from how they phrase this concern. Boethius asks: 'is there any freedom for our judgement or does the fatal chain also constrain the motion of human minds?'[32] Alfred's *Mod* asks 'whether we have any freedom or any power over what we do, what we do not do; whether divine predestination or Wyrd compels us to what they will.'[33]

Boethius is concerned with our freedom to think while Alfred is concerned with our freedom to act.[34] Alfred stresses that God 'rewards everyone justly

---

28. '*We habbað micelne anweald. Nis nan gesceadwis gesceaft þæt næbbe friodom. Se þe gesceadwisnesse hæfð. se mæg deman and tosceadan hwæt he wilnian sceal and hwæt he onscunian sceal. and ælc mon hæfð þone friodom þæt he wat hwæt he wile hwæt he nele.*' See op. cit. [24], ch. 40.

29. '*Ac him is þearfþæt he aredige þone midmestan weg betwyhs þære reþan wyrde and þære liþan ... forþam he ne mæg naðres ungemet adriohan. Ac hit is on hiora agnum anwealde hwaðre þara hi geceosan. Gif hi þonne þone midmestran weg aredian willað. þonne scylan hi selfe him selfum gemetgian þa wynsuman wyrde and orsorgan. Þonne gemetgað him God Þa reþan wyrde ge on Þisse worulde ge on þære toweardan*'. See op. cit. [24], ch. 40.

30. Payne, op. cit. [23], p. 16.

31. Cf. op. cit. [14], I pr. 4 and op. cit. [24], ch. 1.

32. '*Sed in hac haerentium sibi serie causarum estne ulla nostri arbitrii libertas an ipsos quoque humanorum motus animorum fatalis catena constringit?*' See op. cit. [14], V pr. 2.

33. '*hwæðer we ænigne freodom hæbben oððe ænigne anweald. hwæt we don. hwæt we ne don. þe sio godcunde foretiohhung oððe sio wyrd us need to þam hi willan.*' See op. cit. [24], ch. 40.

34. See op. cit. [30], pp. 40–41.

according to his deeds', which places a tremendous amount of autonomy and responsibility on human free will and human action.[35]

Tolkien shares Alfred's emphasis on action rather than contemplation when faced with the problem of evil. In *LotR* the figures of greatest wisdom – Gandalf, Elrond, Galadriel – do not try to convince Frodo that evil is a matter of perception; Mordor is all too real. Instead they advise the free peoples on how best they may oppose Sauron. Think of Imrahil at the last debate asking if they will 'sit like children on sand-castles when the tide is flowing?' (*RotK*, 'The Last Debate', 878). The obvious answer is 'No'. This does not mean Tolkien is a dualist who sees evil and good as independent and equal forces perpetually at war. He maintains the orthodox position that evil is deprivation. As Elrond says: 'nothing is evil in the beginning. Even Sauron was not so' (*FotR*, 'The Council of Elrond', 267). But Tolkien does emphasise the power of evil: Sauron can torture and destroy the very hills (*FotR*, 'The Council of Elrond', 266). As Tom Shippey has pointed out, the Nazgûl are perhaps the best example of Tolkien's balancing of both the emptiness and power of evil.[36] The Nazgûl paradoxically embody evil as absence; exemplified by the Witch-king's crown resting on nothing (*RotK*, 'The Siege of Gondor', 829). And yet they wield tremendous power, both physically and psychologically. Tolkien does not suggest that the power of the Nazgûl could be annulled simply by refusing to believe in their power, as a committed Boethian might have. Instead he has Éowyn and Merry actively face the Witch-king. And though the Lord of the Nazgûl's death is prophesied, and therefore implicitly fated, it is brought about by their choices, which are inherently free. This privileging of choice over fate is perhaps best put by Galadriel. She says to Frodo: 'now we have chosen, and the tides of fate are flowing' (*FotR*, 'The Mirror of Galadriel', 366). Choice comes first.

Boethius' cosmos is highly ordered, practically to the point of determinism. Middle-earth, though providential, is a more dynamic and mutable world. The metaphysics revealed in Tolkien's notes on 'Fate' appear to owe more to the Old English Boethius with its emphasis on a providence that is responsive to human choices. Similarly, Tolkien's depiction of evil is more Alfredian than Boethian.[37] While Boethius may claim that the punishment for evil is to be an evil person, and to be inherently miserable in this world, Alfred looks to God's judgement and the world to come.[38] For Boethius, evil is non-existent because everything in the cosmos is God's order; evil is a matter of perception.[39] For Alfred, evil is nothing

---

35. '*gilt ælcum be þam ryhte æfter his gewyrhtum.*' See op. cit. [24], ch. 42.

36. Shippey, *Author*, op. cit. [10], pp. 213–14.

37. See Shippey, *Road*, op. cit. [10], pp. 141–42 and op. cit. [36], pp. 134–35.

38. Cf. op. cit. [14], IV pr. iv, and op. cit. [24], ch. 39.

39. See op. cit. [14], IV pr. iv.

because it is doomed to be driven out of the kingdom of God, which, unlike this world, will last forever; evil is in the end nothing because it is being destroyed by God's providence, in part through the actions of the good.[40] Tolkien, like Alfred, emphasised freedom but linked that freedom to a responsibility to face the very real challenge of evil and, through willed effort, side with providence.

---

40. See op. cit. [24], ch. 39.

# 'Teaching Leadership and Ethics through Tolkien'

## Laura Miller-Purrenhage

*One of the growing fields of interest in academia is the relationship between leadership and ethics. Tolkien's works, particularly his Lord of the Rings trilogy and mythocosmography, The Silmarillion, afford educators and students an excellent lens through which to study these fields. This paper will discuss how these works can be used in the classroom to explore leadership and ethics. The paper will focus on course construction, methodology, and scenes and characters that yield useful analysis of this topic. The purpose of this paper will be to contribute to the growing pedagogy on leadership and ethics, and on the pedagogy that incorporates Tolkienâ's work into university study.*

Leadership and ethics is a growing field of study in academia and of particular interest at my university. The capstone course we require of all students is a seminar in leadership and ethics and the university has redesigned its student learning outcomes to include these topics. Tolkien's *Silmarillion* and *Lord of the Rings* trilogy afford educators and students an excellent lens through which to study these fields. This paper will discuss how these works can be used in the classroom to explore leadership and ethics. Particularly, the paper will focus on course construction, methodology, and scenes and characters that yield useful analysis of this topic.

Several years ago, I attended a pedagogy conference where the speaker Dr. L.Dee Fink pointed out that one of the significant problems professors have when they create their courses is that they do not start with a specific set of objectives.[1] Such an observation may seem ludicrous to the primary or secondary education teacher who has been taught from early on that goals and objectives are essential to teaching. But the university or college professor often begins with books – textbooks or, in the case of a literature professor, literature. When asked what we will teach this term, we will often rattle off that list of books and, when asked what our objectives are, we will often meet the question with a blank stare and respond, 'well, I will start with Beowulf and move chronologically up through Shakespeare'. We may add in something about improving writing and critical thinking skills. But Fink stressed the need to start one's course construction with

---

1. L.Dee Fink, 'Course Design for Higher Level Learning,' (presentation at Lilly International Conference on College Teaching, Oxford OH, 2005).

more specific thematic and skill-oriented objectives. If we shape every aspect of our course around these specific objectives, the elements of the course cohere, and analysis of the specific themes can become deeper and more nuanced throughout the term.[2]

Tolkien's work can be taught from so many different angles that one's course can become quite scattered. The abundance of scholarly work in this field attests to this fact. So when I created my course on Tolkien, I tried to structure it mainly around the themes of leadership and ethics and around the following skill sets: to improve students' leadership capabilities in groups, to improve their oral and written communication skills, to improve their abilities to closely analyse a text, and to engage in ethical arguments.

Structuring the course around leadership and ethics allowed me to focus on several sub-themes, as well as on the very important elements of the genres myth and epic. Tolkien's *Silmilarillion*, often described as a mytho-cosmography, not only details the origins of the various races and characters we encounter in the more well-known *LotR*, it provides a value system or an ethical foundation for his entire world. So when my class reads this work, we discuss the definition and function of myth, as well as the specific characteristics of Tolkien's myths and how those myths set up the ethical system of his world. *LotR*, on the other hand, possesses many of the characteristics of an epic in prose. Three of the main functions of epic are to explore leadership and/or heroism (which is a category that combines elements of leadership and ethics), the question, 'What does it mean to be human?' and the more complex concern, 'How do we live our lives, knowing that we are mortal and how would we live our lives if we were immortal?' In order to make these elements of the course clear to the students, in the opening remarks on my syllabus, I indicate that the course will explore the genres of myth and epic with those questions in mind. I then tell them that 'the main goal of this course will be to examine the ethical and social dimensions of these questions, with particular emphasis on the following:

- What is our ethical responsibility to ourselves, our community, the world community and our environment?
- What are the responsibilities of the individual when faced with a problem of global proportions and seemingly insurmountable odds?
- What makes a leader and what are his/her ethical responsibilities?
- How do we decide what we value, considering that we are mortal? What helps us uphold those values and what tempts us into abandoning them?

---

2. See also L.Dee Fink, *Creating Significant Learning Experiences: An Integrated Approach to Designing College Courses*, Jossey-Bass, San Francisco CA, 2003.

- What is the relationship between knowledge, power, righteous behaviour and unethical behaviour?

I should mention one other element of course structure. In order to meet the goals of promoting leadership and improving oral communication and close analysis skills, I make the course a seminar. At my university, seminars have an upper limit of roughly twenty students, they place more responsibility for learning on the students, and they require a more extensive project at the end of course. Methodologically, the seminar follows a discussion-format, so the professor almost never lectures and, after the third week of a ten and a half week term, the classes are entirely student-lead.

This methodology requires a certain amount of preparation and out-of-class work to be effective. Particularly, I would stress six elements of teaching student-leadership: discussion of expectations, formalised guidelines of these expectations, professor-directed support and help in class preparation, professor modeling of leadership, minimal professor intervention, and feedback. First, on either the first or second day of class, I conduct a discussion about how to make class discussions successful, and particularly stress the roles of the leaders and participants. This exercise helps students to think about their own role in creating a dynamic discussion. It also helps them see the purpose in participating, since discussions encourage students to analyse the text on their own and thus to develop their critical thinking and their oral discussion skills. It also teaches them to develop a stronger sense of responsibility for their own learning, as they cannot rely on the professor to tell them what the text means.

Second, I have students sign up to lead class in pairs and provide them with a handout that clearly explains the role of the class leaders. In addition to explaining the purpose of the assignment, I explain their responsibilities, which include: reading the assigned text for their day closely and with the course themes in mind, finding and defining three terms that students may not know, but that must be explained in order to understand the content, identifying three quotations from the reading that can spark discussion, and preparing three open-ended questions (connected to the quotations or not) that will lead to a thoughtful, in-depth discussion of the text. On this handout, I also stress that student leaders are responsible for keeping the class on-track, for involving as much of the class as possible, for asking clever and useful follow-up questions, and for providing any other information that could be useful for understanding the assigned text.

Third, I then require that students email me their outline for the class they will lead (which includes all the aforementioned elements) at least twenty-four hours in advance. I comment on their outline and usually offer advice for improved questions. This exercise helps students who have had no training as teachers learn how to run what is, in essence, a group meeting. It keeps my intervention mainly out of the classroom, but it also helps me feel more assured that the student-leaders will focus on elements of the texts I consider important. As a side note, last term, I found that I often needed to remind the students of the course themes and encourage them to think of ways to direct the conversations towards those themes. I had several students in the course who were fans of the books and they often wanted to chat about trivia or speculate about non-theme related issues (such as what Tom Bombadil is – a Valar, a Maiar, what?). So I also found myself helping student-leaders to find ways to redirect conversations when these side-tracks would occur.

Fourth, for the first three weeks of class, I modelled leadership. I prepared study questions on *The Silmarillion*, lectured on a few key issues (such as the definition of myth, the medieval concept of the music of the spheres, and the definitions of myths and various types of heroes), and modelled various ways to lead class discussion (using large groups, small groups, and media support). Fifth, during the class itself, I spoke rarely. But I will say that I noted a few typical moments where a professor's voice became crucial. For example, when a conversation had ranged over several sub-topics of a question that was asked and for many minutes, I would tie the elements of the discussion together. At other times, I found a need to elevate a discussion to point out how a plot piece that had been discussed related to a thematic element. There was a moment when my students were discussing the pros and cons of the hobbits' isolation in *LotR* as presented in *FotR*: 'Prologue', 'The Unexpected Party', and 'The Shadow of the Past', Gildor's comments in 'Three is Company', Aragorn's and Boromir's comments regarding the Shire in 'The Council of Elrond';[3] and in *RotK*, 'Homeward Bound' and 'The Scouring of the Shire'.[4] I found that I needed to intervene and ask, then, what he might be saying about isolationism versus an individual's or a country's need for involvement in the wider world. I also tended to provide commentary or even leadership when the discussions ranged towards topics students found particularly uncomfortable, such as gender and race. My point about teaching leadership, then, is this: Although providing students with an opportunity to lead class is productive, students are still too new and generally unskilled to take on the entire task of leadership. Modelling how to deal with difficult situations and when a leader should step in to a discussion is another form of teaching leadership.

Finally, as students are leading class, I take notes so that I can provide written feedback, both positive and negative, on their performance. I use a grading

---

3. J.R.R. Tolkien, *The Fellowship of the Ring*, Houghton Mifflin, Boston, 1994.
4. J.R.R. Tolkien, *The Return of the King*, Houghton Mifflin, Boston, 1994.

rubric so that I can fill most of it out during the class. The rubric includes their preparation, the quality of the questions, quotations, and definitions they provided, the effectiveness of the discussion format they chose, and their effectiveness at leading and controlling the class discussion. Overall, these six elements to teaching student-leadership are, I believe, crucial to the success of the leading class assignment since they provide a comprehensive approach.

The other assignments of the course also support the goals and objectives. In addition to the class-leadership and daily participation in discussion assignments, students are required to write a weekly journal entry, one three-page paper, one six-page paper, and one final project which requires a minimum of ten pages of writing. In the weekly journals, I ask students to choose a significant passage of their choice and analyse it in a minimum of one hundred and fifty words. Students are required to do this assignment before we discuss the text. Thus, their analytical skills are enhanced because they are analysing a passage before having the help of the professor or the class. But this assignment also helps students improve their leadership skills as it allows them to become very well prepared to speak on at least one passage in the discussion. This tends to be a particularly helpful way to encourage shy students to speak out in class.

I try to gear paper topics toward the leadership and ethics themes. In the first paper, I only require that students engage closely with the text and I ask them to use no outside resources beyond Tolkien's own writing to create an argumentative, analytical essay. At that point in the term, we have only read *The Silmarillion*, so all topics are dedicated towards this text. Some examples of topics include:

One of the main questions *The Silmarillion* poses is how and why people make unethical choices. What draws Elves, humans, or dwarves to make unethical or even evil decisions? This is a very broad topic, so I suggest that students choose one character to examine in detail to help make their case about how and why people are drawn into evil actions. Another option is to choose one way that folks are drawn into evil and demonstrate that more than one character is pulled into evil through that way, flaw, or temptation.

According to Mary Magoulick, one of the main purposes of myth is to 'help establish important values or aspects of a culture's worldview'.[5] Students are asked to closely examine one story from *The Silmarillion* and analyse how Tolkien uses it to help create the value system for his world.

Students may pick one leader in *The Silmarillion* and write an essay in which they claim that this person either is or is not an effective leader. To do so, they

---

5. Mary Magoulick, 'What Is Myth?', *Folklore Connections* <http://www.faculty.de.gcsu. edu/~mmagouli/defmyth.htm> [accessed 1 April 2012].

have to define what they think effective leadership is.

So far, these topics have been highly productive at encouraging students to delve more deeply into the themes of the course. In answer to the question regarding unethical choices, students have discussed the role of covetousness, lust for power, the misuse of gifts such as the fire of one's spirit and free will, pride, and fear. The main characters or groups they have focused on are Fëanor, Melkor, Maeglin, the Noldor who made Fëanor's oath, the Númenóreans, and anyone who came into contact with a silmaril.

The question regarding the value system Tolkien created was also answered with a broad range of responses, and many of them overlapped with the previous question. For example, some students analysed unethical choices as negative examples to demonstrate Tolkien's value system: desire for control over others is unethical, but a desire to create for the good of the whole music of Ilúvatar is good (see particularly *TSil* 'Of Aulë and Yavanna');[6] pride leads to evil ends, while humility and obedience to the Valar and Ilúvatar lead to positive outcomes (compare *TSil* 'Of the Flight of the Noldor' and 'Of the Voyage of Ëarendil and the War of Wrath'). Some focused on concepts not readily connected to the previous question, such as the importance of harmony (see *TSil* 'Ainulindalë' and 'Of the Beginning of Days'); the role of wisdom and the critical difference between it and knowledge, as seen particularly in Fëanor's and Morgoth's behaviour in the chapters just cited; and the roles of love, self-sacrifice, and patience particularly in *TSil* 'Of Beren and Luthien' and 'Of the Voyage of Ëarendil and the War of Wrath'.

In response to the question on leadership, students only focused on the characters of Fëanor, Fingolfin, Thingol and Morgoth. Interestingly, they disagreed on whether or not these leaders were effective, mainly because they were able to provide their own definition of what an effective leader is. Their definitions of effective leadership focused on the character's ability to persuade their followers to follow a specific course of action, their ability to protect their followers, their ability to reason clearly and then make rational decisions. Some required that good leaders think of the greater good of their followers versus their own wants and needs. In short, students who chose to leave ethical behavior out of their definition of effective leadership tended to argue that Fëanor and Morgoth were effective. Similarly, the role of ethics seemed to play a pivotal role in how Thingol was perceived, with some claiming that his obsession with the silmaril and his initial unwillingness to allow his daughter to make her own decisions made him an ineffective leader (see *TSil* 'Of Beren and Luthien' and 'Of the Ruin of Doriath'). Others claimed that these were small blips in an

---

6. J.R.R. Tolkien, *The Silmarillion*, ed. Christopher Tolkien, Houghton Mifflin, Boston, 2001.

otherwise positive reign. So, at this point in their early engagement with the topic of leadership, students are still struggling with what leadership is. For the purpose of this class, I do not mind that they are working out these definitions on their own and, in my responses to their papers, I ask questions to try to help them refine their ideas.

In the second paper, I asked students to write on *The Fellowship of the Ring* and the beginning of *The Two Towers*. I attempted to make the questions more difficult and asked the students to engage with ideas presented by Tolkien scholars. For example, I asked them to engage with a small part of Tolkien's *On Fairy-Stories* to discuss whether or not *FotR* does indeed contain, as Tolkein says in a letter to Sir Stanley Unwin, 'moral and religious truths'.[7] I asked that they engage Agnes Perkins' and Helen Hill's claim that *LotR* is 'a study in power',[8] and examine the relationship between power and responsibility as it is presented in *FotR*. I also asked that they examine Tom Shippey's contention in his book *The Road to Middle-earth*, that Tolkien's work reconciles a Boethian and somewhat Manichean view of evil.[9] Finally, I asked students to analyse whether or not Boromir is a tragic hero, based on the definition that a tragic hero is a good person who makes a catastrophic mistake. In response, several students chose to read the entire article or chapter from which their chosen paper topic came and thus wrote rather stunning essays. Several chose what they must have thought was an easy choice and discussed Boromir. Interestingly, those who decided he is not heroic argued that he was not inherently ethical enough or a good enough leader to be a hero – he thinks only of the good of his people, not the rest of the world, does not use wisdom to make decisions, and desires power and honor too much. But those who argued that he is a hero also argued that he was a good, ethical leader, claiming that his focus is mainly on protecting his city which, in turn, protects the rest of Middle-earth (or so he believes) and on protecting the fellowship.

The question regarding the relationship between power and responsibility probably received the most varied response. Some claimed that having any kind of power makes one responsible to use it wisely and ethically. Some claimed that one only gains power at all by accepting the responsibility for it. Others took a different approach and argued that refusing responsibility for power or refusing to use it responsibly leads to evil or unethical behaviour. Others still examined what the responsible use of power is by comparing and contrasting Gandalf and

---

7. Humphrey Carpenter, ed., *The Letters of J.R.R. Tolkien*, with the assistance of Christopher Tolkien, Houghton Mifflin, Boston, 2000, Letter 130, p. 144.

8. Agnes Perkins and Helen Hill, 'The Corruption of Power', in Jared C. Lobdell, ed., *A Tolkien Compass*, Ballantine Books, New York, 1975, 60–72, p. 60.

9. Tom Shippey, *The Road to Middle-earth*, Houghton Mifflin, Boston, 2003, pp. 140–41.

Saruman in *FotR*: 'The Council of Elrond', 'The Ring Goes South', and *TT*: 'The Voice of Saruman');[10] or Tom Bombadil and Frodo. For this it was useful to compare *FotR*: 'In the House of Tom Bombadil'; comments made about Tom Bombadil during 'The Council of Elrond'; and Frodo's willingness to carry the ring in *FotR*: 'The Shadow of the Past' and 'The Council of Elrond'. In short, for undergraduate students, these questions posed a challenge, but they were able to rise to it and, thus, increase their understanding of the topics of leadership and ethics.

For the final project of this course, I wanted to allow students to explore their analysis of the texts through either a traditional paper or a more creative route. Thus, I allowed students the option of writing a ten-page argumentative, analytical paper on the topic of their choice; or writing fan fiction that incorporated the themes we had been discussing; or using existing music to create a soundtrack for any one of the books, as long as the music explored the themes we discussed; or creating an art museum of existing pieces to explore visually the themes we discussed. The results of this assignment are too broad and varied to discuss in detail here. Instead, I want to focus on the process I used to help students create these projects, as I find that this process is what made the projects successful. First, about six weeks into the eleven week term, I gave students about ten minutes in class to brainstorm an idea with another student. I also made myself available to students who want to discuss their projects during office hours. I think that if I had time, I would require all students to discuss the project with me. In these meetings, I mainly asked questions about how students would incorporate the themes of the course. This is particularly important for those students who want to write fan-fiction, since many of them just want to write about a fun topic and are not thinking about how their story can reflect Tolkien's themes.

Seven weeks into the term, I required that students submit a project proposal, which includes their thesis, if the paper is argumentative, or the list of major themes they planned to discuss, if the project was more creative. I provided written feedback to these. Mostly, I asked questions about how they planned to explore the themes of the text, but I also helped make sure the scope of the project was feasible in the allotted time. On the last day of class, students exchanged completed projects and peer evaluated them using a detailed form that I provided. Because of the length of these projects, I have found that the peer evaluation takes at least two hours, so some of the work must be done outside of class. Students then had three to five days (depending on when our final exam is scheduled) to rewrite the project and submit it to me.

This process is so crucial to student success because it requires them to start

---

10. J.R.R. Tolkien, *The Two Towers*, Houghton Mifflin, Boston, 1994.

their projects early and to examine their ideas through the lens of several different readers and listeners. The revision process then requires that students re-engage with their work. In order to encourage full participation in all of these steps, I grade each part of the process.

Having discussed my course structure, methodology and assignments, I want to touch briefly on the characters and scenes that produce a particularly useful discussion of leadership and ethics. As Tom Shippey noted in his presentation given at the *Return of the Ring* conference in 2012, Tolkien presents a rather large variety of leaders in these books.[11] I tend to focus on Fëanor and Fingolfin in *TSil*, although I also discuss Beren, Lúthien, Morgoth, and Manwë. In *LotR*, I tend to focus on the comparison of the leadership styles. In *FotR*, I mainly study Gandalf, Aragorn and Boromir and particularly like to focus on their behaviour before, during, and right after the Mines of Moria. In *TT*, I focus on Aragorn's development, Théoden, Gandalf and Saruman. In *RotK*, I examine Denethor, Théoden, Aragorn, and Faramir. I find that studying the way that Denethor and Théoden treat Pippin and Merry is particularly enlightening, but I also recommend looking at the way the two men muster and treat their troops, how they prepare their armies for war, and how they interact with Gandalf and their relatives (see particularly *RotK*: 'Minas Tirith', 'The Muster of Rohan', 'The Siege of Gondor', 'The Ride of the Rohirrim', 'The Battle of the Pelennor Fields', and 'The Pyre of Denethor'). The films have tended to skew student opinion of Denethor in a very negative direction, so examining his character in detail and posing essay topics such as, 'Discuss one positive attribute of Denethor's leadership in detail,' can help develop student's close analysis skills.

Scenes that yield particularly useful analysis of ethics are many. I particularly find the following scenes and sections from *TSil* fruitful: the creation of Arda; the discussion on the differences between Men and Elves; Morgoth's interaction with the Noldor; Feanor's oath and the fall of the Noldor; the stories 'Of Beren and Luthien', 'Of Turin Turambar', 'Of the Voyage of Earendil and the War of Wrath'; and the fall of Numenor. From *FotR*: Frodo's decisions to accept and carry the ring in 'The Shadow of the Past' and 'The Council of Elrond'. His struggle in the Barrow Downs; his struggle to resist the effects of the knife wound; Galadriel's tests; Boromir's fall. From *TT*, Frodo and Sam's treatment of Gollum; Gollum's struggles especially in 'The Passage of the Marshes' and 'The Stairs of Cirith Ungol'). From *RotK*, Éowyn's choices; Sam's decision to abandon the quest to save Frodo; Frodo's struggle with the ring across all the books; and the reluctance of the hobbits to resist Sharkey until the heroes return

---

11. Tom Shippey, 'Tolkien on Leadership,' (presentation at *The Return of the Ring: Celebrating Tolkien in 2012* conference, Loughborough, England, 17 August 2012).

in 'The Scouring of the Shire'. Almost all of these scenes allow the class to explore deeply how and why characters are able to resist evil or how and why they cannot resist. They also ask students to explore the characters' obligations to themselves, their community, and their world. Ultimately, they encourage students to think about the value system Tolkien seems to be advocating throughout all of these works.

Overall, my first attempt at teaching the course was very successful and my department has decided to offer it regularly. I found it to be one of the most rewarding classes I have ever taught, particularly because of the new light the lens of leadership and ethics sheds on this beloved author.

**RELIGION AND ITS DISCONTENTS**

# 'Tolkien — Pagan or Christian?
## A proposal for a 'new' synthetic approach'

## Claudio A. Testi

*In this essay I propose an interpretative approach that can avoid the limits of the antithetical positions that consider Tolkien's work explicitly Christian or mainly Pagan. This synthetic proposal is based on the principle that establishes the harmony between nature-grace (fully elaborated during the entire history of Catholic Theology): the same principle can explain how (and why) the pagan world sub-created by Tolkien is at the same time different from historical paganism and from Judeo-Christian Revelation.*[1]

## 1. INTRODUCTION

I want to deal with the question is Tolkien's world is Pagan or Christian? This question has faced scholars and readers since the publication of *The Lord of the Rings* in 1954. Now, in my humble opinion, both the thesis 'Tolkien's work is Christian' and the antithesis 'Tolkien's work is Pagan' have some weak points that the synthesis I would like to propose here is able to avoid.

## 2. THE THESIS: TOLKIEN'S WORK IS CHRISTIAN

Let us start with the approach that considers Tolkien's *Legendarium* a universe containing explicit Christian values, as authors like Pearce,[2] Caldecott,[3] Kreeft[4],

---

1. This text of my presentation at Loughborough has become a more extended article that has been published on *Tolkien Studies*, 10 (2013), pp. 1–47. I would like to thank Professor Verlyn Flieger for her encouragement and suggestions and for permission to publish this text in these Proceedings.
2. Joseph Pearce, 'Foreword' to Bradley J. Birzer, *J.R.R. Tolkien's Sanctifying Myth*, Intercollegiate Studies Institute, Wilmington DE, 2002, pp. ix–xiv. See also his *Literary Giants, Literary Catholics*, Ignatius Press, San Francisco, 2005; *Tolkien: Man and Myth*, HarperCollins, London, 1999; *Tolkien: A Celebration*, Fount, London, 1999.
3. Stratford Caldecott, *Secret Fire: The Spiritual Vision of J.R.R. Tolkien*, Darton Longman and Todd, London, 2003.
4. Peter Kreeft, *The Philosophy of Tolkien*, Ignatius Press, San Francisco, 2005.

West,[5] and Agøy,[6] maintain.

2.1 The first weak point is that this approach contradicts Tolkien's razor. Pearce, for example, says: 'It is not merely erroneous but patently perverse to see Tolkien's epic as anything other than a specifically Christian myth.'[7] But for Tolkien it is extremely important to cut from a myth every explicit reference to Christian religion, because this is fatal to the tale, e. g:

> [The Arthurian cycle] explicitly contains the Christian religion. For reasons which I will not elaborate, that seems to me fatal.[8]

> I have deliberately written a tale, which is built on or out of certain 'religious' ideas, but is not an allegory of them (or anything else), and does not mention them overtly, still less preach them.[9]

The Third Era was not a Christian world.[10]

2.2 The second weak point is that it confuses interpretation with allegory or application. Kreeft, for example, writes:

> even though *The Lord of the Rings* is not an allegory of the Gospels, we can find numerous parallels to the Gospels in *The Lord of the Rings*.... For instance, Frodo's journey up Mount Doom is strikingly similar to Christ's way to Cross. Sam is his Simon de Cyrene. but he carries the cross bearer as well as the cross.... [Christ] is more clearly present in Gandalf, Frodo and Aragorn, the three Christ figures.[11]

But Tolkien carefully distinguishes those concepts:
I have no didactic purpose, and no allegorical intent. I do not like

---

5. John G. West Jr., ed., *Celebrating Middle-earth: The Lord of the Rings as a Defence of Western Civilisation*, Inkling Books, Seattle, 2002.

6. Nils Ivar Agøy, 'The Christian Tolkien: A Response to Ronald Hutton', in Paul E. Kerry, ed., *The Ring and the Cross: Christianity and the Writings of J.R.R. Tolkien*, Fairleigh Dickinson University Press, Madison NJ, 2011, pp. 71–89. See also his 'The Fall and Man's Mortality', *Arda Special* 1, Arda Society, Oslo, 1997, 16–27; 'Quid Hinieldus cum Christo?: New Perspectives on Tolkien's Theological Dilemma and His Sub-Creation Theory', in Patricia Reynolds and Glen H. GoodKnight, eds, *Proceedings of the J.R.R. Tolkien Centenary Conference*, The Tolkien Society and The Mythopoeic Press, Milton Keynes and Altadena, 1995, 31–38.

7. Op. cit. [2], 'Foreword', p. ix.

8. Humphrey Carpenter, ed., *The Letters of J.R.R. Tolkien*, with the assistance of Christopher Tolkien, HarperCollins, London, 1981, Letter 131.

9. Op. cit. Letter 211, p. 283.

10. Op. cit. Letter 165, p. 220.

11. Op. cit. [4], p. 222.

allegory (properly so called: most readers appear to confuse it with significance or applicability).[12]

I think that many confuse "applicability" with "allegory"; but the one resides on the freedom of the reader, and the other in the purposed domination of the author.[13]

So, it is certainly a mistake to consider, for example, Frodo as an allegory of Christ because Tolkien cordially disliked this kind of allegory. However a Christian can certainly 'apply' the figure of Frodo to illustrate Christ's *Via Crucis*, but this is not in any sense an interpretation of *LotR*.

2.3 Third, it confuses source with representation, for Caldecott in fact writes: 'For Tolkien Elvishness and Catholicism were closely related. I think you can detect a 'hidden code' that refers to Catholic themes and ideas, such as the Eucharist and the Blessed Virgin Mary, in *LotR*'.[14] But Tolkien affirms in *On Fairy-Stories* that: 'We must be satisfied with the soup [the products of Fantasy] that is set before us, and not desire to see the bones [the sources] of the ox out of which it has been boiled'.[15] Certainly the Virgin is a source of inspiration for Galadriel (as is Morrigan in the Welsh tales) but Galadriel is not a representation of Mary (or Morrigan).

2.4 The fourth weak point of this approach is that it derives a total identity from a partial similitude. For example, 'The Music of the Ainur' has many similarities with the text of *Genesis*, but these Tolkien critics often overlook the significant differences between them (see 5.2.1 below).

## 3. THE ANTITHESIS

Other authors like Madsen, Hutton or Curry affirm that the Pagan perspective is predominant in Tolkien's secondary world, in opposition to the 'orthodox' Christian vision of life and history; but this approach suffers similar weak points.

3.1 First, it diminishes the importance of the texts that show the fundamental

---

12. Op. cit. [8], Letter 215, p. 279.

13. J.R.R. Tolkien, *The Lord of the Rings*, HarperCollins, London, 1993, 'Foreword to the second English edition', p. xvii. All quotations from *LotR* are taken from this edition.

14. Stratford Caldecott, 'Tolkien's Project', in Stratford Caldecott and Thomas M. Honegger, eds., *Tolkien's The Lord of the Rings: Sources of Inspiration*, Walking Tree Publishers, Zurich and Jena, 2008, 211–32, p. 226.

15. J.R.R. Tolkien, 'On Fairy-Stories', in Christopher Tolkien, ed., *The Monsters and the Critics: And Other Essays*, Allen & Unwin, London, 1983, 109–61, 120. All quotations from *OFS* are taken from this edition.

relation between Tolkien's world and Revelation. Madsen, for instance, considers the epilogue of *On Fairy-Stories*, as well as the 'Tale of Aragorn and Arwen' in *LotR*, only as a sort of *post scriptum*,[16] whereas both the Epilogue and the Appendices are integral parts of the text to which they belong.[17] In a similar way, they often ignore or underrate the letters in which Tolkien affirms the importance of Catholic faith in his works, referring to the alleged incompleteness of the published *Letters*,[18] although they nevertheless unhesitatingly invoke the very same letters when they speak of differences between Tolkien's and the Christian world.

3.2 Second, when proposing a 'Pagan Tolkien', the important differences between Middle-earth and the historical Pagan civilisations, such as human sacrifices in use among Germanic peoples and the Egyptians;[19] relationship between magic and religion; presence of nudity in rituals, etc.[20] are usually not sufficiently remarked.

3.3 Third, this approach wrongly interprets some elements of Tolkien's world as incompatible with Christian Revelation, when in fact they are not. For example, Curry affirms:

> The spiritual word of Middle-earth is a rich and complex one. It contains both polytheistic-cum-animist cosmology of 'natural magic' and a Christian (but non-sectarian) ethic of humility and compassion.[21]

But Tolkien's ecological views can indeed very well be fitted in the frame of a Christian cosmology based on the concept of stewardship, as shown by Matthew Dickerson and Jonathan Evans in *Ents, Elves and Eriador: The Environmental Vision of J.R.R. Tolkien*,[22] and strongly criticised by Curry in his review, and by Siewers.[23]

---

16. Catherine Madsen, 'Eru Erased: The Minimalist Cosmology of *The Lord of the Rings*', in Kerry, op. cit. [6], 152–69, p. 157.

17. Op. cit. [8], Letter 181, p. 237.

18. Ronald Hutton, 'The Pagan Tolkien', in Kerry, op. cit. [6], 57–70, p. 58.

19. See e.g. Simson R. Najovits, *Egypt: Trunk of the Tree*, Algora, New York, 2003.

20. See Ronald Hutton, *The Triumph of the Moon: A History of Modern Pagan Witchcraft*, Oxford University Press, Oxford, 2001, pp. 391–93. See also *Witches, Druids and King Arthur*, Continuum, London, 2006, pp. 193–214.

21. Patrick Curry, *Defending Middle-earth: Tolkien, Myth and Modernity*, HarperCollins, London, 1998 , p. 28. See also p. 110.

22. Matthew Dickerson and Jonathan Evans, *Ents, Elves and Eriador: The Environmental Vision of J.R.R. Tolkien*, University Press of Kentucky, Lexington, 2006.

23. Alfred K. Siewers, 'Tolkien's Cosmic-Christian Ecology: The Medieval Underpinnings'.

TOLKIEN: PAGAN OR CHRISTIAN? 159

3.4 The fourth weak point of this approach is that it derives contradictions between Tolkien's and Christian world from what are only partial differences. A usual argument is to underline the Neo-Platonist inspiration of Arda's Theology (God is often called 'the One'), but this is certainly not in antithesis with the Christian Theology that, from Augustine to Aquinas, has used Neo-Platonist categories to explore the contents of Revelation.

## 4. THE SYNTHESIS: DIFFERENCE OF LEVELS AND POINTS OF VIEW

Now I will try to explain the principles on which my 'synthetic' interpretation is based, whose inspiring authors are Shippey and Holmes. The approach I propose is based on a logic that distinguishes between two points of view from which it is possible to examine the *Legendarium*: the first one from the *inside* of the work, by examining the theological and ethical background within which the characters' storylines are internally developed; the second one from the *outside*, by making, through a meta-narrative analysis, an historically grounded comparison of Tolkien's work and the development of culture within our real world. In addition, my proposal outlines two strictly distinguished conceptual orders, in harmony with each other even if differing in parts:

a) *The plane of Nature*, where actions, knowledge, and products are made by rational beings only in virtue of their own inherent capabilities and faculties (i.e. reason, language, freedom, craftsmanship);

b) *The plane of Grace*, or the super-natural order, where the rational beings receive gifts such as Faith, or revealed truths such as Unity and Trinity, Incarnation and Resurrection of God, belonging to the Judeo- Christian Revelation which would be *impossible to obtain fully* by means of mere natural abilities.

Now, if we apply these distinctions to Tolkien's world, we can avoid the weak points of the previous interpretations, thanks to a synthesis that I can summarise in three propositions: (1) Tolkien's world is internally pagan because devoid of specifically Christian elements, being the expression of a simply natural plane. But (2) it is externally in harmony with the supernatural plane of Christian Revelation. (3) So the co-existence of those aspects in Tolkien's work does express a fundamentally Catholic culture.

---

in Jane Chance and Alfred Siewers, eds, *Tolkien's Modern Middle Ages*, Palgrave Macmillan, London, 2009, 138–53.

# 5. TOLKIEN'S WORLD IS NON-CHRISTIAN BUT IN HARMONY WITH THE REVELATION

Now the arguments to demonstrate the proposition (1) and (2) are of two kinds: general principles affirmed by Tolkien in his critical essays concerning his poetic and hermeneutic, and arguments based on the structure of Tolkien's narrative universe.

5.1 GENERAL PRINCIPLES CONCERNING TOLKIEN'S POETIC AND HERMENEUTICS: Concerning the general principles, in *On Fairy-Stories* it is affirmed:

> Fantasy is a natural human activity. It certainly does not destroy or even insult Reason; and it does not either blunt the appetite for, nor obscure the perception of, scientific verity. On the contrary. The keener and the clearer is the reason, the better fantasy will it make. (*OFS*, 65)

> Fantasy remains a human right: we make in our measure and in our derivative mode, because we are made: and not only made, but made in the image and likeness of our Maker. (*OFS*, 66)

> Redeemed Man is still man. Story, fantasy, still go on, and should go on. The Evangelium has not abrogated legends; it has hallowed them, especially the 'happy ending'. (*OFS*, 78)

These texts state that: Fantasy as a natural (and not super natural) ability of Man; the relation between this natural ability and the Maker (God); the harmony between Fantasy and its products with the supernatural plane of Gospel.

A harmony and continuity in the human condition of a pagan and a Christian is also affirmed in *Beowulf: The Monsters and the Critics*: the *Beowulf* poet is a Christian who admires the pagan times, and in this poem the monsters are considered the enemies of man and of God:

> A Christian was (and is) still like his forefathers a mortal hemmed in a hostile world. The monsters remained the enemies of mankind, the infantry of the old war, and became inevitably the enemies of the one God'.[24]

---

24. J.R.R. Tolkien, *Beowulf: The Monsters and the Critics*, ed. Christopher Tolkien, George

Similar principles concerning the harmony between Pagan culture and Christian revelation are also affirmed in *The Homecoming of Beorhtnoth, Beorhthelm's Son*, and in *Sir Gawain and the Green Knight*, so we cannot be surprised, nor can we misinterpret, the fact that Tolkien defines himself as a '*converted heathen*'.[25]

5.2 EXAMPLES IN TOLKIEN'S WORLD: We can now see how these general statements are concretely realised in Tolkien's world.

5.2.1. ARDA'S THEOLOGY:

PAGANISM: From all the points of views (Elvish, Mannish and Hobbit) it is affirmed in different degrees: the existence of Iluvatar/Eru/The One, the Maker of everything; the existence of the Ainur, made by Eru; the existence of Elves and Men, beings made of soul and body. But these elements do not allow us to consider Arda Theology a Christian one. In fact, also the pagan Greeks (Plato and Aristotle) had already theorised the existence of a principle of all things, of separate spiritual substances and of the immaterial soul of Man. In addition, in Tolkien's *Legendarium* there are no explicit references to the Holy Trinity, to the incarnation and to resurrection of God. Finally, there are considerable differences as opposed to the 'official' Christian theology, like the fact that the world created by Eru had been marred by Melkor's sin, before Elves and Man were created,[26] or that there are angelical entities who associate among each other or with Elves (Melian and Thingol), even, in the latter case, having children. Because of the almost full absence of revealed data and these differences, we have to say that *the theology of the Legendarium is essentially Pagan.*

HARMONY WITH REVELATION: However, this perspective has also a lot of similarities with Christian Revelation, in fact it is different from the polytheism proper of a certain historical Paganism. Least of all does the theology of Middle-earth share anything with atheism of contemporary world: the existence of a Creator cannot be denied, unlike Pullman's *His Dark Materials*. Finally, the most important intuitions of Arda's Theology can find their place in Christian Revelation: both affirm a tripartite order of beings, a monotheistic theology, and the Secret Fire is similar with the Holy Spirit. For these reasons, *the Pagan theology of the Legendarium is in harmony with the Christian Revelation.*

5.2.2. OTHER EXAMPLES: It would be possible to demonstrate the

---

Allen & Unwin, 1983, p. 26.

25. J.R.R. Tolkien, 'English and Welsh', op. cit., p. 162.

26. Op. cit. [8], Letter 212, p. 285.

162                                CLAUDIO A. TESTI

Paganism of Tolkien's world and its harmony with Revelation examining the
problem of Cults, Philosophy of History and the ethics of the Hero in Tolkien's
*Legendarium*; but for limitations of space.

## 6. TOLKIEN'S WORK AND CATHOLIC CULTURE

Concerning the proposition (3) in Section 4 above, it is important to note that
if we want to give a cultural and not confessional definition of Catholicism, we
could say that this interpretation of the Christian message is characterised by
the principle of harmony between the two different planes of Nature and Grace:
*gratia non tollit naturam, sed perficit* reads a famous Thomistic adage. This
interpretation of the Christian message has its foundation in the Holy Bible,
that contains many 'pagan saints' – 'just men' who have not yet received the
Revelation – like Abel, Noah, Melchizedek, the Queen of Sheba, Jonas and
Job (books in part translated by Tolkien), and Saint Paul explicitly affirms
the possibility for the pure natural reason of Man to learn of the existence of
God (Romans 1. 19-20). These principles were theologically proposed by the
Fathers of the Church (Clement of Alexandria. Eusebius of Caesarea, Augustine
of Hippo), who gave a positive judgement of the pagan culture (i.e. the usage
of the Greek philosophical categories in order to understand the content of the
Scripture). St. Justin considered Christians also the virtuous pagan like Socrates
and Heraclitus:

> He [Christ] is the Word of whom every race of men were partakers;
> and those who lived reasonably are Christians, even though they have
> been thought atheists; as, among the Greeks, Socrates and Heraclitus
> and men like them.[27]

The same principles were continuously reaffirmed from Augustine to
Aquinas: he affirms the possibility for natural reason to achieve important truths
for instance that God is, that God is one.[28] The same ideas were established in
many Councils, from the Council of Trent (against the Protestant Reformation)
up to the Second Vatican Council (*Lumen Gentium* n. 16) The Lutheran Reform,
on the contrary, radically refuses the harmony between Reason and Faith (*sola
fide, sola scriptura*, Luther affirmed) to the point that in polemics with Zwingli,
it rejects the very idea of eternal salvation for the 'virtuous Pagans':

---

27. St. Justin, *Apologie*, Rusconi, Milano, 1995, 'First Apology', n. 46.
28. Thomas Aquinas, *Summa Contra Gentiles*, Marietti, Taurini, 1967, I. c. 3.

> Tell me, you who would be a Christian, what need is there of Baptism, the Sacrament, Christ, the Gospel, or the Prophets, and Holy Scripture, if such godless heathen, Socrates, Aristides [and Antigone, Cato and Hercules, mentioned before].... are blessed and saints with the Patriarchs, Prophets, and Apostles in heaven, though they knew nothing of God, Scripture, the Gospel, Christ, Baptism, and the Sacrament, or the Christian faith?... I lost all hope in an improvement of those followers [of Zwingli] (to the point I ceased praying for them).[29]

These ideas were followed by other Protestant theologians emphasising even more the 'Catholicity' of the 'appeal of the pagans'. In this perspective the 'Pagan Man' – meaning all those who do not partake of the alliances of Abraham and Jesus – acquires enormous dignity, because for Catholicism every man has natural abilities that allow him to have access to the Truth and Beauty present in full in the Christian Revelation.

From this point of view, Tolkien's *Legendarium* appears a magnificent literary exemplification of the principle of harmony between Nature and Grace, Reason and Faith. This, in my humble opinion, is the real meaning of his remarks in Letter 142 (too often quoted but rarely analysed in its deep significance), where Tolkien says that his work is 'fundamentally religious and Catholic'.[30] In other words, *the fundamental catholicity of Tolkien's work* is not to be found in explicit confessional elements related to his Faith, but paradoxically *in the quite peculiar non-Christianity of his world*, where the most authentic existential and ethical tensions involving the 'mere natural' Man are represented.

## 7. CONCLUSION

In this essay I hope to have contributed to a debate that has involved (and involves) many great scholars. The interpretation I have here offered does not pretend to be 'original' or 'revolutionary', but only to be synthetic and in some aspects new because, while taking into account previous positions, it is a comprehensive and systematic interpretation of Tolkien's works (section 5 above), based on a small and consistent set of foundational principles (section 4 above). It is able to explain the true difference (Sections 2.1. and 3.2), but also the fundamental relationship between Tolkien's world and Revelation, denying neither (Sections 2.4 and 3.1). For this reason, it differs from explicitly Christian

---

29. Martin Luther, *Dr. Martin Luther's kurzes Bekenntnis vom heiligen Sacrament wider die Schwärmer*, Junge, Ansbach, 1866, p. 6. My translation.
30. Op. cit. [8], Letter 142, p. 172.

or essentially Pagan views of the subject matter, thus avoiding any mistake or reductionism (Sections 2–3). In being based on the idea of a natural plane devoid of chronological contents, it also differs from the simple idea of *praeparatio evangelii* as it has already been propounded by others (Section 4). It strongly affirms the absence of exclusively Christian elements in Tolkien's world, differentiating itself from the most common interpretations that do affirm just an equal coexistence of Christian and Pagan ones. Finally, it explains by the same principles that the sub-created universe of the *Legendarium* is the expression of a 'fundamentally Catholic' culture mainly because of its peculiar non-Christian nature (Section 6).

To conclude, I hope I have helped to show why Tolkien's mythology, as proved by its universal appreciation, is meant neither for a single nation (England) nor a specific religion (be it Christian or Pagan), but for all of Mankind capable of sensing with their natural capabilities that beyond the Circles of the World there is 'more than memory'.[31]

---

31. Op. cit. [13], 'Appendix A', p. 1038.

# 'A Latter-day Saint reading of Tolkien'

# James D. Holt

*This paper explores the religious themes evident in some of Tolkien's writings, most notably The Silmarillion, The Hobbit, and The Lord of the Rings. I will utilise the existing scholarship on Tolkien's religious views, and the imagery already explored, in light of his Roman Catholicism. I will reflect on how these relate to, and can deepen my understanding of, Latter-day Saint beliefs. The paper begins with an exploration of Tolkien's motivations for writing, and his religious beliefs. The two intertwine nicely, and provide a justification, if one is necessary, for the use of his work in a religious context. This does not suggest that LotR can be used devotionally, rather that it can point towards greater truth. The remainder of the paper will explore themes from Tolkien's writings in the Latter-day Saint context.*

Tolkien, especially in the Church of Jesus Christ of Latter-day Saints, is not known as a Christian writer to the same degree as his friend, and contemporary, C.S.Lewis. Within the context of works like Lewis's, and also the more straightforwardly allegorical works of John Bunyan, the writings of Tolkien are less obviously Christian. Indeed, if the religious themes are there the reader has to dig beneath the surface. Perhaps this is the enduring quality of much of Tolkien's myth; it is not immediately recognisable as a religious work, though he might be disappointed by such a claim. To recognise the Christian elements 'absorbed' into the various tales of Middle-earth a person needs to search, and it is perhaps this search that makes the endeavour all the more rewarding. Tolkien was very careful to avoid any possibility that his work could be seen as allegory; he has argued that 'As for any inner meaning or "message", it has in the intention of the author none'. He further rejected any semblance of allegory in the *Lord of the Rings*: 'It is neither allegorical nor topical' (*LotR*, 'Introduction', 6).[1] Bradley J. Birzer argues that 'Tolkien utterly rejected the use of allegory altogether and noted his dislike of it wherever he could detect it. In *The Monsters and the Critics* Tolkien expressed his fear that in making his meaning too explicit an author risks destroying the art and deeper significance of his work.'[2] However,

---

1. J.R.R. Tolkien, *The Lord of the Rings*, HarperCollins, London, 1995. All quotations from *LotR* are taken from this edition.
2. Bradley J. Birzer, *J.R.R. Tolkien's Sanctifying Myth: Understanding Middle-earth*, Intercollegiate Studies Institute Books, Wilmington DE, 2009, p. 40.

there are points within the work, and perhaps throughout the whole history of Middle-earth, where the story does seem allegorical. This may be a result of the fusion of the background of the author and the reader. Middle-earth is much less obviously allegorical than Narnia; it is only when the reader brings their own understanding that the meaning is brought to the fore. Spengler outlines the difference between Lewis and Tolkien's Christian stories in a way that I think outlines Tolkien's genius:

> Tolkien is a writer of greater theological depth than his Oxford colleague C.S. Lewis, in my judgment. Lewis is a felicitous writer and a diligent apologist, but mere allegory along the lines of the Narnia series can do no more than restate Christian doctrine; it cannot really expand our experience of it. Tolkien takes us to the dark frontier of a world that is not yet Christian, and therefore is tragic, but has the capacity to become Christian. It is the world of the Dark Ages, in which barbarians first encounter the light. It is not fantasy, but rather a distillation of the spiritual history of the West.[3]

While it might be possible for Tolkien to keep himself out of his work it would be unreasonable to have the expectation that he does. Indeed in various comments he does recognise the religious nature of his writings. However, Tolkien creates a world where the writing and history works on a number of different levels, not least the level of imagination and enjoyment. The books can, and should, be enjoyed as stories, or myths of a bygone age. It is only latterly that I have begun to explore the Christian depths of Tolkien's writings, and maybe I would not have the same love the stories and characters had I begun to analyse or allegorise them from the outset. If I think about my relationship with *Pilgrim's Progress*, I feel that it is a fabulous religious story but not one that I can read again and again for enjoyment. Middle-earth is a fabulous story that can be enjoyed without any nod to religion, and should only later be explored for its hidden depths. Whether the religiosity of Middle-earth is designed or merely a reflection of Tolkien's subconscious or the reader's bias does not take away from the fact that religious themes can be identified.[4]

---

3. Spengler, 'Tolkien's Christianity and the pagan tragedy', *Asia Times Online*, 24 April 2007 <http://www.atimes.com/atimes/Front_Page/ID24Aa01.html> [accessed 15 September 2011].
4. Ronald Hutton argues that there are as many, if not more, Pagan themes as Christian themes identifiable in Tolkien's legendarium. This argument highlights the argument that the works of Middle-earth can tell us as much about the reader and what they are looking for, as about Tolkien himself. Ronald Hutton, 'The Pagan Tolkien', in Paul E. Kerry, ed., *The Ring and the Cross: Christianity and the Lord of the Rings*, Farleigh Dickinson University Press, Madison NJ, 2011,

One further reason why the myth may not be immediately recognisable as Christian is the use that Tolkien makes of Norse mythology. From a Roman Catholic perspective Tolkien had a very positive view of 'pagan' myth. In an exploration of the Norse or Greek myths some Christians would see them as anathema to the Christian message. These stories are pre-Christian attempts to understand the natural and physical realm. The story of a god who rides a chariot to help the sun rise in the morning may be imaginatively evocative but can in no way relate to the view of God as Lord of the heavens and the earth. Perhaps, this is how Latter-day Saints view the myths of the various cultures of the world. The story of Thor is enjoyable to read, but cannot teach or help a person learn more about their relationship with Heavenly Father, Jesus Christ and the Holy Ghost. This might lead some to suggest that they are of no value at best or dangerous at worst. However, for Tolkien

> even pagan myths attempted to express God's greater truths. True myth has the power to revive us, to serve as an anamnesis, or way of bringing to conscious experience ancient experience with transcendence. But, Tolkien admitted, myth could be dangerous, or 'perilous', as he usually stated it, if it remained pagan. Therefore, Tolkien thought, one must sanctify it, that is, make it Christian and put it in God's service.[5]

Tolkien's Catholicism suggests that Christ is 'the true light that enlightens every man.'[6] As such Christ can be present in pagan myths as they point towards the truths of his person. This might be the view that through apprehension of certain questions or truths in the world, people are led to suggest some answers that are imperfect but a step towards Christ. For Latter-day Saints it might be possible to suggest a similar approach to myth and the presence of the light of Christ. Latter-day Saint teaching about the light of Christ and its revelatory role may support the possibility of general revelation.

> For behold, the Spirit of Christ is given to every man, that he may know good from evil; wherefore, I show unto you the way to judge; for every thing which inviteth to do good, and to persuade to believe

---

57–70.

5. Op. cit. [2], p. xxiii.

6. John 1:9. Latter-day Saints have four books of scripture: *The Holy Bible*; *The Book of Mormon*; *The Doctrine and Covenants*; and *The Pearl of Great Price*. Except for the bible, when a passage is used in this article the associated book of scripture is identified in parentheses. All published by The Church of Jesus Christ of Latter-day Saints, Salt Lake City, 1985.

in Christ, is sent forth by the power and gift of Christ; wherefore ye may know with a perfect knowledge it is of God.[7]

This scripture highlights that the light of Christ is given to humanity with the express purpose of persuading people to believe in Christ. In contrast to the Holy Ghost who does not dwell with the unworthy, the light of Christ is 'the instrumentality and agency by which Deity keeps in touch and communes with all his children, both the righteous and the wicked.[8] The light of Christ is the enticing power through which God encourages individuals 'to forsake the world and come unto Christ' by the placing of 'good desires and feelings … in the hearts of decent people'. The light of Christ is not limited to the sphere of religion:

> It is the medium of intelligence that guides inventors, scientists, artists, composers, poets, authors, statesmen, philosophers, generals, leaders, and influential men in general, when they set their hands to do that which is for the benefit and blessing of their fellowmen. By it the Lord guides in the affairs of men and directs the courses of nations and kingdoms. By it the Lord gives ennobling art, the discoveries of science, and music like that sung in the courts above.[9]

It is sometimes assumed by Latter-day Saints that the beliefs that they hold are the same as those held by the majority of the Christian world. Though there is much truth in this, there is also a note of caution to be sounded, that the way Tolkien understood his relationship with God and Jesus Christ would have been different to a Mormon understanding. There will be places where this article will explore areas of the stories that might relate to Mormonism. In examining the world of Middle-earth it is not my argument that the interpretation I put on events would have been the one that Tolkien intended or understood. I may use his thoughts as a starting place but the interpretation will be distinctly Latter-day Saint; it will view the people, creatures and events of Middle-earth through Mormon spectacles.

*The Silmarillion* begins with the two short stories of 'Ainulindale' and 'Valaquenta' in which is contained much of the myth of creation. Before the creation of Middle-earth, Tolkien describes the creation of the Valar. Elsewhere he has described the Valar as 'angelic powers whose function is to exercise

---

7. Moroni 7:16 (*Book of Mormon*, op. cit.).
8. Bruce R. McConkie, *A New Witness for the Articles of Faith*, Deseret Book Company, Salt Lake City, 1985, p. 259.
9. Op. cit.

delegated authority in the spheres (of Rule and government, *not* creation, making or re-making)'.[10] Once created these Valar participate with Ilúvatar (the One) in the creation of Middle-earth. Creation is not the work of Ilúvatar alone, rather it is a communal experience through which Ilúvatar's supremacy is shown. The description of the creation of Middle-earth is, for me, one of the most evocative passages in literature. It begins with Ilúvatar, the Ainur and a void (into which the world would eventually go). This void was easily transported from both traditions which Tolkien drew upon – Nordic mythology taught that it all began with a void as did the Book of Genesis (where also it begins with pure spirit, God (Ilúvatar) and the angels (Ainur) in the void). The world is imagined through the music of the Ainur:

> Then Ilúvatar said to them: "Of the theme I have declared to you, I will now that ye make in harmony a Great Music. And since I have kindled you with the Flame Imperishable, ye shall show forth your powers in adorning this theme, each with his own thoughts and devices if he will" (*TSil*, 'Ainulindalë', 15).[11]

With the music composed 'the echo of the music went out into the void' then Ilúvatar took the Ainur into the void and said:

> "Behold your music!" And he showed to them a vision ... and they saw a New World made visible before them, and it was globed amid the void … And as they looked, and wondered this World began to unfold its history, and it seemed to them that it lived and grew.[12]

Then he sent forth to Earth across the Void the Flame Imperishable, which belongs to Ilúvatar, alone and necessary to Being. So the Ainur saw the new globe like 'a cloud with a living heart of flame' knew that it had ceased to be a vision and had become a new thing.[13] The Flame Imperishable being 'the visible form of the song of the Ainur, the stuff of creation.'[14]

---

10. Humphrey Carpenter, ed. *The Letters of J.R.R. Tolkien*, with the assistance of Christopher Tolkien, George Allen & Unwin, London, 1981, Letter 131, p. 146.
11. J.R.R. Tolkien, *The Silmarillion*, ed. Christoper Tolkien, Grafton, London, 1992.
12. Op. cit., 'Ainulindalë', pp. 16, 18.
13. Paul Kocher, *A Reader's Guide to The Silmarillion*, Houghton Mifflin, Boston, 1980, p. 18.
14. Timothy O'Neill, *The Individuated Hobbit: Jung, Tolkien, and the Archetypes of Middle-earth*, Thames and Hudson, London, 1979, p. 46.

# JAMES D. HOLT

## THE COMMUNITY OF CREATION

For Latter-day Saints there are points of convergence and divergence in this form of creation. The communal nature of creation is highlighted in the Abrahamic creation narratives:

> And then the Lord said: Let us go down. And they went down at the beginning, and they, that is the Gods, organised and formed the heavens and the earth. And the earth, after it was formed, was empty and desolate, because they had not formed anything but the earth; and darkness reigned upon the face of the deep, and the Spirit of the Gods was brooding upon the face of the waters. And they (the Gods) said: Let there be light; and there was light.[15]

Although reference to the Gods is incompatible with the angels of Tolkien's imagination,[16] the involvement of others in the creation of the universe is a parallel with Latter-day Saint teaching. Joseph Smith, in the King Follett discourse, taught that Heavenly Father created the universe utilising the council of the Gods:

> This is the true meaning of the words ROSHITH [BARA ELOHIM] signifies [the Head] to bring forth the Elohim. If you do not believe it, you do not believe the learned man of God. No learned man can tell you any more than what I have told you. Thus, the Head God brought forth the Head Gods in the grand, head council. I want to simplify it in the English language.
> O, ye lawyers, ye learned doctors, who have persecuted me, I want to let you know and learn that the Holy Ghost knows something as well as you do. The Head One of the Gods called together the Gods and the grand councillors sat in grand council at the head in yonder heavens to bring forth the world and contemplated the creation of the worlds that were created at that time.[17]

What this means is not elucidated, but just as Ilúvatar utilised his creations, Latter-day Saints know that the Father (Elohim) created through his Son, who

---

15. Abraham 4: 1–3 (*The Pearl*, op. cit. [6]).
16. Though interestingly in the earliest drafts of the creation myth, the Valar were described as 'gods'.
17. Stanley Larson, 'The King Follett Discourse: A Newly Amalgamated Text', *BYU Studies* 18, (1978), 190–207, p. 202.

must have been one of the Gods mentioned in Abraham. This suggestion is strengthened when we read further in Abraham that:

> Now the Lord had shown unto me, Abraham, the intelligences that were organised before the world was; and among all these there were many of the noble and great ones;
> And God saw these souls that they were good, and he stood in the midst of them, and he said: These I will make my rulers; for he stood among those that were spirits, and he saw that they were good; and he said unto me: Abraham, thou art one of them; thou wast chosen before thou wast born.
> And there stood one among them that was like unto God, and he said unto those who were with him: We will go down, for there is space there, and we will take of these materials, and we will make an earth whereon these may dwell.[18]

However Joseph Smith described Elohim as the 'head' of the council of the Gods. This suggests that those in council with him were subject to him. This alludes to those who achieved Godhood pre-mortally (the Saviour and possibly the Holy Ghost); and possibly those who are foreordained to receive Godhood after their probation. As such, the scope for some of us to be involved in the creation of the world increases exponentially. This is somewhat speculative, but Joseph Fielding Smith has taught: 'It is true that Adam helped to form this earth. He labored with our Saviour Jesus Christ. I have a strong view or conviction that there were others also who assisted them. Perhaps Noah and Enoch; and why not Joseph Smith, and those who were appointed to be rulers before the earth was formed?'[19] Hyrum Andrus explores this further by suggesting that: 'the great prophets such as Moses…. had exalted themselves to be gods even from before the foundation of the world, and were the noble and great spirits whom Abraham designated as "Gods."'[20]

The communal nature of creation is important for Latter-day Saints, as they seek to emulate the unity of the Godhead and those who worked with them. It is possible to examine Tolkien's Ainur as parallels to help understand how Heavenly Father uses his creations to help in all of his endeavours. Just as Ilúvatar took of the various themes given by the Ainur, the Father takes of individuals' themes

---

18. Abraham 3: 22–24 (*The Pearl*, op. cit. [6]).
19. Joseph Fielding Smith, *Doctrines of Salvation*, ed. Bruce R. McConkie, Deseret Book Company, Salt Lake City, 1999, vol. 1, pp. 74–77.
20. Hyrum Andrus, *Doctrinal Commentary on the Pearl of Great Price*, Deseret Book Company, Salt Lake City, 1970, pp. 106–107.

172                                    JAMES D. HOLT

and efforts 'to bring to pass the immortality and eternal life' of humanity.[21]

## MELKOR'S THEME AND THE ATTEMPTS TO DISRUPT THE PLAN

This use of themes is especially evident when Melkor's contribution and its attempted distortion of the theme are examined. *The Silmarillion* describes how Melkor took his freedom and went against Ilúvatar, however nothing can thwart Ilúvatar's plan. He 'warned all the Ainur, especially Melkor and his adherents that every sub theme or counter theme which they might think was theirs came ultimately from him, and would always be absorbed into his themes making them more wonderful than before (*TSil*, 'Ainulindale', 17). In short, Ilúvatar would always transmute it so as to serve the ends of his divine providence. This can be seen in Latter-day Saint belief when the events immediately following creation are examined.

When Adam and Eve were in the Garden of Eden, Satan sought to destroy the plan of salvation by tempting them: 'And Satan put it into the heart of the serpent, (for he had drawn away many after him,) and he sought also to beguile Eve, for he knew not the mind of God, wherefore he sought to destroy the world.[22] The important part of this scripture in this discussion is that 'he knew not the mind of God'. Satan did not know that by tempting Even he was enabling the plan of the Father to come to fruition. Had Satan really wanted to disrupt the plan all he needed to do was nothing, to leave Adam and Eve in a state of innocence in the Garden. He did not do this and so his supposed disruption to the plan was taken and made glorious. This can be seen in Eve's response to the choices she made in the Garden:

> And Eve, his wife, heard all these things and was glad, saying: Were it not for our transgression we never should have had seed, and never should have known good and evil, and the joy of our redemption, and the eternal life which God giveth unto all the obedient.[23]

God took of what Satan thought were discordant themes and made them more wonderful than before. There is a difference between *The Silmarillion* and the Gospel in the sense that the discordant themes were introduced after creation; though they have their beginnings in the Council and War in Heaven.

Recently a graduate student came to my office for guidance with an essay he

---

21. Moses 1: 39 (*The Pearl*, op. cit. [6]).
22. Moses 4: 6 (*The Pearl*, op. cit. [6]).
23. Moses 5: 11 (*The Pearl*, op. cit. [6]).

was writing. He had decided to explore a particular aspect of Latter-day Saint belief and suggest how that tied into Pentecostal Christian theology. His premise was that as a 'Restoration' movement/Church there has to be a way to account for the fact that God has failed; the failure being the apostasy, or the falling away of the Church established by Christ. I explained to this well-meaning young man that he had missed the entire point of Latter-day Saint theology: God has not failed; humanity has, and the apostasy and Restoration were a part of the plan from the beginning. Latter-day Saints believe the Lord has taken of the 'discordant themes' and made them even more glorious as they serve his ends. To fully appreciate the foretelling of the apostasy and restoration it is possible to use aspects of the Bible: 'For I know this that after my departing shall grievous wolves enter in among you, not sparing the flock. Also of your own selves shall men arise, speaking perverse things, to draw away disciples after them'.[24]

The 'righting' of this apostasy is also taught:

> For the time cometh, saith the Lamb of God, that I will work a great and a marvellous work among the children of men.[25]
> Therefore, I will proceed to do a marvellous work among this people, yea, a marvellous work and a wonder, for the wisdom of their wise and learned shall perish, and the understanding of their prudent shall be hid.[26]

The Restoration, which came about because of the apostasy is, for Latter-day Saints, a 'marvellous work and a wonder'.[27] The restoration of the fullness of the Gospel stands in stark contrast to the confusion of the years of the apostasy highlighted in Joseph Smith's search for truth.

Only two of the themes evident in the creation of Middle-earth have been explored in this paper: the communal nature of creation and the power of the One over evil. There are many other elements that could be explored at a later time; not least the view of God in Middle-earth, the importance of the Flame Imperishable, types of Satan in Middle-earth and an investigation into echoes of a Christ figure.

---

24. Acts 20: 29–30. See also Amos 8: 11 and 2 Thessalonians 2: 3.
25. 1 Nephi 14: 7 (*The Book of Mormon*, op. cit. [6]).
26. 2 Nephi 27: 26 (*The Book of Mormon*, op. cit. [6]).
27. Joseph Smith History 1: 10, 12 (*The Pearl*, op. cit. [6]).

# 'Tolkien's Magic'

## Ronald Hutton

*Magic is a pervasive feature of Tolkien's fiction, and one which gives his work much of its appeal. As a devout Catholic, however, he came to worry about the extent to which it could be reconciled with traditional Christian teaching, and provided a defence that it could. This paper considers the nature of magic in his stories, the sources on which he drew for it, and the question of whether his view of it was indeed orthodox in traditional Christian terms. I will propose that it derived directly from two bodies of literature - medieval legend and fairy tale - of which he was very fond, but which also clashed at times directly with Christian teaching on the matter. As a result, it became one of the heterodox features of his fictional world, and his attempt to defend it as orthodox in fact articulated a position that was directly contrary to traditional Christian doctrine.*

Most readers of Tolkien's fiction would regard it as being set in a magical universe, in which spell-casting and spell-weaving is a routine activity for many characters and pivotal to the action. Most would probably also agree that this glimmer of enchantment which lies over his story-telling is one of its most attractive and distinctive qualities. What is not always appreciated is how remarkable this quality is, for an author as devout and conventional in his Christian faith as Tolkien undoubtedly was. I am not suggesting that devout old-fashioned Christians cannot write stories which feature acts of magic, routinely applied by characters of whom their readers are expected to approve. I am only saying that they need, if they wish to make such acts consistent with traditional orthodox theology, to pay some special attention to the context in which the acts concerned are performed. I have three contentions to make in this paper. The first is that Tolkien himself did not in fact pay such attention when he wrote his fiction, tending instead to write instinctively and to draw in the process on other traditions, more favourable to magic than the established Christian one. The second is that after the publication and initial reception of *The Fellowship of the Ring*, he did become aware that there was a problem, and attempted to confront it. As part of this point I would also argue that he totally failed in this attempt. My third argument is that much of the success of his writing is due to his fidelity to literary sources which are similarly not easy to reconcile with Christian orthodoxy. In many ways his fiction represents a modern extension of

them.

Let me commence with his own attempt to confront the problem. It took the form of a paragraph in a letter which he drafted in September 1954, to thank his fellow novelist Naomi Mitchison for a glowing review which she had published of *FotR*.[1] In this, he confessed that thought that he had been 'far too casual' about his depiction of magic in the book and his characterisation of it. He excused himself by saying that it was a 'large question, and difficult', and that he could not 'burden' his story with a discussion of it. He went on in the letter, however, to supply such a discussion, and to base it on the ancient and medieval distinction between *magia* and *goeteia*. Unfortunately, he did not himself define what he took to mean by these terms, and he does not seem to have followed the conventional meaning of them. Both are Latin words based on Greek originals. *Magia* was simply a neutral term for any magical acts, and is indeed the one from which our modern word 'magic' directly derives. *Goeteia* was always a disreputable form of magic, increasingly identified with the conjuring of evil spirits. Tolkien, however, *seems* to treat the former as meaning 'actual' magic, which creates real physical changes, and the latter as illusion, intended to deceive observers into thinking that real magic was taking place. What is not in doubt is what follows, a ringing statement from Tolkien that neither form of magic was bad in itself, but distinguished by its motivation and use. Both of the opposed sides in his story used both kinds, but Sauron and his followers used it to impose their will on others, and the good characters did not.

In other words, the magic used by the characters on the right side was always employed for benevolent ends, and so it was effectively good. Magic, real or illusory, was to Tolkien simply a mechanism, morally neutral in itself. He then concluded with a further defence of his portrayal of it, and of a different kind: that it was an inherent and natural power in certain species of being, like Elves and wizards, and neither possessed by the humans of Middle-earth nor attainable by them. At this point he hit a snag: that Aragorn, as a hereditary king, had healing powers of a kind that most would regard as magical. He wriggled out of this with two further excuses, that Aragorn was not quite human, having elven blood in him, and that his powers might have rested largely on a combination of good pharmacological knowledge, and hypnosis. The first excuse was entirely reasonable, but the second showed how desperate he was getting. There can be no doubt that Tolkien took the idea that a legitimate hereditary king had healing powers from actual history. In particular, the monarchs of late medieval and early modern Europe, including England, were believed to have a divinely-given

---

1. Humphrey Carpenter, ed., *The Letters of J.R.R. Tolkien*, with the assistance of Christopher Tolkien, Houghton Mifflin, Boston, 1981, pp. 199–200.

power to heal scrofula, the disease nicknamed the 'King's Evil', by touch. To try to explain it away in terms of reason and of natural phenomena was to import an extreme rationality into a fictional world which was deeply magical in virtually every other way. None the less, as an explanation, though a rather disappointing one, it could hold up. Here, however, he remembered a further detail of his own writing which torpedoed his entire argument about the human lack of magic. In the margin of his draft letter he scribbled 'but the Númenoreans used 'spells' in making swords?'. Here, of course, he was absolutely right. When Aragorn examined the daggers taken from the human tomb on the Barrow Downs, and given by Tom Bombadil to Merry and Pippin, he noted that they were 'work of Westernesse, wound about with spells for the bane of Mordor' (*TT*, 'The Departure of Boromir', 405).[2] At this point Tolkien simply gave up. He laid aside the draft letter – which is why it survived among his manuscripts – and sent a new version, which lacked the tricky discussion of magic. Nor, as far as is known, did he ever attempt a consideration of the place of it in his work again.

It is time now to look at definitions of acceptable and unacceptable forms of magic in ancient and medieval Europe, and in Christian theology, to see how those provided by Tolkien matched up to them. The ancient definitions and attitudes have been much studied in the past quarter of a century, by authors including Jan Bremmer, Robert Fowler, Naomi Janowitz, Sarah Iles Johnston, Fritz Graf, Peter Green, Matthew Dickie, and Daniel Ogden, and, in a minor capacity, myself.[3] It is rare for so many historians to agree unanimously on anything, but on the question of ancient definitions they do. Of Tolkien's two terms, *goeteia* was, as I have said, distinctly grubby. It was the manipulation of uncanny power for disreputable purposes. *Magia* was, as I have also said, a more neutral term, meaning just the use of spells, charms and other mechanisms to control supernatural power in order to bring about human desires. What needs to

---

2. J.R.R. Tolkien, *The Lord of the Rings*, HarperCollins, London, 1995. All quotations from *LotR* are taken from this edition.

3. Peter Schafer and Hans G. Kippenberg, eds, *Envisioning Magic*, Brill, Leiden, 1997; David R. Jordan et al., eds., *The World of Ancient Magic*, Norwegian Institute at Athens, Bergen, 1999; Jan N. Bremmer and Jan R. Veenstra, eds., *The Metamorphosis of Magic from Late Antiquity to the Early Modern Period*, Peter, Leuven, 2002; Robert Fowler, 'Greek Magic, Greek Religion', *Illinois Classical Studies* 20 (1995), 1–22; Naomi Janowitz, *Magic in the Roman World*, Routledge, London, 2001; Susan Iles Johnston, 'Magic', in Susan Iles Johnston, ed., *Religions of the Ancient World*, Cambridge, Belknap, Massachusetts, 2004, 139–51; Fritz Graf, *Magic in the Ancient World*, Harvard University Press, Cambridge, Massachusetts, 1997; Matthew Dickie, *Magic and Magicians in the Greco-Roman World*, Routledge, London, 2001; Daniel Ogden, *Greek and Roman Necromancy*, Princeton University Press, Princeton, 2001; and *Night's Black Agents*, Hambledon Continuum, London, 2008; Ronald Hutton, *Witches, Druids and King Arthur*, Hambledon and London, 2003, pp. 87–136.

be emphasised here, however, is that most ancient people who used it did so with as a means of abuse, and with strong disapproval. This hostility to magic only became stronger as the ancient world grew old, and the era of Greek cultural supremacy in the Mediterranean world gave way to the Roman Empire. Magic was disliked for two different reasons. One was simply that it tended to be carried out in secret, and to gratify private wishes. To ancient societies, which were strongly communal, for one or a few of their members to gain apparent supernatural power to achieve their ends was inherently anti-social, and menacing. The other reason was religious, and embedded in the belief that the proper and respectable way to gain such power was to ask a god or goddess for help. Prayer was entirely permissible, because it left the decision over whether or not the end would be accomplished to superhumans, to whose will humans should always submit. To try to take control of the process of wielding supernatural force was to usurp the role of deities, and so added a risk of subverting the divine order as well as the social one. As such, it could easily bring down divine anger on the whole of a community. It should be emphasised that this was specifically a European viewpoint. Across the Mediterranean, in Egypt, was a much older civilisation in which the use of magic, even to control the deities themselves, was considered entirely permissible.[4] In Europe, however, the prejudice against it ran very deep. It was voiced as soon as Greek civilisation took shape, by authors as famous and influential as Plato. On the whole, the pagan Greeks and Romans united to define the magician as somebody on the margins of society, who threatened it as a whole, and had either to be cast out of it or forced to stop her or his activities.

Magic emerged into European culture from the ancient world as a definition of acts that bypassed the ordinary laws of nature. They were propelled by an effort by individual humans, using arcane power and knowledge, to tap into supernatural force for their own personal benefit. Christianity absorbed this definition wholesale, and with it the distrust and dislike that was attached to it. It added, however, a completely new context, of a cosmos ruled by a single, all-powerful, ever-present and completely good god. This caused a redirection of attention, when looking at the use of supernatural power by humans, onto one issue above all: its source. The Bible taught, in both Testaments, that holy people were able to achieve miraculous cures and transformations, if empowered by the true God. All other acts which apparently bypassed the laws of nature, by

---

4. Geraldine Pinch, *Magic in Ancient Egypt*, British Museum, London, 1994; Ian Assmann, 'Magic and Theology in Ancient Egypt', in Schafer and Kippenberg, eds, op. cit. [3], 1–18; David Frankfurter, 'Ritual Expertise in Roman Egypt and the Problem of the Category "Magic"', in Schafer and Kippenberg, eds, op. cit. [3], 115–35; Robert Kriech Ritner, *The Mechanics of Ancient Egyptian Magical Practice*, Oriental Institute of University of Chicago, Chicago, 1993; *Ancient Egyptian Magical Texts*, ed. Joris F. Borghouts, Brill, Leiden, 1978.

definition, had now to be considered the work of the Devil, and his attendant demons. Magicians, who were invariably people operating outside orthodox religious structures, and for personal gain or that of their clients, therefore became inherently satanic. The polar opposite of the magician became the saint, who, as somebody working within orthodox religion, was naturally using powers granted directly by divine favour. Any alleged or presumed act of magic was now a matter for concern to orthodox churchmen. Attitudes to magic in medieval and early modern Christianity have also recently been submitted to intensive study: by Matthew Dickie and myself, again, but also more prominently by Richard Kieckhefer, Michelle Sweeney, Karen Jolly and Valerie Flint.[5] Again, a very large degree of consensus has resulted. It is clear that the only open division of opinion among medieval Christians concerning magic was over the degree to which it could be seen as natural. Natural magic consisted of those powers and essences hidden within the created universe, which, if properly understood, could be manipulated by humans for their mutual benefit. As such, it was barely distinguishable from what we, and indeed medieval people, called science. In general, from St Augustine onward, Christian thought lumped together all forms of magic and divination as harmful, because demonic. It distinguished between the manipulation of material forms for human good and prosperity, which was wholly permissible, and attempts to transcend the limits of the material world using spiritual forces, which were not.

Such considerations were, however, largely confined to a scholarly and political elite of churchmen. There is every sign that ordinary people, until relatively modern times, continued to resort to spells and charms for practical needs, just as they did to material remedies. Specialists in these services, called charmers, or wise folk or cunning folk, remained a feature of local society all over Europe until the twentieth century. What is more, learned magicians also continued to operate all through the medieval and early modern periods. What propelled most people when using magical remedies was simply a matter of cause and effect. If they were believed to work, in practical terms, then they had the same status as any other remedies. The learned magicians, when they attempted to justify their activities at all, used very much the same argument. If

---

5. Dickie, op. cit. [3]; Hutton, op. cit. [3], pp. 137–92; Richard Kieckhefer, *Magic in the Middle Ages*, Cambridge University Press, Cambridge, 1989; Richard Kieckhefer, 'The Specific Rationality of Medieval Magic', *American Historical Review* 99 (1994), 813–36; Karen Louise Jolly, *Popular Religion in Late Saxon England*, University of North Carolina Press, Chapel Hill, 1996; Karen Jolly et al, eds, *The Athlone History of Witchcraft and Magic in Europe*, vol. 3, Athlone, London, 2002; Valerie J. Flint, *The Rise of Magic in Early Medieval Europe*, Oxford University Press, Oxford, 1991; Valerie J. Flint, 'The Demonisation of Magic and Sorcery in Late Antiquity', in *The Athlone History of Witchcraft and Magic in Europe*, vol. 2, Athlone, London, 1999, 277–348.

the results of their rites were beneficial to humanity, then they had to be a part of God's plan. As for the question of their origin, magicians suggested that either the powers used derived from angels, in which case they had to be godly, or from the success of magicians in overpowering demons and forcing them to work for the good of humans. In that case magic counted as a victory against Satan. At all levels, the basic test that was applied to justify magic was the use to which it was put: good or bad. This was never acceptable to established Christianity, but, it may now be recognised, it was the one proposed by Tolkien. There is no sign that orthodox Christian attitudes to magic have altered much over the past few hundred years. The official hostility to it has merely blended with, and been reinforced by, the modern rationalist one, that it is all superstitious nonsense. It must be emphasised that the orthodox attitudes were embedded in texts with which Tolkien was thoroughly familiar. Some, indeed, he edited, such as the poems *The Pearl* and *Sir Gawain and the Green Knight*. Nor has the recent scholarship that I have quoted overturned any earlier scholarly thought about ancient and medieval attitudes to magic, of the sort to which Tolkien would have been used. It has merely amplified it with a greater quantity of data, of a more precise kind.

To see how a different author of fantasy literature handled the same problem in the same period, we need turn only to another member of Tolkien's own literary circle. He was not merely a close friend of his but somebody whom Tolkien himself had helped convert to Christianity. I am referring of course to C.S. Lewis. In his sequence of novels about the land of Narnia, Lewis came to be more and more careful to assimilate his stories to Christian orthodoxy. Like Tolkien, his land was invested with what has conventionally been termed magic, and towards the end of the sequence he defined his stance with regard to that, along wholly traditional lines. In the fourth book, *The Silver Chair*, he has his two current child protagonists discuss how to call on the deity-figure of Narnia, Aslan. One considers invoking him in a magical rite, with circle and incantations. The more experienced and reflective replies that this would seem to be trying to make Aslan do something, when humans should really only ask him.[6] Here we see the ancient distinction between religion and magic. The sixth book, *The Magician's Nephew*, is largely devoted to a condemnation of magic, with a repeated emphasis on the point that magicians are never truly in control of the powers which they release. The only genuine, and good, magical activity, is that of the Creator of Narnia, Aslan. Right from the beginning, however, the Narnia stories embodied one further feature of the hostile European tradition with regard to magic. This was to see its most dangerous and most natural practitioners as being

---

6. C.S. Lewis, *The Silver Chair*, Bles, London, 1953, chapter 1.

female. This runs from the ancient world, with unscrupulous and destructive sorceresses like Circe and Medea, to the procession of villainous enchantresses in medieval romance, of whom Morgan le Fey, Vivianne and Nimue stand at the head. Whereas conventional witches, also from ancient times onward, were usually portrayed as repulsive hags, the sorceresses were physically attractive, and their magic was commonly related implicitly to their sexual power over men. With their sexuality played down, because these are, after all, children's books, such figures feature in four of the six Narnia novels. Jadis, the White Witch is the chief villainess in the first, and almost makes a comeback in the second, before being shown in her younger guise in the fifth. Even more interesting in this respect is the nameless sorceress, referred to vaguely as another of the same kind as Jadis, who is the evil character in fourth book. This is because she can transform herself into a lethal snake, thereby blending the figure of the enchantress with another medieval stereotype of supernatural female menace and allure, the lamia.[7] It makes a dramatic contrast that not merely does Tolkien not engage in any discussion of the theoretical problems of using magic in the course of his fiction, but he has no prominent, unequivocal and obvious, villainous sorceresses.[8] Very strikingly, the mighty enchantress of *The Lord of the Rings* is perhaps the most imposing and admirable female character in the whole of the three books: Galadriel. As if to emphasise this, Tolkien puts into the mouths of some of the other good (or ultimately good) characters – such as Boromir and the Riders of Rohan – doubts about her which echo exactly the bad opinion of female magicians found in medieval romance.[9] The whole point of these is that they are completely misplaced and unjust.

It is time now, in the final part of this discussion, to look at the well-springs of Tolkien's attitude to magic, and treatment of it, and ask why it was so different from the theological norm. It can be said at once that in this matter his difference from C.S. Lewis was completely in character for both men. Although both were equally devout in their Christianity, Lewis, the convert and the Protestant, was much more analytical and conscious in his relationship with it. Tolkien, the Catholic from boyhood, was a much more instinctual and organic sort of believer, less inclined to intellectualise his religion, except when forced to do so in self-

---

7. C.S. Lewis, *The Lion, The Witch and the Wardrobe*, Bles, London, 1950; *Prince Caspian*, Bles, London, 1951; *The Magician's Nephew*, Bodley Head, London, 1955; and op. cit. [6], chapters 10–12.

8. He once toyed with the figure of a wicked human sorceress, in Queen Berúthiel of Gondor, but never developed her story: J.R.R. Tolkien, *Unfinished Tales of Númenor and Middle-earth*, ed. Christopher Tolkien, HarperCollins, London, 1980, pp. 519–20.

9. Op. cit. [2], *The Fellowship of the Ring*, 'The Mirror of Galadriel'; op. cit. [2], *The Two Towers*, 'The Riders of Rohan'.

defence.[10] Furthermore, his attitude to magic must be put into two particular contexts that made the usual application of traditional European attitudes in general, and those of orthodox Christianity in particular, very difficult for him. The first was that, as he occasionally reminded correspondents, although Christians could feel that his imagined world was completely compatible with their own basic ethics and instincts, it was not actually a Christian cosmos. Its supreme deity was a much more remote and less interventionist being than the Christian one, and far more inclined to sub-contract the day-to-day concerns with events on his created earth. As a result, miracles of the Christian kind could not occur, and the opposition between magic and miracle could not exist. The other very unusual feature about Tolkien's stories is that human beings are not at their centre. This space is occupied by hobbits, who happen to be one of the minority of races in their world who do not have any magical abilities. As such, they play out much of the role of humans in most fantasy fiction, of representing the everyday, practical and rational, while struggling to cope with the enchanted and the fantastic. Their presence as the vehicles for the stories in many ways frees at least some kinds of human to become more magical.

The question of the roots of Tolkien's use of magic as a motif can now be addressed directly, and it can be found in the sources which he employed, as a famous medievalist and a consumer of fantasy literature himself. They can be considered with respect to each of the magically-empowered kinds of being which take their place in his fiction. To start at the top, there is no problem at all with the dominant beings actually in his sub-created world, the Valar. Tolkien came to equate them as much as possible with angels, of the supreme deity, but in his earlier writings he referred to them simply and accurately as gods. They may be lesser deities in comparison with the supreme one, but they are still much more active and powerful on their own account than Christian angels. As I have emphasised elsewhere, they form a bickering, dynamic and often badly-behaved pantheon of the sort familiar from most pagan mythologies. They also started by having effective control of the day-to-day management of the world, even if they retired more and more from it with time.[11] Although strictly speaking unable to create anything from new themselves, they could reshape both heavens and

---

10. This impression of their natures is based on their writings, but also their biographies: Humphrey Carpenter, *J. R. R. Tolkien*, Allen & Unwin, London, 1977; George Sayer, *Jack*, Hodder and Stoughton, London, 1988; Colin Duriez, *Tolkien and C.S. Lewis*, Hiddenspring, Mahwah, New Jersey, 2003; Alan Jacobs, *The Narnian*, SPCK, London, 2005; John Garth, *Tolkien and the Great War*, HarperCollins, London, 2003.

11. Ronald Hutton, 'The Pagan Tolkien', in Paul E. Kerry, ed., *The Ring and the Cross*, Farleigh Dickinson University Press, Madison, 2011, 57–70; Ronald Hutton, 'Can We Still Have a Pagan Tolkien?', in Paul E. Kerry, ed., *The Ring and the Cross*, Farleigh Dickinson University Press, Madison, 2011, 90–105.

earth to a very great extent. Effectively, they could even form new species by this process.[12] Their powers are effectively so tremendous that the term 'magic' is really too limited to comprehend them, but sometimes they use apparent magical techniques to achieve their will. The real bad egg among them, Melkor or Morgoth, for example, is described as 'cursing' a captured enemy and his kin, as an act of punishment and vengeance.[13]

The case of the Elves is more interesting, and for our present purposes more significant. Tolkien was so very fond of fairies that he included at points in his fiction virtually every kind of them represented in the traditional folklore and medieval literature of the British Isles. At the one extreme stand his High Elves, who are most similar to the Irish Tuatha de Danaan, themselves originally goddesses and gods, and the British 'high fairies' or 'trooping fairies' (to use the terms of C.S. Lewis and Katharine Briggs), with their royal court and aristocratic lifestyle.[14] At the other, in some of his earlier poems and stories, are small, cute fairies of the kind familiar from Victorian and Edwardian children's books.[15] It is worth stressing quite how anomalous the medieval, northern European fairies, of whom Tolkien was so fond, are in both the classical ancient world and Christian theology. They have no real equivalents in Greek or Roman mythology. They are not deities, and neither are they nature spirits like the water or tree nymphs of the ancient Mediterranean, because they had a royal court, and industries, and went on processions and raids. Nor could a place be easily made for them in the Christian cosmos. Two were attempted in the Middle Ages – to declare them a lesser sort of fallen angel, not quite bad enough to be thrown all the way to Hell, or to declare them the ghosts of unusual human beings. Neither explanation found as much favour with medieval writers as the third one, which was that they were simply baffling, having no obvious origin point in Christian tradition. At the time of the Reformation, many evangelical Protestants dealt with the problem by deciding that they had to be demons pure and simple.[16] That,

---

12. Indeed, of all the races of his world, Tolkien acknowledged that the Creator only made elves and humans directly. Op. cit. [1], Letter 131, p. 147.

13. J.R.R. Tolkien, *The Silmarillion*, Allen & Unwin, London, 1983, chapters 20–21.

14. C.S. Lewis, *The Discarded Image*, Cambridge University Press, Cambridge, 1964, pp. 122–33; Katharine Briggs, *The Anatomy of Puck*, Routledge, London, 1959, pp. 8–43.

15. For example, in his early poem 'Goblin Feet', first published in *Oxford Poetry* in 1915 and since anthologised twice. John D. Rateliff, *The History of the Hobbit. Part One: Mr Baggins*, HarperCollins, London, 2007, pp. 111–21, also notes that in the original version of 'The Tale of Tinúviel', the elvish heroine hides underneath a tall flower, and that *The Hobbit* saw the last appearance of this sort of elf (at Rivendell) in Tolkien's fiction.

16. Minor White Latham, *The Elizabethan Fairies*, Columbia University Press, New York, 1930, pp. 23–64; Briggs, op. cit. [14], pp. 8–43; Katherine Briggs, *The Fairies in Tradition and Literature*, Routledge, London, 1967, pp. 48–57, 105–10; Diane Purkiss, *Troublesome Things*,

of course, was the very last way in which Tolkien regarded them. He adhered faithfully to mainstream medieval tradition by declaring simply that they were another race of being, who were wholly themselves.

A large part of their appeal to him is that, in all traditional bodies of lore, they were inherently magical beings, adept in casting spells and glamours and changing shape. Here his essay on fairy stories, written before he began work on *LotR* and revised as he was near the end of it, serves as a manifesto for his attitude to magic in general. In it he defined a fairy story as any which contains spontaneous and inherent magic, which he opposed directly to the laboured and artificial rites of ceremonial magicians.[17] To him they were tales which embody the marvellous: the property of enchantment, which he called the 'elvish craft', par excellence. To him that property allowed the refreshment of the human imagination which he held to be essential to mental health, as an antidote to the ugliness that he perceived in modern life, but also to the sufferings of life in general. It also, however, served a Christian purpose to him, in keeping the human imagination open to the possibility of the supernatural and the miraculous, and so to the reception of the Christian message. The irony of this argument is to me as breathtaking as its tactical brilliance: after almost two millennia in which orthodox Christianity had looked upon the concept of magic with deep suspicion, Tolkien was suggesting that a love of the magical could be to his religion's advantage. Such an argument could only have potency, however, in a modern and rationalist age in which people were no longer afraid of spells, and no longer relied on them to ward off misfortune or cure disease. It was fitted for one in which people now regarded elves as an entertainment, and not as a potentially serious problem. This is the essence of Tolkien's approach to magic: that his vision of it was essentially a post-industrial, post-rationalist one, but that he drew on very old materials to fashion its products. This was, indeed, exactly what he said that people should do in fairy stories. One further example of it can be given here: that whenever the medieval and early modern British identified elves and fairies as having monarchs, it was more often the queen than a king whose importance was emphasised.[18] That is the true reason why Galadriel is so powerful and so admirable, transcending the stereotype of the

---

Allen Lane, London, 2000, pp. 52–82; Jeremy Harte, *Explore Fairy Traditions*, Heart of Albion Press, Loughborough, 2004, pp. 8–27, 115–50.

17. First published in C.S. Lewis, ed., *Essays Presented to Charles Williams*, Oxford University Press, London, 1947, 38–89, p. 47. Reprinted in J.R.R Tolkien, *Tree and Leaf*, Unwin, London, 1964, 11–72.

18. Latham, op. cit. [16], pp. 65–110; Lucy Allen Paton, *Studies in the Fairy Mythology of Arthurian Romance*, Franklin, New York, 1960; Diane Purkiss, 'Old Wives' Tales Retold: The Mutations of the Fairy Queen', in Danielle Clarke and Elizabeth Clarke, eds, *This Double Voice*, Macmillan, Basingstoke, 2000, pp. 103–33.

dangerous enchantress – she occupies an equivalent position among the Elves of Middle-earth.

The other magical races can be dealt with swiftly. Dwarves, from their first appearances in Tolkien's unpublished fiction, in Beleriand, and their first appearances in his print, in *The Hobbit*, automatically use magic as well as practical skills when making objects. This is simply because that is what they do in the medieval northern texts which Tolkien knew so well. The basic plot of the Niebelungenlied, or of the problems given to the Norse gods by the Brisingamen necklace, would have been impossible without this trait. Wizards changed their nature in the course of the development of his body of legend: or rather, they had their nature better defined, in a way that was more theologically comfortable. When Tolkien's greatest wizard first appears, under the name Bladorthin in the first drafts of *The Hobbit*, there is nothing to indicate that he is not, as wizards have always been supposed to be, a human being who has become expert in magic. He is indeed repeatedly called a man, and continued to be so after he had been renamed Gandalf. None the less, as Gandalf grew more powerful, in successive drafts, Tolkien classed wizards in a letter with supernatural beings.[19] In an earlier unpublished work, the *Book of Lost Tales*, he had already done so, creating a being called a wizard who was also a fairy, and was, after many changes, to become the figure of Sauron.[20] None the less, in print, the status of Gandalf and his fellows long remained ambiguous. It was only in the 1950s that he began to declare roundly that they were not human.[21] He developed instead the concept of wizards as a category of spirit related to the Valar, the Istari, sent out from Valinor to aid Middle-earth.[22] This rescued them completely from association with professional human magicians, a category of person with whom, as explained, European tradition, including the Christian, had always been profoundly uncomfortable. Indeed, in Middle-earth humans are generally devoid of magical powers. Yet, as Tolkien ruefully acknowledged in that unpublished section of letter, he let himself be carried away in the matter of making weapons. How could he resist this, when the use of spells in smithcraft was embedded in some of those northern texts on which he drew primarily for inspiration? One such was Völsunga Saga, in which is described the cutting of magical runes upon a sword, to aid the person who used it.[23] The tradition of ancient northern Europe, that the skill of the smith was at least partly magical,

---

19. Rateliff, op. cit. [15], pp. 28–53.

20. This is Túvo or Tü, in J.R.R. Tolkien, *The Book of Lost Tales I*, ed. Christopher Tolkien, Unwin, London, 1983, pp. 232–35.

21. As in the letter to Robert Murray in 1954: op. cit. [1], Letter 156, p. 202.

22. Op. cit. [8], pp. 502–20.

23. H. Halliday Sparling, ed., *VölsungaSaga*, Scott, London, 1888), p. 71.

ran too deep to be expunged by any fear of magic; after all, it was just that kind of use of uncanny power, for the good of others, which popular tradition (and Tolkien) instinctually approved.

The place of magic in the fiction of J.R.R. Tolkien is therefore a matter of quite considerable complexity. On the one hand, he himself simply loved it, as a motif in stories, and saw it as meeting a crucial imaginative need in modern society, which was of some benefit to Christianity, as it was to any religious faith. On the other hand he was also aware, if belatedly, of a long hostility to, and suspicion of, magic in Christian tradition, which drew on strong and ancient roots. This was offset in turn, however, by other ancient and medieval texts, and a strong folkloric tradition, which not only spoke of the existence of inherently magical races but justified the use of spells by humans in a good cause. These texts, and that tradition, represented some of Tolkien's own greatest sources of pleasure and inspiration. At the last major Tolkien Society conference, I suggested that, culturally, Tolkien's fiction ultimately rested on three main, and different, bodies of material: the Christian, the pagan and the fairy-tale.[24] Much of the time they co-existed in harmony in his own creations, but occasionally there were tensions between them; and these became greater after the publication of *LotR* began, and he became more self-conscious about his writing. I hope that this paper has substantiated this view further, but also taken further the other major point that I made before, that it is precisely the co-existence of these different elements in his work which provides its sheer richness and complexity.

---

24. Ronald Hutton, 'The Pagan Tolkien', in Sarah Wells, ed., *The Ring Goes Ever On: Proceedings of the Tolkien 2005 Conference*, vol. 2, The Tolkien Society, Coventry, 2008, pp. 32–39. See also Hutton, op. cit. [11].

# THE MYTHIC DIMENSION

# 'Cyclic cataclysms, Semitic stereotypes and religious reforms: a classicist's Númenor'

## Pamina Fernández Camacho

*Tolkien's work has rarely attracted the attention of classicists, but investigating the importance of Greek and Roman elements in the framework of Middle-earth can sometimes yield interesting results. This study is centered on the Akallabêth, and it outlines some of the insights obtained in this manner: from Plato's influence on Tolkien, with his theory of sucessive catastrophes and his use of elements from different civilisations, especially Eastern and Semitic, to create the first 'fictional country' on the Western edge of the world, to the figure of Tar-Palantir as a subverted replica of Julian the Apostate and his attempts to restore a Neoplatonic form of paganism to a Roman empire overrun by Christianity.*[1]

In Tolkien's unfinished story *The Notion Club Papers*, as the Club reflects upon the languages of Númenor, the character Lowdham is credited with these words:

'I said Atlantis because Ramer told us that he associated the word Númenor with the Greek name. Well, look! Here we learn that Númenor was destroyed; and we end with a lament: far, far away now is Atalante. Atalante is plainly another name for Númenor-Atlantis. But only after its downfall. For in Avallonian atalante is a word formed normally from a common base talat "topple over, slip down".... Atalante means "She that has fallen down". So the two names have approached one another, have reached a very similar shape by quite unconnected routes. At least, I suppose the routes are unconnected. I mean, whatever traditions may lie behind Plato's Timaeus, the name that he uses, Atlantis, must be just the same old "daughter of Atlas" that was applied to Calypso. But even that connects the land with a mountain regarded as the pillar of heaven. Minul-Tarik, Minul-Tarik! Very interesting.' (*Sauron Defeated*, 249)[2]

This is the only time that Plato's name occurs in roughly one hundred and

---

1. A version of this article has been published in the *Lembas Extra* journal of the Dutch Tolkien Society.
2. J.R.R. Tolkien, *Sauron Defeated*, ed. Christopher Tolkien, HarperCollins, London, 2002.

fifty pages of discussion between learned men about the myth of Atlantis. The lion's share belongs to the Northern *legendarium*, especially Germanic but also Celtic, with which Tolkien desired to connect his version of the story at the time. Plato, in passing, is credited with having received a distorted echo of an older tradition. This affirmation is not discussed further, not even by the Club's appointed defender of the Classics Philip Frankley, who might have been a good foil to these pretensions (Philip 'Horsefriend of Macedon', as Lowdham calls him alluding to his name's Greek etymology and historical connotations, who is said to have 'a taste for Romance literatures and a distaste for things Germanic'). But either he or the young Classics undergraduate that he introduced into the club, John 'Rashbold' who significantly remains silent during the whole affair (intended maybe to represent the young Tolkien who studied Greek as a young man), could have pointed out a few things. Such as, *there is no Greek tradition about Atlantis before Plato.* Atlantis came out of the *Timaeus* and the *Critias* like Athena from her father's head, already grown and armed. Or that Atlantis, the 'insolent power in the West' which sunk beneath the waves in a single day, is completely distinct from the amalgam of 'Western island' traditions found in many different cultures, which are much better identified with Tolkien's Valinor: remote realms of the Blessed with definite otherwordly connotations. None of them sink.

Plato's own characters, of course, declare the story to be 'completely true'. To increase the believability of this 'new myth', his character Critias spins an intricate tale of millennia-old Egyptian records, a tradition transmitted orally through several generations of the same family and even an old and revered lawgiver figure of Athenian tradition, Solon, who is said to have been prevented from writing the tale by the weight of his political obligations.[3] Even today, amateur atlantologists from all around the globe fall for this setting.[4] Tolkien, who employs similar methods to create the setting of his own tale (bringing in legendary and historical characters like St. Brendan, Shield Sheafing and the various Ælfwines, family tradition and mysterious scribbles found in old libraries) should know better. Plato has been called the inventor of Western fiction as such, and his work 'the first piece of deliberately fictional narrative in Greek literature', precisely because of this pastiche and the claim of truth put in his narrator's mouth.[5] In Tolkien's time, moreover, authors like Stevenson, Stoker or Haggard had turned all these devices into a staple setting to create an

---

3. Plat. Tim. 21.

4. P. Vidal-Naquet, *L'Atlantide: Petite histoire d'un mythe platonicien*, Belles Lettres, Paris, 2005.

5. Christopher Gill, 'Plato's Atlantis Story and the Birth of Fiction', *PhandLit* 3 (1979), pp. 64–78.

illusion of authenticity.[6]

It is precisely this search for authenticity which turns this silencing (or 'transforming') of Plato's role into a necessity. Because Plato is, in fact, the creator of Atlantis, to recognise his role as such would have destroyed Tolkien's pretensions to connect it with Northern myth and geography. And this was no mere hobby for the Professor. Both *The Lost Road* and *The Notion Club Papers* are rooted in a very Romantic view of language and national heritage, which harked back to the discovery of Indo-European and the consequent focus on historical grammar.[7] Languages become identified with peoples, and families of related peoples, constituting an expression of their truest character, whose core remains largely unaltered through their evolution. The link between this view and the racialism which also became fashionable in the nineteenth and early twentieth century is evident: the 'Indo-Europeans' or 'Indo-Germans' were primarily a linguistic group which became identified with the 'Aryans', originally – as Tolkien himself points out – only used as an ethnic name by the easternmost, Indian and Persian members of the family.[8] Their opposition to the Semitic group (discovered in the same decade as Indo-European) was also originally linguistic.

Tolkien himself was quite chagrined by the 'French invasion' of the English language, and specialised in Anglo-Saxon. His characters are able to 'remember' certain myths and languages from blood heritage. The fact that he, himself, declared that he had experienced 'the Wave dream',[9] and came by chance upon the linguistic root for 'Atalantë',[10] and, furthermore, the fact that those characters, especially the Alboin of *The Lost Road*, can be seen as having autobiographical traits, proves that his Atlantis was originally meant as the collective memory of a people that lived in Britain 'in old days, very old days, before the Romans, or the Carthaginians (*Lost Road*, 42),[11] and that he felt a personal connection with the people belonging to that place and time. And though the nationalistic use of Atlantis to explain the origins of peoples who have nothing to do with Plato's story is infinitely older than the twentieth century, Tolkien should have been aware of the use of the Atlantis myth in Germany by Nazi ideologists

---

6. M. Saler, *As If: Modern Enchantment and the Literary Prehistory of Virtual Reality*, Oxford University Press, Oxford, 2012.

7. Martin Bernal, *Black Athena: The Afroasiatic Roots of Classical Civilisation*, vol. 1: *The Fabrication of Ancient Greece 1785-1985*, Rutgers University Press, 1987, p. 216.

8. Humphrey Carpenter, ed., *The Letters of J.R.R. Tolkien*, with the assistance of Christopher Tolkien, HarperCollins, London, 2006, Letter 30, p. 37.

9. Op. cit., Letter 163, p. 213.

10. Op. cit. Letter 256, p. 347, footnote.

11. J.R.R. Tolkien, *The Lost Road and Other Writings*, ed. Christopher Tolkien, Unwin Hyman, London, 1996.

like Zschaetzsch, Hermann or Rosenberg, not to mention the ideologists of the Ahnererbe Institut.[12] His description of evil, imperialistic Númenor has been connected to Germany, especially as Christopher Tolkien remarked 'When at this time my father reached back to the world of the first man to bear the name "Elf-friend" he found there an image of what he most condemned and feared in his own.' (*Lost Road*, 84) The very recovery of the notion that Atlantis was not, in fact, a utopia but a dystopia is a symptom of sorts of German misuse of the story at the time.

In this sense, Tolkien's Númenor writings can be compared with two other twentieth century works, Ullman and Kien's opera *Der Kaiser von Atlantis* and Géorges Pérec's *W, or the Memory of Childhood*. The first was written in 1944, a few months before the authors disappeared in a concentration camp; the 'Emperor of Atlantis', whose name is Emperor Overall (a parody of Hitler), declares war on the world and disrupts the natural order of things, which can only be solved by him coming to grips with his own mortality. The second, as the title indicates, is a semi-autobiographical work where the author of *La disparition*, a Polish Jew who lost his parents on the Second World War, mixes childhood remembrances with an account of an island in the far West originally introduced as a fulfillment of the Olympic ideal, where the life of all the inhabitants revolves around sports competitions (one of which is called Atlantics) in a way that recalls the glorification of the 'gods of the stadium' in Leni Riefenstahl's account of the Berlin Olympics. Little by little, the dystopia is revealed in the shape of all sorts of cruel routines and treatments that the athletes are subjected to. *W* is a world where people need to know how to 'get on their knees, stand up. Stand up, get on their knees. Fast, ever faster. Run in circles, lie on the ground, crawl, stand up again, run. Stand up, waiting for inspection, hours, days, days and nights'.[13] At the end of the book, the story of the island is revealed as an allegory of life in the concentration camps, just as Tolkien's earlier drafts of the Númenor under the shadow of Sauron seems an allegory of the development of modern warfare during the German war, as well as the Nazi doctrine of the *Lebensraum*:

> At first he revealed only secrets of craft, and taught the making of many things powerful and wonderful; and they seemed good. Our ships go now without the wind, and many are made of metal that sheareth hidden rocks, and they sink not in calm or storm; but they are no longer fair to look upon.... our shields are impenetrable, our swords cannot be withstood, our darts are like thunder and pass over

---

12. Op. cit. [3].
13. G. Pérec, *W ou le souvenir d'enfance*, Denoël, Paris, 1975, p. 205.

leagues unerring. Where are our enemies? We have begun to slay one another. For Númenor now seems narrow, that was so large. Men covet, therefore, the lands that other families have long possessed.... Wherefore Sauron hath preached deliverance; he has bidden our king to stretch forth his hand to Empire. Yesterday it was over the East. Tomorrow – it will be over the West. (*Lost Road*, 74)

Plato's account of the degeneration of a society that at first seemed good had not inspired previous atlantologists, (and that is all the more true of the nationalistic ones like Goropius Becanus, Rudbeck, Spanuth, Wilford or Mazzoldi.[14]) who tended to see the island only in a positive light. Even today, Trousson still calls Atlantis 'the first utopia'.[15] Still, it cannot be denied that the use of the myth by the Nazis favoured the strong comeback of that element of the story.

Another thing it would have favoured is the condemnation of nationalistic myths involving Atlantis, especially those having a Germanic racial component. Several authors writing about Tolkien have propounded a World War II-related 'acute awareness of the dangers of insisting on ... national purity; he knew how origin and cultural myths could be misused and appropriated,[16] which would be behind a change of direction in his writings in the 1940s. As Renée Vink puts it in her recently published book *Wagner and Tolkien: Mythmakers*:

It was the combination of myth and nation ... that had become tainted after the war; mythology and territory had become very uneasy bedfellows. Through no fault of Tolkien's, the Anglo-Saxon connection had become problematic, and even the idea of transmission via "racial memory" introduced in the "Notion Club Papers" no longer looked innocent. Explicit ties had to be cut.[17]

*The Notion Club Papers* was indeed abandoned in 1946, shortly after the end of the war, and from then on any attempts to root the story of Númenor/Atlantis in English history and legend would cease. Many years later, in 1964, Tolkien would write that he had found that his 'real interest was only in the upper end,

---

14. P. Vidal-Naquet, 'L'Atlantide et les nations', in Vidal-Naquet, ed., *La démocratie grecque vue d'ailleurs: Essais d'historiographie ancienne et moderne*, Flammarion, Paris, 1990, pp. 139–59.

15. R. Trousson, *Voyage aux pays de nulle part: Histoire littéraire de la pensée utopique*. Université de Bruxelles, Brussels, 1999.

16. Dimitra Fimi, *Tolkien, Race and Cultural History: From Fairies to Hobbits*, Palgrave Macmillan, Basingstoke, 2009, p. 130.

17. Renée Vink, *Wagner and Tolkien: Mythmakers*, Walking Tree Publishers, Zurich and Jena, 2012, p. 102.

the *Akallabêth* or *Atalantie*'.[18] However that may be, an attentive reading of *The Lost Road* and, especially, *The Notion Club Papers*, shows an uphill battle to fit, in a context of Germanic and Celtic myth, a story which is anything but. Myths about 'Western Blessed Lands', like Tir-Nan-Og, Hy Bresail or St. Brendan's isle, or legends about divine children coming from the Sea in a boat like that of Shield Sheafing, have, as we mentioned earlier, and in spite of Tolkien's own rewritings, a very tenuous connection with the main matter of the story – which, in fact, follows Plato far more closely than most atlantologists ever did.

But, some might be asking now, to what degree is this true? How does this follow on from the lack of actual mentions of the philosopher in Tolkien's writings and letters, or his supposed 'Northern focus'? Actually, and contrary to the image of a Professor of Anglo-Saxon completely shut to Classical influences, the portrait that emerges from Tolkien's letters is that of a man who remembers his years studying the Classics and uses his knowledge to frequently inform and relate his world to. His Middle-earth is 'archaic English for ἡ οἰκουμένη'.[19] His Quenya is an 'Elven Latin' composed 'on a Latin basis with two other (main) ingredients' that he said, 'happen to give me "phonaesthetic" pleasure: Finnish and Greek'.[20] Latin is one of his favourite languages.[21] Túrin's figure 'might be said ... to be derived from elements in Sigurd the Volsung, Oedipus and ... Kullervo.[22] As a young man, he 'first discovered the sensation of literary pleasure in Homer',[23] which gives a special significance to his definition of both the Rohirrim and their Second Age ancestors as 'Homeric' in his letter to Milton Waldman.[24] He also expresses strong opinions on the state of politics in Classical Greece, comparing them with the politics of his time. In a letter to Christopher Tolkien he toes the traditional line of seeing Alexander the Great's 'orientalisation' as a degeneration that led to disaster and death, and later Greece as 'a kind of Vichy-Hellas',[25] selling postcards about its glorious past. More interestingly, in a letter written in December 1944 (also to Christopher Tolkien), he objects strongly to a politician's affirmations of Greece being 'the home of democracy' in very revealing terms:

δημοχρατία (sic!) was not in Greek a word of approval but was nearly equivalent to "mob rule"; and he neglected to note that the Greek Philosophers –

---

18. Op. cit. [8], Letter 257, p. 347.
19. Op. cit. [8], Letters 152, 154, 183, 211.
20. Op. cit. [8], Letter 144, p. 176.
21. Op. cit. [8], Letters 163, 294, 338.
22. Op. cit. [8], Letter 131, p. 150.
23. Op. cit. [8], Letter 142, p. 172.
24. Op. cit. [8], Letter 131, p. 159.
25. Op. cit. [8], Letter 52, p. 64.

and far more is Greece the home of Philosophy – did *not* approve of it.[26]

This is, in fact, a clear reference to Plato, even without mentioning his name. Plato is the Greek philosopher whose writings have reached us and who did not approve of democracy. Of course, not every philosopher disapproved of democracy, and not everyone who disapproved of democracy was a philosopher. But Plato finds himself in the unique position of having started – apparently following the teachings of Socrates, who did not leave any writings – a school of thought that was radically critical of it, and of having been admired, studied and preserved until our own days in an unbroken line of tradition (giving the false impression that his rather minority party was larger than it actually was).

So, Tolkien was parroting Plato roughly at the same time that he was working on *The Drowning of Anadunë* and *The Notion Club Papers*, and the most striking traits of the story were emerging. To what extent this might not have been a coincidence is something that we will explore as we proposed above, going through each of these traits separately and analysing them in light of Plato's Atlantis story.

## THE TRAITS OF THE STORY

The first element to be analysed will be the origins of Númenor, and those of its royal dynasty. On reading the 'Akallabêth', the resemblance with the origins of Atlantis will rather strike the Platonic scholar. A sea-god (in this case the Maia Ossë, the most similar to Poseidon among Tolkien's Ainur) raises the island from the depths of the sea for Men to live in (*TSil*, 'Akallabêth', 310–11).[27] The first king, Elros, comes from a pair of twins, who are called 'Peredhil' because of their double nature: they have the blood of mortal Men, and at the same time the blood of the Eldar and the Maiar. In Plato's story, the concept of twins constitutes a reinforcing symbol of a similar double nature, the nature of the sons of Poseidon and the mortal maiden Kleito who would rule Atlantis. The oldest twin of the first pair – there are five – is the overlord of the island; he would leave the kingship to his oldest son, so the inheritance would always be passed in the male line.[28] Eventually, it is this double nature of the rulers that would bring the moral decay of Atlantis, as Plato explains:

> For many generations, and while the nature of the god was still dominant in them, the kings paid heed to the laws and remained

---

26. Op. cit. [8], Letter 94, p. 107.
27. J.R.R. Tolkien, *The Silmarillion*, ed. Christopher Tolkien, HarperCollins, London, 1999.
28. Plat. Criti. 114c.

attached to the divine principle, to which they were themselves related…. But, as the divine element was diminished, being mixed with the mortal, and as human character prevailed, then, unable to withstand their present prosperity, they fell into shameful behaviour.[29]

Tolkien's story follows Plato in seeing the degeneration of the ruling line as a symbol for the decay of the whole kingdom. The influence of their non-mortal side is symbolised by their long life; as the 'shadow grows' in Númenor the rulers start dying earlier and earlier, until Gimilkhâd's shocking 198 years of life (*TSil*, 'Akallabêth', 322). This goes hand in hand with the development of imperialism, their moral decay and, eventually, their worship of Melkor.

This whole storyline, however, had several stages of development. It was not part of Tolkien's earliest draft (*Fall of Numenor 1*); in *Fall of Numenor 2* it is Elrond who is the first ruler of Númenor, and there is no mention of the dwindling lifespan. Elros as the ruler of Númenor and as the twin brother of Elrond who chose mortality emerges in *Fall of Numenor 3*, then disappears throughout the various versions of the *Drowning of Anadunë* except for a mention in one sketch.[30] But the whole correlation between the foundational twin element, the double nature and the decay of the line being perceived as, and related to, a gradual dilution of the Elven/Maia trait of long life, was the conclusion of a laborious process of expounding which does not become evident until the version published in *The Silmarillion*. The fact that the more he wrote about it the more his story became like Plato's, is, in my opinion, evidence of the shift of priorities that would further and further remove Númenor from the frame of Northern nationalistic atlantology.

## THE SECOND ELEMENT

Following Plato's outline in the matter of the dilution of a 'divine element' (which would have suited Tolkien's general tendency to depict his world's history in degenerative terms, not to mention his obsession with heritages), would, as we have mentioned earlier, naturally result in turning Númenor into a dystopia, as in the original Platonic myth, and unlike the greatest majority of elaborations on the subject. Degeneration turns what was originally positive into something negative, and, in both cases, destruction is invoked as the ultimate consequence of this. In Tolkien, the outline has become clearer: moral corruption turns into a desire to grasp what does not belong to oneself, culminating in the ultimate sin:

---

29. Op. cit. 121a–b. The translation is mine.
30. Op. cit. [2], 'Sketch III', p. 403. On the variants of 'The Fall of Númenor', see op. cit. [8].

sailing against the land where the Valar live to grasp immortality from them. The sinking of Númenor happens because the Valar agree to lay down their rule and call upon Ilúvatar to solve the conflict.

Plato is less clear: though the element of the assembly of the gods deciding what to do with corrupted Atlantis, under the authority of Zeus, the 'god of gods',[31] and the cataclysm which sinks Atlantis under the waves,[32] are both clearly there, they do not belong to the same dialogue or to the same sequence of events, and only the later interpreters (among them Tolkien) have joined both together. The tale of the assembly is, in fact, interrupted just as Zeus is about to speak; the *Critias* remained unfinished forever. It is clear, though, that Zeus does not plan on destroying Atlantis completely.[33] On the other hand, we already know, because it was advanced in the *Timaeus*, that Atlantis would sink, but not before they launched a great invasion on the Mediterranean and were soundly defeated by the Ancient Athenian army. Ancient Athens is the utopia fighting the dystopia, but in spite of its victory, brought on by its ultimate moral superiority, both are equally swallowed by a cataclysm.

My interpretation of how those threads can be put together would be to reconstruct the sequence of events according to a well-known pattern of Athenian tragedy and historiography: the gods, when they want to bring ruin upon someone, bring madness and hubris upon them so they are incited to actions that will end in disaster. What the gods would have decided in their assembly, following this pattern, would have been to push the Atlantians to start an unjust war that they would not win – exactly the role that *Sauron* would have in Tolkien's version. The cataclysm, on the other hand, would belong to a different order of circumstances, and have no moral significance whatsoever: as Plato points out earlier in the *Timaeus*, through the wise Egyptian priest of his tale, such cataclysms are periodical happenings on Earth which bring on a restart of human civilisation, and they cannot be avoided.[34]

Plato, however, was working with a set of morals and philosophical principles and interests which Tolkien would not have shared. He was thinking in terms of political systems, and the political unity is, as the word indicates, the *polis*, the city-state. A city with the perfect laws, like that of the *Republic* and Ancient Athens (the rival of Atlantis in the story) could never degenerate in a million years, because that would have been a symptom of the political system not being wholly good *ab initio* (as it was with Atlantis, which, as commentators have pointed out, carries from the beginning the seeds of its future destruction). So the

---

31. Op. cit. [28], 121c.
32. Op. cit. [3], 25d.
33. Op. cit. [28], 121b–c.
34. Op. cit. [3], 22.

cataclysm would be the only narrative device capable of explaining why Athens has become so different and has no remembrance of its past.

Tolkien, on the other hand, prefers to see history in terms of individuals, and, for him, every human soul is marred from the Fall. There can be no perfection in Arda Marred, so the corruption of Númenor-Atlantis (kept at bay for a long time by the goodness and wisdom of the civilisation symbolised by Elven blood and contacts with Elves) is rather the natural order of things. Therefore, there is no Tale of Two Cities here, only of one: the same thing which starts as good will end as bad. It is no coincidence that the great refoundation of Númenorean civilisation, Aragorn's unified kingdoms of Arnor and Gondor, was expected to start rotting before the last generation to remember the War of the Ring died (*Peoples*, 465–79).[35]

Still, to a degree, both stories use the device of the cataclysm, taken from much older sources. There is no need to detail the various Deluge traditions, which both Plato and Tolkien knew quite well. Plato integrates those into a general theory of the world which also incorporates the old Myth of the Ages, formulated in Hesiod's *Works and Days*, which postulates the successive existence of several races of rational beings, each becoming extinct after its allotted time on Earth. Therefore, in Plato's myth, the world is struck by a series of cataclysms which will periodically destroy every vestige of civilisation on the face of Earth, which then has to start anew. Evolution becomes cyclical, as each new cycle is unable to build on any prior knowledge.[36]

Tolkien's work shows clear evidence of these conceptions, though they are, once more, given a particular bent. There is an Age of Men, opposed to an earlier time of the Elves, who were designed to awake first and then fade to give way to the Secondborn. Cataclysms are, too, an integral part of his *legendarium*, and they are the major reason for the destruction of great lands and civilisations like Beleriand and Númenor, not to mention Earth's primitive state of grace symbolised by the Spring of Arda. The world of the First Age ends with a great cataclysm provoked by the War of Wrath, while the Númenorean cataclysm not only destroys the island, but also the whole concept of mythical geography. Still, though it could be said that the first puts an end to the kingdoms of Elves and the second to the greatest kingdom of Men, there is no total discontinuity here. There are Elves who remain in Middle-earth until the Fourth Age, and Men who flee the wreck of Númenor to bring their civilisation elsewhere. The races are further mixed via the three Elf-Man marriages. The cohesive thread of transmission and heredity, which was one of Tolkien's dearest themes even after he abandoned

---

35. J.R.R. Tolkien, *The Peoples of Middle-earth*, ed. Christopher Tolkien, HarperCollins, London, 1996.
36. Op. cit. [3], 22b.

his idea of writing a mythology for England, is never wholly severed. This is not favoured by Plato's own tale, but it is favoured by other atlantologists's interpretations of Plato, and not only the Nazis. I am thinking here, for example, of Ignatius Donnelly, who, in a book published in 1882 which became widely popular, theorised that the survivors from the disappeared continent of Atlantis had founded the great civilisations on the East and West coasts of the Atlantic Ocean, and brought with them stories about the catastrophe which became distorted into the different Flood traditions.[37] This would have left a place in mythic history for the Shield Sheafing tradition which Tolkien loved so much.

## THE THIRD ELEMENT

Though they may diverge in the historical, the *geographical* consequences of this cataclysm are, however, remarkably similar in both Plato and Tolkien's tales. 'For that sea could be bridged back then', so the Atlantis story begins.[38] The island of Atlantis stood between the shores of the *oikouméne* and an unknown continent that lay beyond. The cataclysm that sunk it under the sea provoked a far-reaching geographical change: the Ocean became 'impassable and unsearchable, being blocked up by the shoal mud created by the island as it settled down'.[39] This mud represents a popular motif in Classical tradition, and it can be found in many authors (such as Pindar, Avienus or Aristotle) as the reason why no ship could cross the Ocean to find what lay beyond. The cataclysm also affected other lands, like Ancient Attica (where Ancient Athens stood), which used to be a very fertile and bountiful land and became a barren skeleton of its former self.[40] Plato, who was quite interested in geological processes, theorised that the great number of small islands to be found in the Aegean Sea were vestiges of this land which had disappeared beneath the waves.[41] Likewise, Tolkien was fixed upon the idea of a worldwide geographical upheaval of this sort, by which 'all the coasts and seaward regions of the western world suffered great change and ruin in that time, for the sea invaded the lands, and shores foundered, and ancient isles were drowned, and new isles were uplifted' (*TSil*, 'Akallabêth', 336). This, in turn, provoked a rift which forever barred the way to the land beyond the Ocean, though the modern Tolkien gives a metaphysical spin to it that Plato did not need: the flat Earth of legend becomes the round Earth of modern physical reality, and the world that is hidden forever is the Blessed Realm. This idea brings

---

37. I. Donnelly, *Atlantis: the Antediluvian World*, Harper & Brothers, New York, 1882.
38. Op. cit. [3], 24e.
39. Op. cit. [3], 25d.
40. Op. cit. [28], 111
41. Op. cit. [28], 111b.

to mind a much-mocked Christian treatise written in sixth-century Alexandria, known as the *Christian Topography of Cosmas Indicopleustés* (literally 'He-who-sailed-to-India'). This work attempts to prove that the Earth is flat, as stated in the Scriptures, and does so by discussing a great number of past sources, both Biblical and Classical, putting its own spin to them. For instance, Cosmas claims that Plato's Atlantis story is just a distorted account of the biblical Flood, and that the ignorant Greeks had been wrong to place it West instead of East.[42] Discussing this Flood, he also claims that, while the water levels were high, Noah's Ark drifted from an unknown Eastern continent beyond the Ocean (where Plato had placed Atlantis and the Bible had placed Paradise), so Noah and his family became the first people to reach our Middle-earth by its Eastern shores and inhabit it. Now, Tolkien himself remarked upon the Noah-Elendil connection; it is apparent that his interpretation of the flight of the Faithful could owe more to this misunderstood defender of the mythic shape of the Earth than to any Northern kings coming from the Sea in ships. This Eastern bent of the legend could also help us understand what happened afterwards in Tolkien's mind.

## THE FOURTH ELEMENT

Tolkien's original idea was to connect the Atlantis legend with the mythology of the British Isles. As he developed the story for *The Notion Club Papers*, however, a new and discordant element seems to have hijacked his mind. This element is Adûnaic, the tongue of Men spoken in Númenor. Before that point, the matter of languages had barely been addressed; there is just one conversation in *The Lost Road*,[43] where Amandil and Herendil remark obscurely that abandoning the tongue of the Elves to go back to an 'ancestral tongue of Men' was part of Sauron's agenda of evil. But from the moment that Adûnaic first appeared, it was there to stay. It would become a major political symbol for the sundering of Númenorean and Elvish civilisations, and Tolkien would start building a nomenclature and writing an Adûnaic grammar. He eventually had to leave it unfinished, having been urged to finish *LotR* at the time, but this language, 'somewhat reminiscent of Semitic' (*Sauron Defeated*, 415), would remain a part of the story, giving it a strong Oriental flavour that seemed quite at odds with the purported North-Western location of the legend. Tolkien would explain it through the influence of the language of the Khazad (that is, Dwarvish, a Semitic-inspired language),[44] however, in two letters written in 1954 and 1958, respectively, he himself

---

42. Cosm. 12: 2–8.
43. Op. cit. [11], pp. 75–76.
44. Op. cit. [8], Letter 144, p. 175.

compares the Númenóreans to Jews.[45] Names with Semitic components like *-bel, -bal, -adun, -nimru* or *-gimil* are given alongside Quenya equivalents in the annals of the kings. This is a great game-changer. It is also a return to Plato whose Atlantis, though a Western country, is a deeply Orientalised construct. As Bidez puts it at the same time that Tolkien was busying himself with these endeavours, 'Plato's fiction does not direct us towards the West except in appearance … it is on the Eastern empires that it really dwells upon … on the degeneration and luxury of a Persian empire allied to the sea-power of the Phoenicians'.[46] To these two, which were deeply enmeshed together in the mind of the Athenians who had faced the great Phoenician navy at the service of the Persian conquering power in the battle of Salamis, could be added a third, the proverbial antiquity of an Egyptian temple-civilisation which preserved the ancient records of the story.

The Atlantis legend is, therefore, built of elements taken from those three sources, which interact to form the model that Plato wanted. Plenty of things have been written about Plato's use of Herodotus's description of the Persian empire and its cities, and his account of how its pride led to the unsuccessful wars on the brave 'underdog' Greeks, as a model of his Atlantis story.[47] Persia, however, was a land power, needing the alliance of the Phoenicians to do battle by sea. At the time of the Second Persian War two different Phoenician fleets, one composed by ships from Tyre and Sidon and working on the behalf of the Persians, and the other belonging to Carthage, were assailing the Greek world from East and West in Himera and Salamis. 'Sea-power' and 'Phoenician' were related words at the time, and so was 'Far West', as it was the Phoenicians who had first sailed the Ocean and established cities there. One of the two elder twins who founded the kingdom of Atlantis bears two names, like the Númenorean kings after Ar-Belzagar, one in Greek (*Eumélos*) while the other, its supposed equivalent in 'the language of the country', is Gádiros,[48] from the root GDR, which was also the name, in the Semitic language known as Phoenician, of the westernmost Tyrian colony in the Atlantic Ocean, *Gadir* or *Gádeira* in Greek (present-day Cádiz). Atlantis, like Númenor, also speaks a tongue 'reminiscent of Semitic'.

Plato's motives, however, went beyond mere word-building. He was using those cultural traits to establish a negative paradigm whose connotations (such as 'threatening fleet' and 'invading power vowed to ultimate defeat because of an excess of hubris') would resonate with his audience, and the ultimate function

---

45. Op. cit. [8], Letters 156, 211.

46. J. Bidez, *Eos, ou Platon et l'Orient*, Hayez, Brussels, 1938, app. 2.33.

47. See for example, op. cit. [4] and J.-F. Pradeau, *Le monde de la politique. Sur le récit atlante de Platon, Timée (17–27) et Critias*, Sankt Augustin, Academia Verlag, Berlin, 1997.

48. Op. cit. [28], 114b.

of this paradigm was to criticise something that he did not approve of. And this something was not Persia, or Phoenicia, or anything in the East, but the social and political developments of his own city of Athens. The imperialism of Persia and the sea-power of the Phoenicians, joined in the evil nation of Atlantis, were meant to underline the immorality of the two pillars of Athens's democratic regime: imperialism (as head of the two successive Attic-Delic Leagues, Athens had become unpopular by demanding tributes from other Greek cities and invading them if they revolted, installing puppet democratic governments), and reliance on a large fleet, which was the instrument through which the poorer classes could have a part in the defense of the city, which in turn gave them the right to participate in its government. This negativity was, in turn, opposed by the positive paradigm of Ancient Athens, which was not at all like Plato's Athens: an inland power, with no ships or fleet, rigidly divided into castes and ruled by the perfect laws of the Republic.

Now, these are all things which are present in Tolkien´s account of Númenor, if, as always, in their own way. The Orientalisation process of the story is clear, and it roughly involves the same cultures as Plato's account. Tolkien himself remarks upon the Egyptian traits of his Númenoreans, mentioning precisely the 'interest in ancestry and tombs',[49] that is, their ability to *preserve* the past, which is the trait referenced in the Atlantis story, while in the name of Ar-Pharazôn one would be tempted to detect the influence of the Pharaoh of Biblical fame, which would be opposed by the Moses-figure of Elendil who would take his people into exile. The crown of Gondor was also described as 'Egyptian', though the wings bring to mind the helmet-crowns of the Persian kings, especially of the Sassanid Dynasty, where they were a symbol of Ahura-Mazda, one of the ancient gods which comes closest to the monotheistic ideal. Tolkien mentions having 'read a great deal about Mesopotamia',[50] and also ps.-Mesopotamian are the names 'Zigûr' and 'Istar' given to Sauron and Ar-Zimraphel. The lion's share, however, belongs to the Semitic element, which has here incorporated a strong Jewish element. Númenoreans practice the monotheistic religion of the Jews, centred around the Meneltarma, the Pillar of Heaven that Lowdham identifies with Mt. Atlas. When they become corrupted they worship Melkor, a god of human sacrifices which brings to mind the so-called god Moloch of the Bible (probably a derivate of MLK, 'king', cognate to the word *molk* used for a type of Carthaginian child sacrifice, whose horrors left a strong impression in the mind of many late-nineteenth-century Europeans from the lavish descriptions of Gustave Flaubert´s Orientalising novel *Salammbô*.)

---

49. Op. cit. [8], Letter 211, p. 281.
50. Op. cit. [8], Letter 297, p. 384.

Martin Bernal, in his *Black Athena*, pointed out how much of this Carthaginian bashing of the eighteenth and nineteenth centuries was French-based and anti-English in nature.[51] The historian Michelet saw the Punic Wars as a fight to the death against the sea power of the 'perfidious' Semites, the Phoenicians.[52] But this is also a model for something else. This becomes clearer as he exclaims: 'How many Tyres or Carthages could be piled up to reach the insolence of titanic England?' The English are the new 'kings of the Ocean'. They did not reject the comparison themselves; at least not immediately. William Gladstone, G. Rawlinson, Mathew Arnold, and T.S. Eliot all wrote about Phoenicians in positive terms. According to the second, a respected historian, the Phoenicians were the people with most traits in common with the English. There was a popular tradition according to which they had come to Cornwall in their Atlantic travels and influenced the indigenous element. In the building of the Royal Exchange in the City of London, a painting by Lord Leighton depicts Phoenicians landing on a British beach and trading their wares with a group of primitive Britons. As Bernal puts it, Victorians identified with that entrepreneurial nation of overseas traders in cloth, who spread civilisation around while reaping benefits in exchange. The Phoenicians were, to a degree, at home in the British Isles.[53] Certainly, neither the Victorians nor Tolkien would have found anything negative in this sea-power paradigm which Plato had so strongly cautioned against. Navigation is usually depicted as positive in Tolkien's world, and the only time when the land versus sea opposition is established, the *Tale of Aldarion and Erendis*, he certainly does not take Erendis's side.[54]

On the other hand, even if it is the tongue of Men, the use of Adûnaic has negative connotations. It becomes the symbol of the abandonment of another tongue that was 'more august, more ancient and, well, sacred and liturgical' (*Sauron Defeated*, 241), which Tolkien calls 'Elven Latin'. These words, 'Latin' and 'liturgical' hold the key to the real nature of Tolkien's own paradigm, beyond the criticisms of Germany or the modern world in the older versions of the tale. It was a religious one, and the abandonment of a Latin-like 'liturgical' tongue in favour of the vernacular, as well as the introduction of new practices probably point to the existence of a Catholic versus Protestant reform opposition in his mind. The Adûnaic language brings to mind a well-known context where the original monotheistic beliefs of a chosen people were continuously jeopardised by the Jezebels and Manassehs who brought foreign cults from Phoenicia or

---

51. Op. cit. [6].

52. J. Michelet, *Histoire Romaine*, Belles Lettres, Paris, 1831, pp. 203–204.

53. Op. cit. [7], p. 322.

54. J.R.R. Tolkien, *Unfinished Tales of Númenor and Middle-earth*, ed. Christopher Tolkien, George Allen & Unwin, London, 1980.

Assiria and introduced human sacrifice in Israel and Judah. And, at the same time, it also brings to mind the Protestant spirit of defending the primacy of the Jewish Bible over the Latin liturgy of the Catholics. Tolkien felt that his mother had been persecuted for her beliefs and even died because of it which made her, and him, into Faithful.[55] The paradigm changes, and the moral changes with it, but Orientalism (especially Semitism) remains a tool for criticism, being able to reference things from the author's own time and place. Tolkien has played in Plato's sandbox, only arranging the toys in a way that Plato would not understand.

To sum all this up, I would say that Tolkien's Atlantis is, ultimately, Plato's Atlantis: not a paradise, an abode of the gods, or an isle of the Blessed, but a human kingdom that becomes an evil imperialistic power and is engulfed by a cataclysm. By cutting the context in which he had been trying to root it, Tolkien would free his story from the trappings of a *legendarium* where it did not fit. From then on, there would be no further need to tone down the Platonic inspiration – nor, indeed, of keeping the non-Englishness of the tradition at bay. The imaginary Middle-earth, where this Atlantis would become rooted, as shown in Tolkien's own comments about bringing the Númenorean matter into relation with his main mythology,[56] is a freer place where concepts like racial and linguistic heritage as well as the chronology and geography of the Primary World will lose the precise, and sometimes uncomfortable meaning they once had. At the same time, however, the influence of this world, and the things which the Author did or did not like in it would remain in a transformed, allusive way. In this, he also followed the path of Plato, who, even as he spoke about long-forgotten civilisations which had perished in a cataclysm long before his time, was ultimately thinking, as Bartoli puts it so expressively, about 'the Athenians, always the Athenians, and the Athenians once more'.[57]

---

55. Op. cit. [8], Letter 267, p. 268.
56. Op. cit. [8], Letter 257, p. 347.
57. Giuseppe Bartoli, *Essai sur l'explication historique que Platon a donnée de sa République et de son Atlantide*, Stockholm, 1779, pp. 224–25; cited in op. cit. [47].

# 'From 2012 AD to Atlantis and Back Again — Tolkien's Circular Journey in Time'

## Xavier de la Huerga

*I offer evidence that Tolkien did somehow accomplish some form of time-travel, or what could be termed pre-cognitive and retro-cognitive insights in writing The Notion Club Papers, from the uncanny prediction of the Great Storm of 1987, to the odd coincidences that connect the story with the Mayan Long Count Calendar, and other enigmatic facts. I will finish with my conclusions regarding the profound the implications. I will also show how auto-biographical The Notion Club Papers is and how it can be read as a 'metaphysical manifesto' of sorts, revealing Tolkien's innermost visionary experiences, often going deep into the realm of mysticism and the paranormal.*

This paper covers some facets of Tolkien's life and work that defy conventional explanations. The focus is on his unfinished time-travel novel *The Notion Club Papers*,[1] which reveals much about the metaphysical nature of Tolkien's sources of inspiration.

Whilst we have hundreds of articles and books tracing the possible sources of Tolkien's ideas back to some cultural traditions, persons, events, works of literature, art and so on. I am setting my sights instead, on the more subtle and intangible forces that Tolkien spoke about in his essay *On Fairy-Stories* when he said: 'behind the fantasy real wills and powers exist, independent of the minds and purposes of men',[2] not to deny the worldly influences, legacies and experiences that undoubtedly shaped Tolkien's life and might have made their way into his works; but to honour Tolkien, by sounding the poignant depths of the Mystery that permeates his labour of love.

Ever since I first read *The Lord of the Rings* and became immersed in its evergreen magic, I felt that Tolkien's creative processes must have been anchored in some kind of visionary, mystic ground. Years later, I received confirmation for this intuition when I read some of his published letters, in which he repeatedly acknowledges that he is but 'a chosen instrument' for the writing of the stories and that he never felt as if he was inventing, but recording (Letter 328, p.

---

1. J.R.R. Tolkien, *Sauron Defeated*, ed. Christopher Tolkien, HarperCollins, London, 1992.
2. J.R.R. Tolkien, 'On Fairy Stories', in *Tree and Leaf*, George Allen & Unwin, London, 1964, p. 21.

413)[3]. I also came across his profound essay: *On Fairy-Stories*, where much is said about the indescribable Realm of Fairy and the elusive sources of true sub-creation, although in fittingly obscure terms. But it was *The Notion Club Papers* that thoroughly blew the lid off, revealing the full extent of the mystic dimension underlying Tolkien's work. For I consider *NCPs* as a deeply intimate autobiographical work. In fact, I have come to regard it as a 'Metaphysical Manifesto' of sorts, where Tolkien wrote extensively about his innermost visions, experiences and insights.

## BACKGROUND WORD RADIATION

I would like to start by calling attention to a *leitmotiv*, a repeated element appearing at the inception point of so many creation myths all over the world, in which the Cosmos is brought into manifestation by the sheer power of word, song or sound. We see this universally recurring, archetypal theme arise in the biblical account of the Genesis, as 'In the beginning was the Word'; in the Vedic tradition, with Brahma's utterance of the primordial syllable 'Aum'; in ancient Egypt's cosmogony, where Atum-Ra first breaks the silent emptiness of the Void with a great cry; among the Hopi, in the Song of Creation, sung by Father Sun and Spider Woman; with the Maori God Io, who speaks light into being; or the Mayan Lightning God Triad, saying in unison the word 'earth', which instantaneously manifests the world; and on and on.... Even in Tolkien's own *legendarium*, the creation of Ea (the Universe) is accomplished by the Music of the Ainur. Then, reflecting on Tolkien's background we see that he started his *legendarium*, his mythology from that very same raw material: from sound, from word, from language. He started creating first the languages and then, his Secondary World arose, the stories came forth. It was all built on a foundation of euphonic words, of beautiful sounds.

If you think about it, it is a pretty obvious thing to do. That is why Tolkien's Secondary World is so convincing; he actually got the best of all possible head-starts by realising that there was a 'common sonic denominator' to most creation myths and then, applying it to his own creative process. Tolkien surely thought: 'There must be something about this ever-present sonic element in all these cosmogonies. This could be the secret ingredient for a successful sub-creation. I should give it a try. Let's start by inventing some beautifully-sounding words, see if a credible Secondary World arises.' And it did!

Of course, Tolkien never set in any purposeful manner to create his stories

---

3. Humphrey Carpenter, ed., *The Letters of J.R.R. Tolkien*, with the assistance of Christopher Tolkien, George Allen and Unwin, London, 1981.

from a sonic/linguistic basis. He started to construct languages very early on in life, in a playful manner, and it was completely unintentional that this activity ended up precipitating the manifestation of an entire universe. Tolkien's words: 'chosen instrument' keep reverberating in my mind when I consider how incredibly appropriate, how powerful, how logical even, from a mythopoeic point of view, it would have been to lay such a conceptual foundation stone for the creation of nothing less than a reality within reality. But it was not Tolkien's conscious choice.

In fact, the 'sonic seed' that was to grow into the very first poem and tale of his *legendarium*: the equivalent of the primeval 'Aum' in Tolkien's sub-creation was not 'uttered' by Tolkien himself (i.e., it didn't come from his invented languages). It was the word 'Earendel', a name for Venus as morning star, found in the eighth-century Anglo-Saxon poem *Crist* by Cynewulf, which Tolkien had encountered in the course of his early studies. 'Earendel' left him in awe of its euphonic intensity, and the two short verses where the word was embedded (*éala éarendel engla beorhtast / ofer middangeard monnum sended*: 'Hail Earendel, brightest of angels, over Middle-earth to men sent') had instantaneously awaken haunting resonances deep within the young Tolkien and prompted his first steps on a road he would never leave again; eventually, the tale of 'Earendil the Star Mariner' turned out to be at the very centre of Tolkien's mythology.

So, from the beginning Tolkien was led in his creative endeavours by his innate predisposition and enormous sensitivity towards the sonic dimension of language; which takes us on to one of Tolkien's earliest insights in his quest to understand his own predicament. An idea he was going to develop, quite fully, in his valedictory address for Oxford University, published later as an essay titled 'English and Welsh'. This was the idea of the genetic inheritance of what he called a 'native language', to differentiate it from 'mother tongue'. That is, if your mother tongue is the language that you learn after you are born. Then, native language can be defined as a language spoken by some of your ancestors, of which you might have a 'genetic memory' that could manifest as different levels of affinity and predisposition towards that language. Tolkien believed that he possessed such a memory and the 'native language' was Middle English, which would have been passed down by his mother, who was of Mercian descent. That is why he had said: 'I took to Middle English as a known language'.[4]

Let us look again now at the young Tolkien and at the precise moment when he first chances upon the *Crist* verses to find a very intriguing description of his reaction:

---

4. Humphrey Carpenter, *J.R.R. Tolkien: A Biography,* HarperCollins, 2002, p. 178.

I felt a curious thrill, as if something had stirred in me, half-waken from sleep. There was something very remote and strange and beautiful behind those words, if I could grasp it, far beyond ancient English.[5]

'[F]ar beyond ancient English': was Tolkien implying that those verses had somehow managed to half-awake the faint memory of a language much older than 'ancient English'; a memory, as in the cellular/genetic memory of a 'native language' that Tolkien's thesis proposed? If so, what other language could that be? Realisation starts to dawn when we find out that the above description of Tolkien's reaction upon encountering the *Crist* verses appears in two places. The first one happens during 'Night 66' of *NCPs*, at a meeting of the Notion Club, when those *exact* words are spoken by Arundel Lowdham, the main protagonist of the tale. The second occasion is in Tolkien's authorised biography by Humphrey Carpenter when those very words – which Tolkien had put in Lowdham's mouth more than thirty years before the biography was published – were transcribed verbatim, word by word, from the text of *NCPs* to Carpenter's biography, when Carpenter tells us about Tolkien's reaction to the Earendel verses. This is another clear indication about both how deeply autobiographical was *NCPs* and also, strikingly, about Tolkien's beliefs – perhaps we should say intuitions – regarding the true nature of his languages and their ultimate source in some form of ancestral memory. But ancestral memories do not seem to stop at the linguistic level with Tolkien.

## THE RESURRECTION AND SECOND COMING OF ATLANTIS

The sinking of Atlantis is a perfect element to include in a time-travel novel that aims at fusing myth and history, and to provide a nexus between the Primary World and Tolkien's Secondary World. Having been surrounded for centuries by such unequalled controversy regarding its historicity or else its mythic nature, Atlantis can be assuredly classed as the most powerfully ambivalent scenario that one can possibly draw from antiquity when faced with a task of this kind – even though no hard proof of its existence has ever come forward. An easy choice for Tolkien, one could say. Perhaps, but, then it was not a choice purely of his own, but one influenced by a strange occurrence in his life. By the time he started writing *NCPs*, he had already been led to attempt the retelling of the Atlantis story, as a way to exorcise a disturbing recurrent dream that went back to his earliest childhood: 'the dream of the Great Wave', which he also called

---

5. Op. cit., p. 92.

## TO ATLANTIS AND BACK AGAIN

his 'Atlantis Complex'; in which he saw a huge towering wave, inexorably swallowing the land. Not only did this recurring dream go back to his earliest memories, but Tolkien thought that he had inherited it from his parents. In fact, he found out one day that his second child, Michael, had indeed inherited the dream.[6]

We can see now that a pattern starts to emerge here. Not only are we contemplating the possibility of some form of linguistic memory being somehow passed down the generations, but also of recurrent dreams being inherited. So, if Tolkien believed that a form of genetic memory of language was possible, did he also believe that other things, maybe traumatic events (Like the experience of a cataclysmic event) could also be imprinted somehow in our genetic architecture and their memory passed along the millennia by members of the same bloodline? Is that what he was thinking about, when he spoke of his 'dream of the great wave' having been inherited? Did Tolkien believe that the sinking of Atlantis had been a real event and that he had inherited a memory of that catastrophe from some ancestor who had lived through it?

That question cannot be answered with absolute certainty. However, we can be one hundred percent certain that that is exactly what the two main protagonists of *NCPs* experience: the sinking of Atlantis as a disturbing memory from their Atlantean ancestors. And if *NCPs* is autobiographical then this would hint to a possible answer for our question. I will summarise very briefly the central part of the *NCPs* story:

> The two protagonists are present at a meeting of The Notion Club in Oxford. Suddenly, they enter a trance in which they find themselves re-living the sinking of the island continent of Númenor (one of Tolkien's names for Atlantis). The other members of the Notion Club watch in amazement as their two colleagues go wild shouting and crying (both in Númenorean and English) at the horror only they can see, all of it eerily timed with the first menacing growls of a rapidly approaching storm. As the massive storm explodes over Oxford in a blinding fury of lightning and rain, they run madly out of the meeting and into the raging chaos. Then, they wander around for days in a daze of which little is remembered; they get a boat; set sail and eventually end up mooring in Porlock where, again in a dream-like trance, they re-live past events experienced by some other ancestors back in ninth-century England. These past selves sail to Ireland and then further West into the Atlantic, until they find

---

6. Op. cit. [3], Letter 163, p. 213.

the 'Straight Road' and get a glimpse of the shores of the Immortal Lands (the narrative of *NCPs* stops here). The Straight Road is Tolkien's device to convey the last tenuous link between the world and the Immortal Lands (home of the Valar and the Elves). It appears immediately after and as a result of the sinking of Númenor/Atlantis.

It all sounds pretty much like past life memories and reincarnation, but Tolkien left some notes indicating that he envisioned this process, of re-living or remembering ancestral memories, as happening only along the same bloodline. So, the protagonists would have been descendants of the same characters they experience as their past selves. Does this make sense? Well, Tolkien's explanation sounds somewhat forced and it might be that he was trying to find a 'solution' that wouldn't collide with his Catholic orthodoxy. Verlyn Flieger hypothesises similarly along these lines in her insightful essay *The Curious Incident of the Dream at the Barrow: Memory and reincarnation in Middle-earth.*[7] If this was the case, then this would be quite a proposition: that Tolkien not only believed in reincarnation, but that he did so because he had had some personal experiences or memories that he could only explain in this way.

But there are many more strange fish swimming around inside the kaleidoscopic bowl of *NCPs*. Indeed, *NCPs* seems like a veritable collection of supernatural happenings, altered states and psychic, paranormal phenomena of all kinds known and many more to be yet classified; otherworldly visions of sublime beauty, time-warps, visitations by extra-dimensional aliens; languages that change as swiftly as sunlight rays under water; Elves weaving human perceptions into works of art; interplanetary out-of-body travelling, dreams within dreams, crystal entities. Some accounts, like the experience of mineral sentiency and geological eras, or the dilated cosmic consciousness pertaining to a meteorite, verge on the bizarre. It is as if a veil has been lifted allowing a glimpse into the infinite potential of the mind.

In most instances, if not all, the accounts of these extraordinary visions and happenings have the distinct ring of truth. Indeed, some of them are attested by Christopher Tolkien in the notes to *NCPs* as being genuinely autobiographical. It seems as if Tolkien had to let a treasure trove of numinous experiences out of his chest, and the only way was to put them into a fictionalised setting where he could give the right answers to the right questions – to his own questions in some cases, I believe – because some of those experiences would have been very puzzling.

---

7. Verlyn Flieger, 'The Curious Incident of the Dream at the Barrow: Memory and reincarnation in Middle-earth', *Tolkien Studies* 4 (2007), 99–112.

# TO ATLANTIS AND BACK AGAIN

The Inklings (the literary club that Tolkien co-founded with C.S. Lewis and other brilliant minds) were a tremendous source of raw inspiration and encouragement for Tolkien. But I believe that, when the Notion Club was imagined into written life, Tolkien created a 'perfected', idealised version of the Inklings that allowed him to explore and express all those numinous experiences, far beyond anything that could have happened during an Inklings meeting in the Primary World. And if I am correct, that would make *NCPs* into a 'Metaphysical Manifesto' of sorts. That is, an exegesis and record of Tolkien's innermost convictions and metaphysical insights. And there is yet one more layer of anomalous facts within *NCPs*, this time concerning what we could class as precognition or synchronicity.

## STORMING INTO THE FUTURE

We find the first anomalous fact related to the great storm at the centre of the narrative. It is as if the 'ghost' of Atlantis had come back to haunt the modern world, coalescing into a monstrous storm that acts as its physical vehicle, to forcefully irrupt into the Oxford of *NCPs* and into the lives of its protagonists. Its appearance in the story lends an ominous bridge between the future and the distant past, between history and myth and, to all effects, between the Primary World and Tolkien's Secondary World. The date for this storm is given in *NCPs* as 12th June 1987; a date forty-two years into the future from Tolkien's perspective – he was writing in 1945. And in the Primary World forty-two years after Tolkien wrote *NCPs* the greatest storm in living memory hit the South of England, on the 16th October 1987; Oxford was pretty much across its central path. So, it seems that Tolkien 'predicted', forty-two years into the future, a mega-storm with an error of just four months. As weather forecasts go in this part of the world that is not a bad projection. The weather is so unpredictable in the British Isles I do not think the Met Office could have bettered that!

In fact, the Great Storm of 1987 went by scandalously unpredicted (for which BBC weatherman Michael Fish, due to a misunderstanding, unjustly blamed in the public eye). Equally, the 'Atlantis storm' of *NCPs* goes completely unpredicted – a fact remarked upon by a Notion Club member. Both storms are similarly labelled for their unprecedented magnitude 'the greatest storm in living memory', and both have a very similar path and effects. Finally and most oddly, we read in a fictive *Note to the Second Edition* by *NCPs'* fictive editor: 'I am now convinced that the Papers are a work of fiction; and it may well be that the predictions (*notably of the Storm* (my emphasis)), though genuine and not coincidences were unconscious: giving one more glimpse of the strange processes of so-called literary "invention", with which the Papers are largely concerned.'[8] So, how conscious was Tolkien of his 'unconscious predictions'?

The other anomalous fact concerns the year 2012, which is when the manuscript of *NCPs* is fictively found 'after the summer examinations of 2012', on a non-specified day that could have been ... today [Note: this paper was given on 18th of August 2012].

## AN UNFINISHED TIME-TRAVEL STORY
## AT THE END OF THE WORLD

Why did Tolkien choose 2012 AD as the time for *NCPs* to be (fictitiously) discovered? Is this just an arbitrary, random date? For many here, the year 2012 will at least ring a bell. It signals the end of the Mayan Long Count; a calendrical cycle spanning 5,125 years. Nowadays, the date 2012 has spawned a whole genre of its own, and as the date gets closer, the controversy over its meaning rages on. If we listen to what the present day Maya Daykeepers and Elders have to say about it (after all, it is their ancestors' calendar), a time of unparalleled transformation is upon us; humankind is at a crossroads and must radically change their ways or face dire consequences. Without going any further into the subject, the fact is that 2012 is nowadays widely associated with ancient prophecy, the shifting of World Ages and apocalyptic scenarios. In a word: 2012 AD is a very convenient date to insert in a time-travel story like *NCPs* for reasons obvious to us – dwellers of the second decade of the twenty-first century. However, was the significance of 2012 AD and its relation to the Mayan Calendar, known to Tolkien at the time when he was writing *NCPs*, back in 1945-46?

I would like to mention here, again, Verlyn Flieger's insightful essay about Tolkien and reincarnation, where she suggests that Tolkien might have read the Popol Vuh – a sacred book of the Quiche Maya – and learned about the 2012 AD date through it. Pointing to what she considers as an 'oblique reference' to the Popol Vuh in a draft of *NCPs*, this is a very logical conclusion to draw. For the inclusion of 2012 by Tolkien in *NCPs* seems too perfect a choice to be just a coincidence. However, the truth is that the chances for Tolkien to have known about the 2012 AD date in connection with the Mayan Calendar are basically none, regardless of whether he read the Popol Vuh or not. Firstly, because there are no dates whatsoever in the Popol Vuh; neither in Mayan, nor in Gregorian calendar reckoning. And secondly, the first correlations between the Mayan Long Count and our Gregorian calendar did not actually appear until the 1960s (And even then, most had calculation errors that gave 2011 AD as the end date for the Long Count, not 2012 AD). So, once more, there seems to be no conscious choice

---

8. Op. cit. [1], p. 158.

by Tolkien regarding the inclusion of a very convenient element (i.e., the date 2012 AD) in his time-travel novel. However, what about the 1987 date? Should this date not also be equally meaningful and relevant? Is there a connection between the sinking of Atlantis/Númenor, the end of the Mayan Long Count cycle in 2012 AD, and the events on 1987 AD?

## SYNCHRONIC TRIANGULATION: THE GREAT STORM, HARMONIC CONVERGENCE AND THE BLACK MONDAY CRASH

It was in 1987 that Jose Arguelles launched the 2012 Mayan Calendar date into mass awareness with the publication of his book *The Mayan Factor: Path Beyond Technology*,[9] which became an instant best-seller. Arguelles was also instrumental in convening Harmonic Convergence on 17th August of the same year. This event was the world's first globally synchronised meditation for world peace, with a focus on 2012 as a window of opportunity for a positive shift away from the prevalent self-destructive trend of humanity. The timing for Harmonic Convergence was chosen because it was both a significant prophetic date in the Mayan, Tibetan, Cherokee and Seneca calendar traditions, all of which tell of a twenty-five year transition period or 'crossing' before 2012 (2012 – 25 = 1987), and also because it marked the beginning of a rare planetary alignment. It received worldwide coverage in the mainstream media and thus it pushed 2012 further into the foreground. So, here we have the first connection: 1987 is both the year when the Great Storm hit the South of England and the year when the 2012 Mayan Calendar date storms into global mainstream awareness.

But 1987 was also the year of the Black Monday stock market crash, which happened just three days after the Great Storm, on the 19th of October. Twenty years after Black Monday, in 2007, financial analyst Mike Estrey issued a retrospective report about the causes behind the crash where he wrote:

> A final factor was the Great Storm of 1987 in England, which occurred on the Friday before the crash. At that time, most dealing was done by phone, and brokers had to physically get to work in London to carry out deals. That morning, many routes into London were closed and consequently many traders were unable to reach their offices in order to close positions by the end of the week. This added to the panic selling which occurred on the following Monday.[10]

---

9. José Argüelles, *The Mayan Factor: Path Beyond Technology*, Bear and Company, Rochester VT, 1987.

10. Mike Estrey, 'The 1987 Crash – What Was That All About?' <http://ezinearticles.com/?The-1987-Crash---What-Was-That-All-About?&id=826333> [accessed 11 November 2015].

Whilst this shows conclusively that the Great Storm did its part to bring about the Black Monday crash, we also have a direct link between Harmonic Convergence and Black Monday. This comes by the hand of yet another financial analyst: Arch Crawford.

Crawford is a highly rated investment advisor, whose newsletter was ranked at number one during 2008 and 2009 by the Hulbert Financial Digest. He is famous not only for having a high rate of success with his stock market predictions, but also because he uses Astrology as the basis for his own method of market analysis. He actually made his name in Wall Street with his prediction of the Black Monday. In an interesting online interview Crawford talks about his methods and recounts how he came to predict the crash of 1987:

> An acquaintance of mine – the late John Nelson – was a radio propagation specialist for RCA back in the '40s. The company knew that sunspots and solar flares created magnetic storms that would disrupt shortwave radio signals on earth. They would have to re-route transmissions during those times. So, they asked John to research ways to predict those solar events. Now, John had absolutely no interest in astrology. But after finding little success early on, someone suggested he take a look at planetary alignments around the sun. So he gave it a shot. He took the thirteen worst radio disturbance days on record at RCA and looked at the charts for those times ... and he was shocked to find that they coincided with very complex astrological planetary interactions. He eventually came out with a book called Cosmic Patterns, and was able to show that planetary alignments relative to the sun could help time sunspot activity.
> Is it inconceivable that these same alignments may have effects on the earth? Or that they could affect those of us living here as well? I've taken my methods to the scientific community and they won't look at it. They're superstitious in the negative form ... because they know these ideas could have major implications. On the other hand, when I take this information to Wall Street, they say, "What's your record?" When I show them, they buy it. They're concerned with results.[11]

Crawford then recounts how he heard about Harmonic Convergence and its

---

11. 'We've never seen anything like this summer: an interview with Arch Crawford', *The Daily Crux*, 25 July 2010 <https://quantumpranx.wordpress.com/2010/07/29/weve-never-seen-anything-like-this-summer%E2%80%A8-an-interview-with-arch-crawford/> [accessed 11 November 2015]. Subsequent quotations are taken from this source.

attendant planetary alignment.

> Some of your readers might remember the so-called "harmonic convergence" that was celebrated by the New Age people that Summer. Without getting into too much detail, the theory behind these kinds of planetary alignments is that they can cause changes in the earth's energy. And these changes can manifest themselves in the way groups of people interact, how the stock market trades, and even in natural phenomena like earthquakes. The harmonic convergence was supposed to be a big one. It was also a Mayan calendar date.

Crawford became curious about the astrology of Harmonic Convergence and using astronomy software he studied the planetary alignment around the date and found out that, seven days after Harmonic Convergence, on August 24th, there occurred the tightest five-planet conjunction in at least eight hundred years, which according to his method led him to predict that:

> the market would peak on August the 24th, give or take three days, after which we would have a horrendous crash. If you go back and look, the high close was actually August 24, 1987.... On October 6, just before the lunar eclipse – which probably triggered the huge 1987 California earthquake by the way – you had the biggest down day in history in points in the Dow Jones Average. And that started the slide into the crash.

And crash the stock market did. So thoroughly in fact, that it has never recovered. Going back to Mike Estrey's article, he says regarding the magnitude and after-shocks of the crash that:

> it felt to some like the end of the financial world was upon us ... Indeed, despite efficient market theory suggesting that falls of the magnitude seen on Black Monday are a once in a lifetime (possibly a millennium) occurrence, we have since seen some hefty falls on a daily basis in the last twenty years.

Implicit in this statement is the acknowledgement that the stock market had never been the same after the crash. Not only that, Estrey was writing in 2007, what happened the next year? We all know what happened in 2008, we are still experiencing it and the problem is not going to go away easily. Because at the heart of the current economic crisis, there is the profound failure of a financial

# XAVIER DE LA HUERGA

system operated by greed and rooted in the perpetuation of debt and the myth of endless economic growth. An economy that is not economy at all – to see real economy we have to look at the biosphere, at nature. That is Economy, absolutely everything is endlessly recycled and nothing is wasted. Our current financial system is in fact, the complete antithesis of economy.

## CONCLUSION

We truly are seeing the end of an age and the beginning of another. What ends on 2012 is a cycle, an era; not the physical world, but a worldview. As such, the current collapse of the financial system is a most telling symptom of this shift, since it is at the very foundation of the worldview that is passing. This worldview has been predominant during the last five thousand years approximately (coinciding with the historical period), which is the length of the cycle the Mayan calendar tracks, itself part of a greater cycle of 26,000 years: the Precession of the Equinoxes, or what the ancient Greeks called the Great Year. So, just as we do not expect trees to shed all their leaves at once and the fields to be blanketed in white by sudden snowfall, precisely at, let's say, 11:11am on the 21st of December. Even less, we should expect the millenary tides of time to shift abruptly at an appointed hour and day of a particular year, as if a door had been closed and another one opened. That said, there are storms in nature, and those can bring overnight great changes in the landscape.

I fully concur with Tolkien's perception of his role as a 'chosen instrument' or 'scribe' and I believe *NCPs*' tale effectively bridges Tolkien's sub-created Universe with the Primary World. I also concur with Mr. Howard Green, the fictive discoverer and editor of *NCPs*, in that the predictions are genuine, whether conscious, subconscious, meta-conscious or something else altogether. Tolkien effectively accomplished time-travel, not in the sense that many imaginations, embedded in our machine-driven civilisation and spoon-fed by Hollywood, often envision, e.g.: by jumping into a contraption driven by an ego and its attendant material wants and needs, and then speeding up and down the motorway of time. But in a very subtle and true way: Tolkien's fuel was imagination; his vehicle: syntax; and 'behind the wheel' were those 'wills and powers', the archetypes that populate what has been variously called the Collective Unconscious, the *Mundus Imaginalis* or *Alam al-Mithal* of Sufi mysticism, the *Nagual* of Mesoamerican shamanism, the Australian Aboriginal Dreamtime, or what Tolkien himself called the Realm of Fairy. All of them are names for that Pool of Mystery that all human beings share and drink from: our very Soul, collective by definition.

# 'The Notion Club Papers: A Summary'

## David Doughan

*After the Oxford Summer Examinations of 2012, the manuscript of The Notion Club Papers will have been discovered, according to The History of Middle-earth vol. 9. Therefore this seems like a good time to look at this work. Tolkien's various drafts for this project are an interesting if inchoate mixture of learned chat, wrangling over the mechanism of travel in space and time, enigmatic visions and a further development of the tale of Númenor. This paper is intended to start discussion of these fragments, looking initially at three points: the extent to which the conversations reflect what actually happened at a regular Inkling, whether or not the characters are actual portraits; and in literary terms, at these conversations as the last appearance of Ælfwine; the tale Númenor between The Lost Road and The Lord of the Rings and its linguistic aspects, particularly the genesis and nature of Adûnaic.*

It is late 1945, and you are weary after six years of war, with its associated devastation and discomfort, with material deprivation continuing unrelieved. You have recently moved into an important new post that involves considerable disruption and the difficulty of adjusting to new systems and tasks, while simultaneously attempting to clear up backlogs from your previous position. Moreover, you have been committed for seven years to a major project which also is desperately behindhand, and which has in fact been hanging fire for more than a year. Additionally, you have increasing problems with your physical and mental health. So how do you set your priorities for resolving all of the above? Simple, if you are J.R.R. Tolkien: you embark on a completely new project.

2012 was of course a significant year for that new project, *The Notion Club Papers*, for according to the fiction they were discovered after the summer examinations of 2012 – in other words at about the time this paper was given at Loughborough.[1] They consist of several incomplete drafts, presented in two parts, which initially appear to be based on Inklings' meetings or their descendants in the then future 1980s, though they rapidly take an unusual turn. Some references are fairly obvious – for example, Franks or Frankley seems to be based on C.S. Lewis, Lowdham is Hugo Dyson, etc., though a major character, Ramer, though

---

1. J.R.R. Tolkien, *Sauron Defeated*, ed. Christopher Tolkien, HarperCollinsPublishers, London, 1992, p. 155.

a philologist and probably originally intended to represent Tolkien himself, seems to have become a character with composite inspirations. In fact seeking out equivalences with the historical Inklings is probably the least productive approach to the Papers, which soon move from being a simple account of discussions and rapidly take a similar path to that which Tolkien had first embarked on with *The Lost Road*, suggested by his division of fictional territory with Lewis,[2] when in about 1936 Lewis said to Tolkien: 'Tollers, there is too little of what we really like in stories. I am afraid we shall have to try and write some ourselves. We agreed that he should try "space-travel" and I should try "time-travel"'.[3] However, although Lewis's *Out of the Silent Planet* was fairly quickly written and published, Tolkien's experiments with time in *The Lost Road* met with considerable difficulty, and were eventually abandoned. In *NCPs* he attempts to revive them, but in a somewhat different form.

Time-travel was of course not a new concept in the 1930s. Interest had been aroused by the publication in 1887 of Edward Bellamy's *Looking Backward: 2000-1887*, a utopian vision of a sort of socialist progress.[4] This provoked a considerable number of responses and different views of the future, most notably William Morris's *News from Nowhere*,[5] which envisions a very different kind of socialist utopia to that foreseen by Bellamy, and H.G. Wells's dystopian *When the Sleeper Wakes*.[6] Despite their differences, Bellamy's work and the reactions to it have in common the means of time-travel, which in all cases is a prolonged sleep, distinguishing them from the purely technological means invoked by Wells in his *The Time Machine*.[7] Tolkien, who took an interest in science fiction (for instance, he enjoyed reading Asimov),[8] would almost certainly have been aware of these highly political visions of the future; however, in *NCPs* he refers not to that strand but to a different work by a different author, dealing with what is, although our future, in fact the narrator's remote past: Olaf Stapledon's *Last Men in London*, published in the 1930s.[9] Stapledon looks backward, at our time and later ones, not from the perspective of a few centuries, but from 2,000,000,000

---

2. J.R.R. Tolkien, *The Lost Road*, ed. Christopher Tolkien, HarperCollins, London, 1987, p. 9. All quotations from *Lost Road* are taken from this edition. Humphrey Carpenter, ed., *The Letters of J.R.R. Tolkien*, with the assistance of Christopher Tolkien, HarperCollins, London, 1995, p. 257.
3. Op. cit., Letter 294, p. 378.
4. Edward Bellamy, *Looking Backward 2000-1887*, Houghton Mifflin, Boston, 1889.
5. William Morris, *News from Nowhere (or an Epoch of Rest)*, London, 1890.
6. H.G. Wells, *The Sleeper Awakes*, London, 1910.
7. H.G. Wells, *The Time Machine*, London, 1898.
8. Op. cit. [2], p. 377, note.
9. Olaf Stapledon, *Last and First Men: a Story of the Near and Far Future*, Methuen, London, 1930.

years in the future, through the eyes of a representative of the eighteenth (and, as it turns out, last) species of humanity: the Last Men on Neptune, who have developed a means of exploring not the future, but the past, by means of what Tolkien's character Ramer feels is ultimately an unsatisfactory a method:

> I thought it worked pretty well, though it was too vague about the *how*. If I remember rightly, the Neptunians could lie in a trance and let their minds travel. Very good, but *how* does the mind travel through Space or Time, while the body is static? (*Sauron Defeated*, 175)

Speculations of how the past may be viewed, or recovered, form part of Verlyn Flieger's *A Question of Time*. Flieger cites not the usual science-fictional subjects but such matters as the enigmatic vision of Charlotte Moberly and Eleanor Jourdain at the Trianon, and especially the theories of J.W. Dunne, author of *An Experiment With Time*,[10] which attracted a certain amount of interest in intellectual circles, and which involves putting oneself in environments where consciousness might be freed, which comes perilously close to the Neptunian method that Ramer rejects. What he suggests instead is dreams.

Dreams have a considerable significance in Tolkien's work, and Flieger discusses some of them in detail in relation to the experience of time. Frodo's dreams are particularly interesting; they partake as much of 'visions' as of dreams. Some are apparently retrospective, like the vision of Gandalf pacing on Orthanc, while at least one other turns out to be prophetic: that of the far green country under a swift sunrise. Flieger also calls our attention to 'The Sea-Bell', originally 'Looney'. All these show a degree of dislocation from the non-dream world, but except possibly in the last case the visions are kept separate from reality as experienced. However, in the *Notion Club Papers*, one dream is of key importance – a dream that Tolkien called his 'Atlantis-haunting':

> This legend or myth or dim memory of some ancient history has always troubled me. In sleep I had the dreadful dream of the ineluctable Wave, either coming out of the quiet sea, or coming in towering over the green inlands.... It always ends by surrender, and I awake gasping out of deep water.[11]

This has obvious resonances with certain European legends; apart from

---

10. Verlyn Flieger, *A Question of Time: J.R.R. Tolkien's Road to Faërie*, Kent State University, Kent OH, 1997.
11. Op. cit [2], Letter 257, p. 347.

222                                 DAVID DOUGHAN

Plato's story of Atlantis, many places (particularly on the Atlantic coast) have traditions of drowned lands, cities going beneath the wave, and underwater cathedrals: for example, the Welsh Cantre'r Gwaelod (the Lowland Hundred), Cornish Lyonesse, and the Breton city of Ker-Is. So Tolkien's dream fits in a tradition, yet is very much his own, and it is on this dream-experience, and its influence on reality, that much of the matter of the *NCPs* will hinge.

Initially, however, the *NCPs* contain a great deal of discussion that does not seem altogether germane, and even when its purpose as establishing a framework for what follows is established it frequently seems (and is) unnecessarily verbose. Therefore I think it is worthwhile to give an outline of the main proceedings.

## PAPERS: PART 1

As mentioned above, the Papers fall into two distinct parts, presented as records of proceedings on various nights on which the club met; Part 1 consists of Nights 54-61, and Part 2 Nights 62-70 (at which point the draft degenerates into what are eventually notes to Tolkien himself for further development). In Part 1, the main participant is Ramer, who among other things is revealed to have been born in Magyarország. i.e. Hungary; and Night 60 is the first substantial entry. After a slow start, there is a substantial discussion dealing with the mechanics of space and time travel, especially the latter, as indicated above. Although this discussion is unconscionably long, and continues on Night 61, it is important in setting the frame of the story that follows by establishing the 'machine' used for time-travel or space-travel; as Ramer puts it, 'the machine sets the tone'. The 'machine' on which Ramer finally settles is by putting himself into a trance-like dream state: what he calls 'falling wide asleep', and reaching the sort of visions he needs by training himself to get 'deeper down'. After a couple of interesting, enigmatic but relatively familiar dreams, or visions, he gets into more exotic territory. First come fragments, especially the Green Wave, towering above green fields, and three tall trees; then distinct worlds, states of being, apparently distant in space, 'beyond the Fields of Arbol', i.e. outside the Solar System, one of a number of references Ramer makes to terms used by Lewis in his Cosmic Trilogy.[12] He has, it emerges, already told the company of one of these worlds, called by a name in Hungarian style: Emberü (in an early draft, Gyönyürü),[13] a sort of blessed land; and in more detail he describes another semi-paradisal world: Ellor

---

12. Fields of Arbol: the Solar System; hnau: sentient being. See C.S. Lewis, *Out of the Silent Planet*, Pan Books, London, 1938; part of his '*Cosmic Trilogy*' with *Perelandra*, Pan Books, London, 1945; and *That Hideous Strength*, Pan Books, London, 1945.

13. 'Gyönyürü' is standard Hungarian, meaning 'beautiful'. 'Emberü' appears to be related to Hungarian 'ember' = 'human being'.

Eshúrizel, which appears to be inhabited by people called the En-keladim, who are elvish, yet not elvish; and further out yet Minal-zidar the Golden, and the world of crystals Tekel-mirim. Then he experiences a sort of wrenching gear-change, a shift of scene to a sort of flux, a repulsive vision of a whirling formless land, steadying to become a small river, and small buildings rapidly growing and disappearing like fungus, with ant-like creatures rushing about; as he gets closer and the motion slows down he sees form in the buildings, particularly one 'thing like a great fluted mushroom with an odd top' – which turns out to be the Radcliffe Camera in Oxford, and the previous chaotic scene has been a sort of time-lapse vision of the Thames Valley.

## PAPERS: PART 2 – NIGHTS 62-67

The main focus now shifts from Ramer, with his Hungarian birth and his travels in space to Lowdham, his Germanic (not to say Anglo-Saxon) orientation and his attraction to times long past. And another interesting development: as early as Night 63 he starts speaking, apparently involuntarily, in another persona, provoked by the sight of the Radcliffe Camera, which, as will become apparent, bears a remarkable resemblance to an ominous temple in a far-off time; and later out of the blue he curses one Zigur, and continues; 'Behold the Eagles of the Lords of the West! They are coming over Númenor!' He increasingly appears subject to possession, as his vision begins to intrude on 'reality', and it is revealed that his father, named Edwin, who had thought of calling him 'Aelfwine', disappeared while sailing in a ship named *The Éarendel*. A discussion of this name and its possible meaning and origins leads into linguistic speculations and discoveries, particularly relating to Old English (as well as two other languages as yet only in vestigial form), especially cryptic verses in that language, one line in particular meaning 'A straight way lay westward, now it is bent'. Then on Night 67 matters take a dramatic turn. Lowdham, recounting his visions, brings some examples of writing in the two languages of 'Avallonian' and Adûnaic, the latter name making its first appearance. There is a recurrence of the name Zigur which now seems to act as a trigger for strange utterances on the part of Jeremy (who has previously only had a minor role) and Lowdham, who start calling each other Abrazân and Nimruzîr; they seem to be experiencing another reality, involving eagles, an abyss and general ruin, which however is also intruding forcefully on Oxford in 1987 in the form of a storm of gathering ferocity. Jeremy and Lowdham go out into the storm and out of knowledge, though Ramer seems to have some inkling(!) of what is happening: that their discussions have resulted in stirring something up, and, as Ramer fears, it is something (an Atlantean event?) that may have disastrous effects on Britain. Myth seems to be dissolving into

224 DAVID DOUGHAN

history, or rather into present reality in a way that recalls Charles Williams in such works as *The Greater Trumps* or *The Place of the Lion*, or even Lewis in *That Hideous Strength*; and of course, the mention of Edwin and Aelfwine Lowdham reminds us of *The Lost Road*.

## PAPERS: PART 2 – NIGHTS 68-70

Some months later, Jeremy and Lowdham have sent a letter telling that they are safe and sound. Meanwhile, Ramer has a page of strange writing (Tengwar) that he hands to old Professor Rashbold at Pembroke, who deciphers it as a piece of Old English, dealing with Zigur, Tarcalion and the downfall of Númenóre. Then Jeremy and Lowdham return; Frankley produces a poem on the Death of St. Brendan (later revised and published as *Imram*), with its theme of a voyage to mysterious lands, the sight of the Cloud, the Tree and the Star, and the old road that leads away from the round world. Lowdham starts to recount where he and Jeremy have been since the storm: travelling from Land's End eventually to Ireland, where they hear from a local inhabitant of men coming ashore in the aftermath of the great wave, apparently associated with the Great Storm and a meteorological disturbance in mid-Atlantic; and then to Porlock, in Somerset, on the Bristol Channel, also called the 'Severn Sea' (Welsh 'Môr Hafren'). Here they find themselves transformed as Old Englishmen, Aelfwine and Treowine, in the company of King Eadward, in the tenth century, expecting an attack from roving Danish, i.e. Viking, ships. Ælfwine (Lowdham) on the king's bidding recites some verses in standard Old English: 'Hwæt! Eadweard cyning Ælfredes sunu', 'Monath modes lust mid mereflóde ...' and 'Hwæt! We on geárdagum of Gársecge ...', and then tells the tale of King Sheave, much as it has already appeared in *The Lost Road*. There follows a fragmentary account of the Danish attack on Porlock and its repulsion; then, as indicated above, the Papers peter out into a collection of notes for presumed further work.

## LANGUAGE(S)

There are two important elements in Part 2: the downfall theme, and the matter of languages (although these often overlap). In fact it will also occasionally be necessary to refer to the text following *NCPs* in *Sauron Defeated*, namely *The Drowning of Anadûné*. Matters linguistic play a considerable part here, stemming partly from Ramer's suggestion in Part 1 that we have a 'native language', which is not necessarily the one in which we are raised.

However, leaving aside fleeting hints of Hungarian, the majority of what is discussed comes from Lowdham, in particular pieces of Old English, which fall into three categories: 'classical' Old English, of the sort students are used to; then what appear to be archaic Mercian forms, such as that in which a version is given of the poem later declaimed in 'classical' Old English by Ælfwine. The version that appears in Lowdham's vision begins: 'Monath modæs lust mith meriflóda ...' (compare with Ælfwine's version above). But then comes the original form of the gnomic utterance about the straight road being bent: 'Westra lage wegas rehtas, wraikwas nu isti.' This appears to be an extremely archaic ancestor of Old English, and indeed of the Germanic group of languages to which it belongs, and this sentence would indeed be, as Lowdham says, of great interest to philologists in that it contains forms that are unattested, but that can be deduced, such as the final vowels of 'lage' and 'isti', which have already been dropped in the earliest known forms of Germanic. Here Tolkien seems to be hinting that extremely early on ancestors of the Germanic peoples had some knowledge of, and possibly contact with, Númenor, which would link in with King Sheave, and the Langobardic elements in *The Lost Road*. Other Old English words are of philological interest: The translation of Númenor as 'Nowendaland' (= shipmaster land) is unexceptionable, and 'Fréafíras' for 'lordly men', Númenoreans, is a regular coinage; however 'Regeneard' appears to contain the element 'regn-', cognate with Old Norse 'regin', gods, and to mean 'God-home', i.e. Valinor. Then there is the entirely unattested 'Midswipen' which appears to be cognate with Gothic 'midja-sweipains' – flood of middle-earth. Lowdham reckons the 'Wihawinia' is 'very antique' – so antique indeed that even Christopher Tolkien does not venture a gloss (elsewhere Nelson Goering suggests among other possibilities 'blessed plain').[14] In any case, there is a lot of philological speculation going on here.

On another track, though still a Germanic one, there is Lowdham's extensive Old English texts. Here the language is unproblematic, being standard Old English; however the script in which it appears, and which old Professor Rashbold deciphers, is very different, being in fact Tengwar of a usual *tehta* mode.[15] As far as I am aware, this is the first extended example of Tengwar in the *legendarium*.

And so we come to Lowdham's 'ghost languages', the languages that have no apparent connection to known human languages. The first, with words like 'Númenor(e)' and 'Atalante', turns out to be Quenya (here called 'Avallonian'), which by now had become a regular feature of Tolkien's writings. However, the second has a very different look from the 'limpid' quality of Quenya, with phrases like 'Kado zigurun zabathán ...' It turns out that this is Adûnaic, the language of

---

14. Nelson Goering (as 'Lord of the Rings'), 'Lord of the Rings Fanatics Plaza Night 66', 28 October 2012, *Lord of the Rings Fanatics Plaza* <http://www.lotrplaza.com/archive/index. php?t-24138.html> [accessed 11 November 2015].

15. Op. cit. [1], pp. 319–27.

Númenor (Anadûne, the Yôzâyân), and it has a very different structure from that of the Elvish languages, since many of the words have a tri-consonantal base. In this, and this only, it resembles Semitic languages like Arabic and Hebrew, e.g. 'kalab' = fall; 'akallabêth' = the downfallen. Tolkien gives an overview of its phonology and grammar and explains more in *The Downfall of Anadûne*.

## DOWNFALL, AND OTHER THEMES

By the end of the Papers, certain recurrent themes have emerged. As already indicated, a major such theme is that of the Great Wave, not only sweeping over the drowned land, but casting a ship and its exiled mariners on the shores of mortal lands. Another is that of land to the West, whether mortal (Anadûne, Númenor) or elvish (Avallóne, Valinor), and the men from it – and above all the way to these lands, which was formerly straight, but is now bent. There is also the person of Zigur/Sauron, and the domed temple, apparently to Melkor, that he has constructed. In short, we have here the beginnings of what would come to be the story of Westernesse and the Númenorean kingdoms in exile, founded by Elendil and his sons.

## TO SUM UP

So this was what Tolkien was devoting his creative energies to in late 1945 and early 1946. Why he embarked on this instead of the various urgent tasks that awaited his attention at this time is debatable. Possibly it was simply displacement activity, Tolkien being notoriously 'dilatory and unmethodical', as Lewis put it,[16] or it could have been a form of self-therapy, as suggested by Bruce Charlton,[17] the verbosity especially of the early parts representing a sort of 'talking cure', a healing conversation with himself. Be this as it may, whatever this might have meant for Tolkien's personal life, there is no doubt about its effect on the *legendarium*. It seems to have cleared a block, and opened a new straight road that resulted in a satisfying conclusion for *The Lord of the Rings*. Finally, the *NCPs* are an interesting repository of ideas worth considering in their own right, as well as giving an insight into the thought-processes of an author who quite unwittingly came to redefine what is understood by 'fantasy.' It is a rare instance of Tolkien showing us at least some of the bones from which he made his very individual soup.

---

16. Warren H. Lewis, *The Letters of C.S. Lewis*, ed. Geoffrey Bles, London, 1966, p. 399.
17. E.g. in *Beyond Bree* July 2012. *Beyond Bree: Tolkien Special Interest Group: Newsletter of American Mensa,* ed. Nancy Martsch, Sherman Oaks, CA, 1981 to present.

# 'Myth-Making: How J. R. R. Tolkien Adapted Mythopoeia from Old English'

## Zachary A. Rhone

*In a form of adaptation, Tolkien extracts text from the Old English elegies The Ruin, The Seafarer, and The Wanderer for the purposes of recreating timeless sentiments within his own sub-creative work. By analysing Tolkien's use of such adaptation, we may discover key examples of Tolkien's creation of mythology: Creation, Fall, and Mortality. This paper will describe Tolkien's adaptations from Old English to his Middle-earth texts in order to reveal greater depths of Middle-earth.*

'His own mind and imagination had been captivated since schooldays by early English poems such as *Beowulf, Sir Gawain and the Green Knight*, and *Pearl*, and by the Old Icelandic *Völsungasaga* and *Elder Edda*,' writes Humphrey Carpenter of J.R.R. Tolkien in *The Inklings*.[1] Tolkien believed the early English texts to be a source of learning and study beyond language alone. As Verlyn Flieger reminds readers in 'There Would Always be a Fairy-Tale: J.R.R. Tolkien and the Folklore Controversy,' Tolkien found fault in those who studied stories for data, failing to recognise the enchantment, or *faërie*, of fairy-tales.[2] In defense of his view, Tolkien argued for the value of old fairy tales in such academic works as *The Monsters and the Critics* and *On Fairy-Stories*. As a result, *Beowulf* and other early English texts are currently studied across the discipline of literary studies.

While critical to his scholarly and creative background, *Beowulf* is not the only Old English text that Tolkien studied. Tolkien is credited to have performed a co-translation with E.V. Gordon of *Sir Gawain and the Green Knight* and further planned to translate *Pearl, The Wanderer*, and *The Seafarer*, but the translations proved to be more by Gordon with Tolkien as a consultant.[3] The two collaborated on a translation of *Pearl* for a while, but Tolkien left the work at a standstill when he became inundated with writing *The Lord of the Rings*, ultimately resulting in

---

1. Humphrey Carpenter, *The Inklings*, HarperCollins, London, 1997, p. 25.
2. Verlyn Flieger, 'There Would Always be a Fairy-tale: J.R.R. Tolkien and the Folklore Controversy', in Jane Chance, ed., *Tolkien the Medievalist*, Routledge, New York, 2003, 26–35.
3. For more detail on their collaboration and friendship, see Douglas A. Anderson, '"An Industrious Little Devil": E.V. Gordon as Friend and Collaborator with Tolkien', in Jane Chance, ed., *Tolkien the Medievalist*, Routledge, New York, 2003, 15–25.

228 ZACHARY A. RHONE

the posthumous publication of Gordon's translation by his widow, Ida.[4]

Regardless of whether or not Tolkien completed translations of these Old English texts, Tolkien's study of the poems shed light on influences other than *Beowulf* in Tolkien's writing. Tom Shippey admits, 'Tolkien was trying continually to extend the frontiers of style beyond the barbed wire of modern opinion. In this endeavour he thought he had the backing of the great poets and romancers, like Sir Thomas Malory or the anonymous authors of *Pearl* and *Beowulf* and *The Wanderer*';[5] however, poetic influences other than *Beowulf* have received considerably less critical attention for the effect that these works have on Tolkien's creative fiction. Because of the limited attention given to some of the smaller Old English texts, this talk focuses on the ways in which Tolkien adapted *The Wanderer*, *The Ruin*, and *The Seafarer* into his fiction.

For instance, Tolkien chose to adapt *The Seafarer* in *The Lost Road*, an incomplete work that prequels *The Lord of the Rings* as one of the histories of Middle-earth. As Shippey notes, one of the characters, Ælfwine, chants an adaptation of *The Seafarer*.[6] The scholarly work of Shippey, which points out adapted texts, is significant to the study of Tolkien's construction of tales—that is, to understand what influenced Tolkien and where examples appear; however, in this discussion, I am concerned not only with *what* and *where* Tolkien adapted Old English texts but also with *how* and *why* Tolkien used the texts within his creative works. Tolkien sheds some light on these questions when he wrote about *The Seafarer* as well as *The Wanderer* in some unpublished notes:

It is, perhaps, not surprising that the reflective poetry of a people

---

4. Humphrey Carpenter, *J.R.R. Tolkien: A Biography*, Houghton Mifflin, Boston, 2000, pp. 144–45. Several reports point to lone, unpublished translations by Tolkien of Old English texts such as *Beowulf* and, at least, portions of Old English elegies from the *Exeter Book* like *The Wanderer* and *The Seafarer*, but unfortunately, few texts have been released.

5. Tom Shippey, *J.R.R. Tolkien, Author of the Century*, Houghton Mifflin, New York, 2002, pp. 181–82.

6. See op. cit., p. 299. In regard to *The Seafarer*, Miranda Wilcox discusses how Tolkien abandoned his project of the 'The Lost Road' in which he incorporates a portion of the poem before beginning 'The Notion Club,' another incomplete text in which two Oxford dons travel back in time prior to the time of *The Silmarillion*. Wilcox asserts that Tolkien could not let go of his desire to include text from *The Seafarer*, for Lowdham, one of the dons in 'The Notion Club,' dreams that he hears Old English lines derived from *The Seafarer* – calling it 'that strange old poem of longing' (quoted in Miranda Wilcox, 'Exilic Imagining in *The Seafarer* and *The Lord of the Rings*', in Jane Chance, ed., *Tolkien the Medievalist*, Routledge, New York, 2003, 133–54, p. 137). Wilcox, perhaps, offers the best close reading on Tolkien's textual adaptations of *The Seafarer*. From various examples in both texts, Wilcox draws five main themes which she believes Tolkien adapted into his Middle-earth mythology: themes of exile, wave images, seabirds, hesitancy to leave, and Spring as a stimulus to act.

with the traditions of the cold north seas, frozen in winter, should show two elegiac poems, in which the sorrows of the lonely seafarer are a leading theme, and a symbol of desolation of spirit. These two remarkable poems of individual sentiment, are also preserved in the Exeter Book, and are now usually known as *The Wanderer* and *The Seafarer*.[7]

Tolkien, thus, adapts from one text to another not simply to show *influence*; rather, as in the case above, he is interested in adapting the *sentiment* conveyed by the Old English texts. Tolkien adapted Old English literature not only in text but also in theme, character, and style, to name a few. Where previous research, for the most part, simply cites textual elements that Tolkien adapted, I will continue the text-centered approach of unlocking Tolkien's adaptation in order to recover the sentiments (i.e. Creation, Fall, and Mortality) which Tolkien adapted from Old English poems into his fantasy texts. Furthermore, through the themes of the giants, ruin, and free will versus fate, I will show how and some of the reasons why Tolkien may have chosen to adapt these particular Old English texts.

## GIANTS AND THE MACHINE

Dimitra Fimi observes that in an early outline of *The Lost Road*, Tolkien cites Tir-nan-Óg, 'the otherworldly land of Irish tradition' which Tolkien parallels to Valinor in a poem called 'The Nameless Land'.[8] With the Celtic otherworldly realm compared to Valinor, the land of Middle-earth's gods, Tolkien undoubtedly correlated the mythology of Britain to Midde Earth, and given that the Celtic people were established in England before the coming of the Angles and Saxons, Tolkien must have had reasons for developing Valinor within the tradition of Celtic Britain.

In a similar comparison, Judy Ann Ford, in 'The White City,' offers a historical correlation between the restoration of the Roman Empire via Britain to the rise of Gondor in *LotR*. Among other conclusions, Ford posits, 'Not only does the kingdom of Gondor in the present of the novel mirror Rome of the fifth and sixth centuries, but its past also parallels that of the Roman state in many ways'.[9] The past of Gondor, in parallel to Roman Britain, is essential to

---

7. Stuart D. Lee, 'J.R.R. Tolkien and *The Wanderer*: From Edition to Application', *Tolkien Studies* 6 (2009), p. 189–211, p. 194.

8. Dimitra Fimi, 'Tolkien's "Celtic' type of legends": Merging Traditions', *Tolkien Studies* 4 (2007), p. 51–71, p. 55.

9. Judy Ann Ford, 'The White City: *The Lord of the Rings* as an Early Medieval Myth of the Restoration of the Roman Empire', *Tolkien Studies* 2 (2005), p. 53–75, p. 62.

understanding one of Tolkien's uses of Old English elegies: the giants.

In *The Wanderer* 'The Creator / of men thus wrecked this enclosure [the wine hall], / until the old works of giants stood empty, / without the sounds of their former citizens'.[10] Giants, perhaps figuratively, built the Roman baths in the poem; however, in Tolkien's use of giants, the term is quite literal when applied to the giants who helped to create Middle-earth: the Valar. In the *The Silmarillion* the Valar function as a form of giant – if not necessarily in size, then, at least, in spiritual design, for 'Men have often called them gods' (*TSil*, 'Valaquenta', 25).[11] Some, however, are attributed with a giantlike size. Ulmo, 'the King of the Sea was terrible, as a mounting wave that strides to the land' (*TSil*, 'Valaquenta', 26–27), and my personal favorite, Tulkas, who fills Arda with laughter and 'whose anger passes like a mighty wind, scattering cloud and darkness before it' (*TSil*, 'Valaquenta', 35), among other Valar, exemplify the giant-likeness of those creators of Middle-earth.[12]

The significance of the giant-like Valar extends beyond their physicality to their creations in the Middle-earth realm. In Old English mythology, the magical island of Avalon exists off the coast of England.[13] Avalon presents a world better than the culture of England and Europe but not good enough to be paradise. In *The Silmarillion*, 'A land was made for the Edain to dwell in, neither part of Middle-

---

10. 'The Wanderer', in Joseph Black et al, eds, *The Broadview Anthology of British Literature*, vol. 1, Broadview Press, Toronto, 2006, 84–87.

11. J.R.R. Tolkien, *The Silmarillion*, ed. Christopher Tolkien, 2nd edn, Houghton Mifflin, Boston, 2001, p. 25. All quotations from *TSil* are from this edition.

12. Another note of the giant quality appears in the Númenórean (or Dúnedain) lineage. The Númenóreans 'dwelt under the protection of the Valar and in the friendship of the Eldar, and they increased in stature both of mind and body.... [T]hey were tall, taller than the tallest of the sons of Middle-earth' (*TSil*, 'Akallabêth', 261–62). The Númenóreans grow in stature because they grow into the likeness of the taller, giant-like Valar and Elves.

13. In *A History of the Kings of Britain*, Geoffrey of Monmouth historicises Avalon as the place that wounded King Arthur 'was borne thence ... for the healing of his wounds, where he gave up the crown of Britain unto his kinsman, Constantine'. Geoffrey further expands on the Arthurian legend of Avalon in *The Life of Merlin*:

> The island of apples which men call 'The Fortunate Isle' gets its name from the fact that it produces all things of itself; the fields there have no need of the ploughs of the farmers and all cultivation is lacking except what nature provides. Of its own accord it produces grain and grapes, and apple trees grow in its woods from the close-clipped grass. The ground of its own accord produces everything instead of merely grass, and people live there a hundred years or more. There nine sisters rule by a pleasing set of laws those who come to them from our country.

Geoffrey of Monmouth, *A History of the Kings of Britain*, in Joseph Black et al, eds, *The Broadview Anthology of British Literature*, vol. 1, Broadview, London, 2006, p. 155. Geoffrey of Monmouth, *The Life of Merlin*, trans. John Jay Parry, <http://www.sacred-texts.com/neu/eng/vm/vmeng.htm> [accessed 27 April 2011].

MYTH-MAKING

earth nor of Valinor, for it was sundered from either by a wide sea; yet it was nearer to Valinor' (*TSil*, 'Akallabêth', 269).[14] Like Avalon of the primary world, Númenor exists neither in the verisimilitudinous realm of Middle-earth nor in the paradisiacal locale of Valinor. Tolkien, thus, adapts Avalon into Númenor. And, similar to the Arthurian legend of great knights, the Númenóreans have a famous descent of Dúnedain warriors – of whom Aragorn is a part.

Like the giants of Middle-earth who built Middle-earth and Númenor for humans to live, the giants of Celtic and Roman origin built England. Tolkien, of course, did not write the history of Middle-earth as an allegory of England's history, but he was forced to use allegorical language, as he iterates in a letter to Milton Waldman in 1951: 'I dislike Allegory – the conscious and intentional allegory – yet any attempt to explain the purport of myth or fairytale must use allegorical language…. Anyway all this stuff is mainly concerned with Fall, Mortality, and the Machine'.[15] The *Machine* is, of course, magic or art but, in Tolkien's case, was his own sub-creation of Middle-earth: his art of a literary form frequently referred to as *mythopoeia*, or myth-making which is reflective of ' a splintered fragment of the true light'.[16] Tolkien's adaptation of Old English texts helps to create the splintered fragment in his literature that reflects the divine truths he aspires to convey. His mythology of Middle-earth requires his own sub-creation and mythopoeia, and the giants – the Valar – of Middle-earth need to be sub-creators, as well. Without the Machine of Tolkien outside of the text and the Valar within the text, the mythology cannot have the other two elements: the Fall and Mortality.

## THE RUIN OR THE FALL

The Fall is inevitably accompanied or signified by some form of ruin, and all around Middle-earth, views of ruin may be found. Gondolin, Númenor, Osgiliath, Khazad-dûm – each of these cities once stood as glorious cities; each fell, and all that remains is ruin. That Tolkien would use the Old English elegy *The Ruin*, then, is not surprising. Shippey notes that Legolas' lament of the stones in *The Fellowship of the Ring* is an adaption of this elegy.[17] In the passage, Legolas states, 'But the Elves of this land were of a race strange to us of the sylvan

---

14. The Edain are those men known as Elf-friends in the realm of Beleriand; however, Ilúvatar uses the term generally for men.

15. Tolkien defines the *Machine* as magic or art: '[Magic's] object is Art not Power, sub-creation not domination and tyrannous re-forming of Creation'. Christopher Tolkien, 'From a Letter by J.R.R. Tolkien to Milton Waldman, 1951', in op. cit. [11], p. xiii.

16. See op. cit. [1], p .43.

17. See op. cit. [5], p. 33.

folk, and the trees and the grass do not now remember them. Only I hear the stones lament them: *deep they delved us, fair they wrought us, high they builded us; but they are gone*. They are gone. They sought the havens long ago' (*FotR*, 'The Ring Goes South', 276).[18] While Shippey's keen observation points out the adaptation, I would like to consider the *how* and the *why* Tolkien adapted *The Ruin* in this passage, or, specifically, how it evidences the Fall motif in Tolkien's construction of myth.

The first significant element is that the ruin Legolas observes is that of Hollin, originally called *Eregion*. When the place of ruin was known under the name of Eregion, Noldor lived there – those Elves who refused to journey into the West to Valinor.[19] The Noldor 'desired ever to increase the skill and subtlety of their works. Moreover they were not at peace in their hearts, since they had refused to return into the West' (*TSil*, 'Of the Rings of Power and the Third Age', 287). As a result of their unrest and eagerness for greater skill and knowledge, the Noldor accepted the dark Lord Sauron's guidance, and they forged nineteen Rings of Power. After Sauron forged the One Ring in the fires of Mt. Doom, all of the rings were subject to the power of the One Ring. Sauron pursued those who possessed the Rings of Power and acquired all but three. Although the story continues from here, this point in the narrative is significant, for 'From that time war never ceased between Sauron and the Elves; and Eregion was laid waste' (*TSil*, 'Of the Rings of Power and the Third Age', 288). The ruin which Legolas laments is the ruin that continues to destroy Middle-earth – the ruin brought by Sauron. Furthermore, the three elvish rings that survive are important to the theme of ruin:

> Narya, Nenya, and Vilya, they were named, the Rings of Fire, and of Water, and of Air, set with ruby and adamant and sapphire; and of all the Elven-rings Sauron most desired to possess them, for those who had them in their keeping could ward off the decays of time and postpone the weariness of the world. (*TSil*, 'Of the Rings of Power and the Third Age', 288)

In essence, the three surviving rings are rings which deny ruin, and ironically, when the three rings leave Eregion, the city falls to ruin.

The adaptation of ruin, however, is not solely from one elegiac poem. In *The Wanderer*, for example, a famous *ubi sunt* passage appears: 'Where has the horse

---

18. J.R.R Tolkien, *The Fellowship of the Ring*, Houghton Mifflin, Boston, 1994.

19. Known as the 'Deep Elves,' the name *Noldor* means 'the Wise' in the Quenya language. *Wise* here means that the elves possess great knowledge rather than sound judgment. Op. cit. [11], p. 344.

# MYTH-MAKING

gone? where is the rider? where is the giver of gold? / Where are the seats of the feast? where are the joys of the hall?'[20] In *The Two Towers*, Tolkien adapts this ubi sunt into the first two lines of a song sung by Aragorn: 'Where now the horse and the rider? Where is the horn that was blowing / Where is the helm and the hauberk, and the bright hair flowing?' (*TT*, 'The King of the Golden Hall', 497).[21] In both cases, the *ubi sunt* passage signals a lament for what is no longer present; that is, the narrator wonders where something has gone that was once there. Tolkien adapts the language barrier of the Old English to modern English translation, as well, for Aragorn 'began to chant softly in a slow tongue unknown to the Elf and Dwarf; yet they listened, for there was a strong music in it' (*TT*, 'The King of the Golden Hall', 497). Legolas observes, despite the language barrier, 'I cannot guess what it means, save that it is laden with the sadness of Mortal Men' (*TT*, 'The King of the Golden Hall', 497). One of the *why*'s of Tolkien's adaptation is clear: he desired to capture the sentiment of sadness encapsulated in the Old English text. He wanted to articulate the universal feeling of sadness over ruin only felt by those laden with the gift of mortality. Only when Aragorn translates the passage for Legolas and Gimli into the 'Common Speech' do the companions understand the content.

To clarify, Tolkien certainly would not have called his adaption of the *ubi sunt* passage a translation of the original, for he had objections to certain translators for their attempts to 're-create' a text.[22] Rather, in Bodleian Library manuscript (A 38, f. 12v), Tolkien claims:

> I have never attempted to "re-create" anything. My aim has been the basically more modest, and certainly the more laborious one of trying to make something new. No one would learn anything valid about the "Anglo-Saxons" from any of my lore, not even that concerning the Rohirrim; I never intended that they should. Even the lines beginning 'Where now the horse and the rider,' though they echo a line in "The

---

20. See op. cit. [10], lines 92–93.

21. J.R.R. Tolkien, *The Two Towers*, Houghton Mifflin, Boston, 1994.

22. Tolkien was allergic to Burton Raffel's philosophy of translation as recreation. In response to Raffel, in Bodleian manuscript A30/1 (at f. 121), Tolkien states his distaste:

> But if I were to venture to translate 'The Wanderer' – the lament of the lonely man withering away in regret, and the poet's reflexions upon it – I would not dare to intrude any sentiment of my own, not to disarrange the order of word and thought in the old poem, in an impertinent attempt to make it more pleasing to myself, and perhaps to others. That is not ' re-creation' but destruction. At best a foolish misuse of a talent for personal poetic expression; at worst the unwarranted impudence of a parasite.

Stuart D. Lee, 'J.R.R. Tolkien and *The Wanderer*: From Edition to Application', *Tolkien Studies* 6 (2009), 189–211, p. 204).

Wanderer," are indeed … not a translation, re-creative or otherwise. They are integrated (I hope) in something wholly different, the only excuse for the borrowing: they are particular in reference, to a great hero and his renowned horse, and they are suppose\d/ to be part of the song of a minstrel of a proud and undefeated people in a hall still populous with men. Even the sentiment is different: it laments the ineluctable ending and passing back into oblivion of the fortunate, the full-lives, the unblemished and the beautiful. To me that is more poignant than any particular disaster, from the cruelty of men of the hostility of the world.[23]

Tolkien, thus, resists the idea of recreating a text through translation; rather, he adapts the Old English text in order to borrow the sentiment of a lament for a missing great hero and horse.

A second *why* Tolkien adapted the *ubi sunt* passage was to help to create a literary tradition in Middle-earth which establishes a historical and traditional sentiment of ruin. In *The Lost Road* and *The Notion Club*, Tolkien establishes the framework for a literary history in Middle-earth which includes *The Seafarer*; likewise, part of the *ubi sunt* in *The Wanderer* lives in the literary tradition of Rohan. After his chant, Aragorn contextualises the poem: 'Thus spoke a forgotten poet long ago in Rohan, recalling how tall and fair was Eorl the Young, who rode down out of the North; and there were wings upon the feet of his steed, Felaróf, father of horses. So men still sing in the evening' (*TT*, 'The King of the Golden Hall', 497). Richard W. Fehrenbacher recognises this *why* when he writes, 'Of course, the elegiac 'sadness of mortal men' is precisely what the ubi sunt motif takes for its theme, and to Tolkien this marks the ultimate limit of unenchanted Rohan's literature (and Beowulf's *Weltanschauung*)'.[24] Tolkien, thus, creates a literary tradition for Rohan like the literary tradition of England which includes *The Seafarer*, *The Wanderer*, and *The Ruin*. He develops a canon of Rohan from which the people have a collective memory of the Fall and of ruin.

For Tolkien, then, these Old English representations of ruin are timeless in sentiment despite their antiquated foci. *The Wanderer* 'remembers hall-holders and treasure-taking,' but 'that joy had all faded'.[25] The wise wanderer laments the ruin of former glory. Tolkien's adaptation, likewise, possesses a sentiment of inevitable destruction but, simultaneously, requires the speaker to have a perspective from the future in order to recognise and envision impending ruin.

---

23. See op. cit.

24. Richard W. Fehrenbacher, 'Beowulf as Fairy-story: Enchanting the Elegiac in *The Two Towers*', *Tolkien Studies* 3 (2006), 101–115, p. 107.

25. Op. cit. [10], lines 34–36.

MYTH-MAKING

In Tolkien's own words,

> In the Wanderer the poet passes before the end of the poem to the vision of a ruin, and a lament for the days devoured by time, a poignant expression of a dominant Anglo-Saxon mood: with this epitaph on antiquity, I will end this brief echo of the now long-vanished Anglo-Saxon days.[26]

Ruin, thus, is a way of looking back: a way of remembering the Fall as the stones do in the lament and the *ubi sunt* passage recognises the absent horse and rider of oral tradition. The 'epitaph' is on the past – on time, itself – and the Creation of the giants. And after this Fall and this ruin, the final element of Tolkien's myth construction remains: Mortality.

## MORTALITY: THE WYRD AND THE WILL

Two key lines of *The Ruin* summarise Tolkien's creation of mythology: 'Wondrous is the foundation – the fates have broken / and shattered this city; the work of giants crumbles'.[27] What was once wondrous and created by the giants falls into ruin, but age is not the culprit; rather, fate – the structure of mortality – shatters creation. Thus, after themes of creation and ruin in adapted passages, Tolkien addresses the final theme of Mortality in the language of fate and free will. Flieger, in 'The Music and the Task,' asserts that Tolkien 're-configured the borrowed material to fit his new context',[28] for 'Tolkien did more than color in a blank space; he invented a cosmology whose operation depends on a paradox, a challenging teleological contradiction'.[29] In other words, Tolkien's Middle-earth incorporated adaptation to connect the elements of myth on a complex, problematic level. Accordingly, the third and most difficult theme to understand is Mortality, for Tolkien discusses Mortality via the complicated task of finding one's way through life—in terms of the ' teleological contradiction' of fate and free will. Flieger quotes Tolkien in some unpublished notes that reveal the paradoxical aspect of fate and free will in *LotR*:

> They would probably also have said that Bilbo was "fated" to find the

---

26. See Lee, op. cit. [22], p. 194.
27. 'The Ruin', in Joseph Black et al, eds, *The Broadview Anthology of British Literature*, vol. 1, Broadview, Toronto, 2006, lines 1–2.
28. Verlyn Flieger, 'The Music and the Task: Fate and Free Will in Middle-earth', *Tolkien Studies* 6 (2009), 151–81, p. 153.
29. Op. cit., p. 151.

Ring, but not necessarily to surrender it; and then if Bilbo surrendered it Frodo was fated to go on his mission, but not necessarily to destroy the Ring – which in fact he did not do…. Just as when Frodo's will proved in the end inadequate, a means for the Ring's destruction immediately appeared – being kept in reserve by Eru as it were.[30]

In this passage Tolkien reconciles the apparent contradiction of *fate* and *will*. Further in this passage of unpublished notes, Tolkien equates *fate* to 'Eru's plan'.[31] For this reason, the ring is fated to be destroyed, but the means of the ring's destruction is open to decision – a result of each character's chosen path. In Tolkien's cosmology, fate and free will are not contradictory – having only one truth; rather, fate and free will are paradoxical, allowing for two or more valid but opposing truths.[32]

Ilúvatar calls fate and the world of Middle-earth into being by the song of the Ainur, yet on page fifty-nine of *The Book of Lost Tales I* Ilúvatar 'devised that Men should have a free virtue whereby within the limits of the powers and substances and chances of the world they might fashion and design their life beyond even the original Music of the Ainur that is as fate to all things else'.[33] Humans have a free will to choose fate; the Elves and other creatures, on the other hand, are bound by fate. For this reason, the race of humans remains on Middle-earth; the Elves, on the other hand, must leave Middle-earth and diminish into the West.

To accompany Ilúvatar's establishment of fate and free will in the beginning of Middle-earth, Tolkien incorporates *The Seafarer* into the mythology of Middle-earth. 'The Seafarer', in *The Lost Road*, is a poem chanted in a king's court. Although Shippey argues that the use of the poem in the court is 'highly inappropriate',[34] Tolkien offers a clue as to where the Old English poem connects to his mythology, especially with his alteration of lines 3 and 4. While lines 1 and 2 read, 'The desire of my spirit urges me to journey forth over the flowing

---

30. Op. cit. [28], p. 158.
31. Op. cit. [28], p. 158.
32. Tolkien discusses this more fully in his essay, 'Fate and Free Will':

On a journey a man may turn aside, choosing this or that way – e.g. to avoid a marsh, or a steep hill – but this decision is mostly intuitive or half-conscious (as that of an irrational animal) and has only an immediate object of easing his journey. His setting-out may have been a free decision, to achieve some object, but his actual course was largely under physical direction – and it might have led to/or missed a meeting of importance.

J.R.R. Tolkien, 'Fate and Free Will', ed. Carl F. Hostetter, *Tolkien Studies* 6 (2009), 183–88, p. 185.
33. Op. cit. [28], p. 162.
34. Op. cit. [5], p. 299.

sea,' Tolkien alters 'that far hence across the hills of water and the whale's country I may seek the land of strangers' to 'that I seek over the ancient water's awful mountains Elf-friends' island in the Outer-world'.[35] Tolkien's Seafarer, or adventurer, has a final goal set for the Undying Lands or the West – for Valinor, or as previously discussed, the heavenly realm. The sentiment of the poem has one's spirit set forth on a path of fate, but for humans, one must decide whether or not to stay on the path of fate. Humans have a will to change fate so that they may simply die or find a new life in Valinor.

Tolkien's adaptation of Old English poetry demystifies his mythology further with *The Wanderer*. The fate-changing free will of humans appears in Tolkien's adaptation of *The Wanderer* which functions similar to the modified passage from *The Seafarer*, but at the same time, *The Wanderer* clarifies a key factor in the fate versus free will discussion. In 'J.R.R. Tolkien and *The Wanderer*: From Edition to Application,' Stuart D. Lee asserts that Aragorn functions like 'The Wanderer' in *LotR*,[36] 'for he is a Ranger ... though, of course, again he is not aimlessly wandering'.[37] In *The Wanderer*:

> There still stands in the path of the dear warriors
> a wall wondrously high, with serpentine stains.
> A storm of spears took away the warriors,
> bloodthirsty weapons, *wyrd* the mighty,
> and storms batter these stone walls,
> frost falling binds up the earth,
> the howl of winter, when blackness comes,
> night's shadow looms, sends down from the north
> harsh hailstones in hatred of men.
> All is toilsome in the earthly kingdom,
> the working of *wyrd* changes the world under heaven.[38]

A path for the warriors lay before them along with a dangerous obstacle – the high wall in the North. The fate versus free will discussion works fine paradoxically until *wyrd* enters the poem. *Wyrd* is a personified mighty fate which takes away warriors.[39] In terms of fate versus free will, then, fate may be

---

35. Op. cit. [6], p. 299.

36. Lee summarises, from collections of Tolkien's notes, how Tolkien uses and critiques *The Wanderer* over the course of nearly forty years in his scholarship: op. cit. [22].

37. See op. cit. [22], p. 203.

38. See op. cit. [10], lines 97–107.

39. This line could also be interpreted with *wyrd* as a verb rather than a personification. In which case, the mighty are 'wyrded,' or acted upon by fate. In either case, however, *wyrd* is active.

divided into two parts: *fate*, which is the path which all creatures follow through life and which humans have a will – a choice – as to what path to follow; and *wyrd*, a form of fate which acts upon all creatures, and none have the power to change.[40]

To return to the example of the ring-bearer, Bilbo was fated – *wyrded* – to find the Ring, but his weakness of will decided whether or not he surrendered to it. His fate with the ring, thus, is decided by his free will or lack of free will. Because Bilbo at least asserts enough free will to surrender the ring to Frodo, Frodo has his choice in fate: to succumb to its power or destroy it. In either case, however, fate in terms of 'Eru's plan' is a matter of *wyrd*, and the ring's destruction is part of the *wyrd* in the text. Hence, when Frodo's free will fails to follow the alignment of his fate and Eru's *wyrd*, Gollum bites off Frodo's finger and falls into the fire, completing the *wyrd*: 'But for him, Sam, I could not have destroyed the Ring. The Quest would have been in vain, even at the bitter end. So let us forgive him! For the Quest is achieved, and now all is over' (*RotK*, 'Mount Doom', 926).[41] The Ring's destruction is fated in the sense of *wyrd*, for when the Quest is inadequately supplied by the free will of Frodo, Gollum's step too far completes the required destruction of the Ring.

The Ring's destruction is, in fact, necessary for Tolkien's conception of mythology. Perhaps the most unique element Tolkien created out of the concept of *wyrd* is of his own terminology, *eucatastrophe*. In his essay *On Fairy-Stories*, Tolkien writes, 'In its fairy-tale – or otherworld – setting, [eucatastrophe] is a sudden and miraculous grace: never to be counted on to recur'.[42] Tolkien argues that the eucatastrophic tale is to fairy-story what tragedy is to drama—the truest form. The eucatastrophic tale requires 'the consolation of fairy-stories, the joy of the happy ending: or more correctly of the good catastrophe, the sudden joyous turn (for there is no true end to any fairy-tale),' writes Tolkien (*OFS*, 152). This sudden and joyous turn to the happy ending is exactly the conclusion of *LotR*. While mixed with the unfortunate fall of Gollum, the fate of Middle-earth is turned by eucatastrophe; however ironically, eucatastrophe functions like a form of *wyrd* which causes joy. The world subjected to eucatastrophe experiences a joy imposed by an active fate.

---

40. Melkor may be an adaptation of the northern evil found in *The Wanderer* and other Old English texts, for 'in the north Melkor built his strength, and he slept not, but watched and laboured,' constructing a fortress and armory called Angband (*TSil*, 'Of the Coming of the Elves and the Captivity of Melkor', 47). Etymologically, as well, *Melkor* means 'He who arises in Might' (*TSil*, 'Index', 340) – an adaptation of '*wyrd* the mighty' in line 100 of *The Wanderer*.
41. J.R.R. Tolkien, *The Return of the King*, Houghton Mifflin, Boston, 1994.
42. J.R.R. Tolkien, 'On Fairy-Stories', in Christopher Tolkien, ed., *The Monsters and the Critics and Other Essays*, HarperCollins, London, 2006, 109–61, p. 152.

MYTH-MAKING

In terms of the Ring's demise, then, Frodo's choice of a different fate is over-written by a *wyrd* – a eucatastrophic intervention – in which Gollum steals the Ring and falls into the fires of Mount Doom. The event certainly contains a sense of sorrow for Gollum's failure to recover and survive. Eucatastrophe ' does not deny the existence of *dyscatastrophe*, of sorrow and failure: the possibility of these is necessary to the joy of deliverance; it denies … universal final defeat and in so far is *evangelium*, giving a fleeting glimpse of Joy, Joy beyond the walls of the world, poignant as grief' (*OFS*, 152). The Ring's destruction, at once, possesses a dyscatastrophe of Gollum's death and Frodo's failed will, yet because of the *wyrd* that the Ring would be destroyed, the event is eucatastrophic in the greater narrative of Middle-earth, thus, eliciting a 'fleeting glimpse of Joy.' Sam, for instance, 'In all that ruin of the world for the moment he felt only joy, great joy. The burden was gone. His master had been saved; he was himself again, he was free' (*RotK*, 'Mount Doom', 926). In the realm created by the giant Valar, Sam survives the ruin of the Fall to a point of great joy – of *wyrd* – of eucatastrophe.

## CONCLUSION

Tolkien creates a mythology of Middle-earth in the tradition of past myth-makers through adaptation. He extracts text from the Old English elegies *The Ruin*, *The Seafarer*, and *The Wanderer* for the purposes of recreating timeless sentiments within his own sub-creative work. By analysing his use of such adaptation, we may discover key examples of Tolkien's creation of mythology: Creation, Fall, and Mortality. The giants of the Old English world are reborn in the Valar of Middle-earth mythology; the Fall is represented in the recurrent ruin throughout Middle-earth; and Tolkien represents Mortality vis-à-vis terms of free will and fate, including both a fate of choice and that of predetermination (*wyrd*). Out of the concept of *wyrd* comes Tolkien's conclusion to Middle-earth, his view of fairy-tale essentials. More specifically, Tolkien adapts *wyrd* from the Old English to term the quintessential fairy-tale ending: the joyous, eucatastrophic ending which elucidates 'splintered fragments of the true light' – the core of Tolkien's mythopoeia.

# 'J.R.R. Tolkien's Mythopoeia and Familiarisation of Myth: Hobbits as Mediators of Myth in The Hobbit and The Lord of the Rings'

## Jyrki Korpua

*Tolkien's creative method uses myths, activates them, modernises them, and familiarises them. This paper discusses Tolkien as a mythographer of English language and his Mythopoeia creative myth making. I will focus on the concept of myth; and the questions of familiarisation (Heimlich) and defamiliarisation (Uncanny, Das Unheimliche) in Tolkien's legandarium, and how these activate the pre-modern myths for the contemporary audience.*

The topic of this article is J. R. R. Tolkien's mythopoeia and the familiarisation of myth; mythopoeia in this case meaning a creative myth-making for artistic purposes. Tolkien used the term in his poem *Mythopoeia*, and the term has later been connected with authors of fantasy fiction who integrate mythological themes and archetypes into fiction. Tolkien's *legendarium* – his collection of books dealing with Middle-earth – is undoubtedly one of the central examples of mythopoeic vision in literary history. My main focus is on the familiarising element of hobbits in *The Hobbit: or There and Back Again* (1937) and *The Lord of the Rings* (1954-55). I discuss how hobbits – as a literary element – function as mediators of myth for the twentieth and twenty-first century audience.

Literary texts use elements which create a sense of 'familiarity' for the reader. In the case of Tolkien's texts these elements could be interpreted as, for example, creating a coherent fictive world by overlapping realistic imagery of familiar flora and fauna or milieus, and realistic narration, or, by Tolkien's use of linguistic skills, as for example modern English language. This effect of reality is used in order to familiarise Tolkien's fantasy world for the reader.

On the other hand, theoretically familiarisation could be approached from the juxtaposition of defamiliarisation, or unfamiliar. The term 'defamiliar', or 'the uncanny', is first identified in Ernst Jentsch's article 'On the Psychology of the Uncanny' (1906). Sigmund Freud popularised the term in his essay 'Das Unheimliche' (The Uncanny, 1919), where he expanded Jentsch's views and added many new perspectives to the term. In the literature theory, the term 'defamiliarisation' is often connected to both Russian formalism (especially Viktor Shklovsky) and to modern and post-modern theories as an artistic

## 242 JYRKI KORPUA

technique forcing the audience to see common things in unfamiliar or strange way – for example in related theories, such as in Bertol Brecht's Distancing Effect, 'making strange', alienation, or even defamiliarisation. In Tolkien's texts, defamiliarising effects are usually those elements weird or alien for both the protagonists and the reading audience, or, especially in the case of *The Hobbit* and *LotR*, unfamiliar for the mediators of hobbits.

Freud thought that the subject of the 'defamiliar' is in a province of aesthetics. It is undoubtedly related to what is frightening – to what arouses dread and horror.[1] Freud describes the etymology of the German word '*unheimlich*', which is obviously the opposite of '*heimlich*' (homely), '*heimisch*' (native) – the opposite of what is familiar – and writes that we are tempted to conclude that what is 'uncanny' is frightening precisely because it is not known and familiar. Freud writes that naturally not everything that is new and unfamiliar is frightening.[2] In my view, the most interesting parts of Tolkien's *legendarium* are those that at first are unfamiliar for the reading audience, but are effectively familiarised in the text from the point of the view of more familiar protagonists, such as hobbits.

## TOLKIEN'S MYTHOPOEIA

Tolkien used mythopoeia – invented and familiarised myths. He wanted his *legendarium* to be a body of more or less connected legends ranging from the large and cosmogonic to the level of romantic fairy-story,[3] which has been also claimed by many scholars, such as Verlyn Flieger and Carl F. Hostetter in the study *Tolkien's Legendarium*.[4]

In my view Tolkien's objective was to create a fictional literary history using the mythopoeic envisioning and re-imagining of myths. In a way, he succeeded in this by creating *The Hobbit* and *LotR* and his work was finished posthumously by *The Silmarillion* (1977) and *The History of Middle-earth* series (1983-96). My view of Tolkien's *legendarium* is that it is a thematic collection of fictional myths of middle-ages that are based on the pre-modern myths of the 'western culture'. Tolkien's texts could be seen as a crucial example of twentieth-century

---

1. Sigmund Freud, *Art and Literature*, ed. Albert Dickson, Penguin Books, Harmondsworth, 1989, p. 339.
2. Op. cit. [1], p. 341.
3. Humphrey Carpenter, ed., *The Letters of J.R.R. Tolkien*, with the assistance of Christopher Tolkien, George Allen & Unwin, London, 1981: Letter 131, p. 144; Letter 190, p. 250; Letter 213, pp. 288–89.
4. Verlyn Flieger and Carl F. Hostetter, eds, *Tolkien's Legendarium. Essays on The History of Middle-earth*, Greenwood Press, Westport, pp. xi–xiii.

transformation of pre-modern myths and contemporary literature, and Tolkien's *legendarium*'s mythopoeia could be seen as a familiarisation of pre-modern myths.

I see Tolkien as a mythographer of English language, which has already been suggested by other scholars. Verlyn Flieger in her study *Interrupted Music: The Making of Tolkien's Mythology* sees Tolkien as a part of a continuum of a long tradition of mythmakers in the history of English literature, such as Edmund Spenser, John Milton and William Blake.[5] Tom Shippey in his study *The Road to Middle-earth: How J. R. R. Tolkien created a New Mythology* sees Tolkien's creative writing as grown out of his love of fable and of his love for language, and sees Tolkien's *legendarium* in comparison with, for example, such classical works of English language as *Beowulf, Pearl*, or *Sir Gawain and the Green Knight*.[6] Northrop Frye in *The Secular Scripture* finds traditional similarities between William Morris's, Lewis Carroll's and George MacDonald's Victorian fantasy and Tolkien, but finds similarities also in the level of language (archaistic and 'invented') between Tolkien and Walter Scott's historical novels and James Joyce's modernist novels.[7] Verlyn Flieger also sees similarities between Tolkien's and Joyce's mythmaking, although they are using the myths in different modes.[8] This unsuspected resemblance between Tolkien and modernism in the level of mythopoeia can also been seen in Jed Esty's study *The Shrinking Island: Modernism and National Culture in England*, where Esty compares Tolkien with a canonical writer, T.S. Eliot, who also used myths in his writings.[9] Then again, I see that even though Tolkien is a British twentieth-century writer, he turned his attention and affection towards a much older history of literature and in his texts integrated pre-modern myth and legends for the contemporary audience. Tolkien's texts reflect myths and stories from many different periods of history, for example ancient, medieval and renaissance literature, and familiarise these materials by the use of contemporary literary tools.

In 1951, in his letter to publisher Milton Waldman, Tolkien writes that his basic passion '*ab initio* was for myth – and for fairy-story, and above all for heroic legend on the brink of fairy-tale and history'.[10] Tolkien noticed that there

---

5. Verlyn Flieger, *Interrupted Music. The Making of Tolkien's Mythology*, Kent State University Press, Kent OH, 2005, pp. ix–x.

6. Tom Shippey, *The Road to Middle-earth*, rev. edn. Houghton Mifflin, New York, 2003, p. 5.

7. Northrop Frye, *The Secular Scripture: A Study of the Structure of Romance*, Harvard University Press, Cambridge MA, 1976, pp. 4, 42–43.

8. Op. cit. [5], pp. ix–x.

9. Jed Esty, *A Shrinking Island: Modernism and National Culture in England*, Princeton University Press, Princeton NJ, 2004, pp. 121–23.

10. Op. cit. [3], Letter 131, p. 144.

were for example Greek, Celtic, Roman, Germanic, Scandinavian and Finnish legends, but – in his view – nothing purely English. For Tolkien, the Arthurian interculturally-coloured mythological world did not count as English. Therefore Tolkien's texts aim at first to create a new mythology 'dedicated for England'.

Fundamentally, Tolkien's *legendarium* is fantasy fiction deriving from the 'world' of myths. Tolkien's creative method uses myths, activates them, 'modernises' them, and familiarises them. There are some appropriate points: Tolkien as a twentieth-century writer romanticised his view of anti-anthropomorphic mythology, constructed for the contemporary audience, an audience that Tolkien saw foremost as English. In the myths Tolkien used, some part are certainly religious elements deriving from the Christian sources, but there are also myths deriving from other sources, such as Finnish, Scandinavian and Germanic mythologies, or ancient myths, such as, for example, Platonic myths of Atlantis and the Ring of Gyges.

It is possible to point out that Tolkien ranged his *legendarium* from the mimetically 'lower' fairy-story of *The Hobbit* to the higher fantasy of *LotR*, and still higher to the cosmogonical and cosmological mythology of *The Silmarillion*, where myth and fictional 'history' is vital. Tolkien writes that *The Silmarillion* 'begins with cosmogonical myth: the *Music of the Ainur*', and moves into the '*History of Elves*', and that his *legendarium* 'ends with a vision of the end of the world'.[11]

This 'change of tone' is easily detected in Tolkien's *legendarium*, which could be seen as functioning in different genres and modes. *The Hobbit: or There and Back Again* could be seen as a simplest form of fairy-story, or even as a story for children and younger audiences. *The Hobbit*'s literary tone is a tone of romantic fairy-story, and it is still mainly considered to be a children's book. Then again, Tolkien's mythopoeia and the aspects of the *legendarium* also overlap *The Hobbit*: some scenes, elements and references link it to other texts of the *legendarium*. When Tolkien started to write *LotR*, it at his publisher's wish, as a sequel to *The Hobbit*. Tolkien's tone in the beginning of *LotR* is still pretty much the same as in *The Hobbit*, but it changes as the story grows, and moves towards the literary tone of *The Silmarillion*.

Tolkien's mythopoeia uses different tools to integrate pre-modern myths and legends. An important familiarising effect is the usage of 'modern' literary tools, such as modern English language and the choosing of familiar protagonists in *The Hobbit* and *LotR*. In *The Silmarillion*, where the protagonists are harder to find and the characters are defamiliar for the contemporary reader, the book becomes unreadable, or harder to read, for most parts of the reading audience.

---

11. Op. cit. [3], Letter 131, p. 149.

Thus, the questions of familiarisation and defamiliarisation become relevant in understanding the popularity of the *legendarium*.

## HOBBITS AS MEDIATORS

On the subject of familiarisation I focus on the race of hobbits as a literary tool for Tolkien to familiarise his *legendarium*'s 'pre-modern' myth and romance for the contemporary reading audience. Tolkien's Middle-earth is a coherent and complex *Secondary Creation*, where encounters and conflicts between fictive ethnic groups and races are commonplace in the narrative. Tolkien populates Middle-earth with characters ranging from different human societies – with different languages and habits – to other humanoids and fantasy creatures; such as elves, dwarves, orcs, or hobbits.

My main point is that hobbits work as a familiarising object for the readers, but at the same time are 'outsiders' to the surrounding milieu, the Middle-earth outside the Shire: outside the idyllic home of the hobbits. Northrop Frye has stated that most romances move in their narrative development from the idyllic to the higher mythic tone, and then back.[12] Richard F. Hardin discusses the same when he claims that in romance, an effect of moral dualism is that romantic heroes and villains inhabit, respectively, a happy world above the muddle of every-day life and an exciting, dangerous, or 'demonic night world' below it.[13] That is also the case in Tolkien's *The Hobbit* and *LotR*, where hobbit protagonists move from idyllic and homely (*familiar*) milieus of their homes to the surrounding, sinister world where they at times feel themselves as 'outsiders'. Narrative methods are the same even though *The Hobbit* is originally written as a children's novel and *LotR* could be described more likely as an epic romance.

Hobbit protagonists could be seen as an answer to the question of familiarisation in Tolkien's *legendarium*. In *The Hobbit* the main character Bilbo Baggins, a hobbit, resembles a 'homely', early middle-aged, middle-classed Englishman living comfortably alone in his bachelor house in the idyllic, rural countryside of the Shire, which in close ways echoes the English countryside of the eighteenth or nineteenth century before the industrial revolution. In the story, Bilbo is forced out from his comfortable life on a dangerous and adventurous quest with the wizard Gandalf and the dwarves to claim back the dwarves' treasure which an evil dragon, Smaug, has stolen. After a variety of different kinds of tasks and quests, the hobbit protagonist evolves in a fairy-story way from an incapable character

---

12. Northrop Frye, *Anatomy of Criticism: Four Essays by Northrop Frye*, Atheneum, New York, 1957, p. 43.
13. Richard F. Hardin, *Love in a Green Shade: Idyllic Romances Ancient to Modern*, University of Nebraska Press, Lincoln, 2000, p. 145.

into a hero: Bilbo Baggins becomes the only one of the book's characters brave enough to even converse with the terrible dragon.

At the end of the book, revealingly sub-titled 'There and Back Again', Bilbo Baggins returns to his idyllic home as a changed and transformed character. The idyllic countryside of the Shire resembles England, but the other parts of the book's milieus have older and more mythical appearances. Danger is lurking everywhere, and even if the book is written in a fairy-story mode it has a kind of a medieval tone in the story-telling, especially in the latter part of the book.

The familiarisation of pre-modern myths, locations and milieus is even plainer in *LotR*. The book starts as a sequel to *The Hobbit*, but the writing tone changes from early on to more adult and more epic style. The main protagonist in *LotR* is once again a hobbit, Frodo Baggins, who starts a dangerous and difficult quest with his fellow hobbits Sam Gamgee, Peregrin 'Pippin' Took and Meriadoc 'Merry' Brandybuck. The four hobbits in the book represent Tolkien's contemporary Englishmen, simplified and caricatured.

In the *LotR*, the more contemporary perspective of the hobbits is put in contrast with – for example – the old-English, Anglo-Saxon, way of life of the Rohirrim, the mythical fairy-story livelihood of the Elves in the milieus of Rivendell and Lothlórien, and traditionally orientated milieu of Gondor resembling a kind of mixture of ancient Egyptian, Greek and Roman cultures. These milieus are defamiliar for the characters of hobbits, and readers relate to the unfamiliar surroundings from the perspective of hobbit characters. Unfamiliar surroundings and milieus, and Tolkien's fantasy's horror elements of beast, monsters and mythological creatures act as defamiliarisation for the contemporary reader, but the characters of hobbits acts as a familiarisors or 'middlemen'.

In a fictious tone of Bakhtinian *heteroglossia*, basically meaning 'differentiated speech', Tolkien even writes in different styles depending on the surrounding milieu. For example Tom Shippey has pointed out that the language and the names of Rohirrim in the second part of *LotR* are deriving from both old Gothic language and Old English.[14]

## HOBBITS AND US?

Tolkien's *The Hobbit* has on occasion been compared, quite surprisingly, to another twentieth-century novel from a different literary genre, Sinclair Lewis' *Babbitt* (1922). Understandably the relevance has been seen in the similarities of the titles (*Hobbit* and *Babbitt*), but also in the themes of those novels. Lewis' *Babbitt* is a satire of American culture, society and behaviour, criticising middle-

---

14. Op. cit. [6], pp. 15, 114–16, 122–23.

class American life and individuals. Although the story is very different to *The Hobbit*, some similarities can be seen in the main characters. Both Tolkien's Bilbo Baggins and Lewis' George F. Babbitt undergo a drastic change of character when drawn out of the comfortable middle-class, idyllic life. Tolkien's Bilbo Baggins – as well as Babbitt – can be seen as a representation of a modern middle-classed, comfort-seeking western man.

Tolkien himself, as a middle-aged, middle-classed, comfort-seeking Englishman compared himself to a hobbit. In 1958, in a letter to Deborah Webster Tolkien writes:

> I am in fact a Hobbit (in all but size). I like gardens, trees and unmechanized farmlands, I smoke a pipe, and like good plain food (unrefrigerated), but detest French cooking; I like, and even dare to wear in these dull days, ornamental waistcoats. I am fond of mushrooms (out of a field); have a very simple sense of humour (which even my appreciative critics find tiresome); I go to bed late and get up late (when possible). I do not travel much.[15]

This passage is of course revealing also in its anti-modernistic tone. *LotR* could be seen as an anti-modernistic and anti-industrialist book. in *which* mechanical devices and modern inventions are declared evil, for example in the case of Saruman's inventions in *The Two Towers*, or once again in *The Return of the King* chapter 'The Scouring of the Shire'. That is not a new point in epic literature, the same tone against modern inventions could also be seen in John Milton's *Paradise Lost*, where Satan in the Sixth Book invents 'devilish machines' against his enemies for the War in Heaven.

Joseph Pearce writes about the 'hobbitness' and the Englishman behind the myth in his *Tolkien: Man and Myth*, and sees hobbits in *The Hobbit* and *LotR* as an imaginative incarnation and personification of 'Englishness'.[16] According to Humphrey Carpenter, Tolkien once told an interviewer that in his mind, the hobbits represent English people, saying that '[h]obbits are just rustic English people, made small in size because it reflects the generally small reach of their imagination – not the small reach of their courage or latent power'.[17]

And the milieu of the Shire, where the hobbits in the books live, resembles England. In 1956 Tolkien wrote to Rayner Unwin, his publisher, that the Shire is based on idyllic rural English countryside:

---

15. Op. cit. [3], Letter 213, pp. 288–89.
16. Joseph Pearce, *Tolkien: Man and Myth*, HarperCollins, London, 1999, p. 153.
17. Humphrey Carpenter, *J. R. R. Tolkien: A Biography*, Houghton Mifflin, Boston, 1977, p. 176.

248          JYRKI KORPUA

> The Shire is based on rural England and not any other country in the world -- The toponomy of The Shire -- is a 'parody' of that of rural England, in much the same sense as are its inhabitants: they go together and are meant to. After all the book is English, and by an Englishman.[18]

Hobbits in *LotR*, and 'a hobbit' Bilbo Baggins in *The Hobbit*, could be seen as mediators from the 'world of myths' towards Tolkien's contemporary twentieth century audience. In a way, Tolkien's mythopoeic vision in the books aims to familiarise the *legendarium*'s epic world for the reading audience, but at the same time the hobbit protagonists are unfamiliar (*defamiliar*) for the other characters of the *legendarium*, and the surrounding Middle-earth is usually defamiliar for the hobbits.

This can be seen many times in the narrative. For example, in *LotR*, when the hobbits feel themselves unfamiliar in milieus such as Bree, Lórien, Minas Tirith, Rohan, or most likely Mordor; or in the adventurous, nearly perilous, trips such as way from Bree to Rivendell, or, from Rivendell to Lórien, and later to Minas Tirith. Even at the end of *LotR* the once so familiar Shire has become defamiliar for the protagonists. And in the end, Frodo Baggins – a changed and transformed character – is no longer a familiar fellow hobbit, but defamiliar for the other hobbits in the Shire. Frodo becomes alienated from his people, and – because of his 'traumas' – leaves Middle-earth. In the end Frodo becomes a mythical character, a hero – quite like 'a King Arthur of hobbits', leaving for his Avalon.

On the other hand, one of the most interesting characters dealing closely with familiar and defamiliar elements is of course Gollum, who functions by both familiarising and defamiliarising effects. In *The Hobbit*, in the first encounter with him in the chapter 'Riddles in the Dark', Gollum functions as defamiliar, frightening opposition for the uncomfortable and frightened Bilbo Baggins. It is a 'foe' in the dark. Later in both *The Hobbit* and *LotR* Gollum could be seen as both comical and pitiful, but also as a sad and nostalgic character. Gollum is a sorrowful example of the power and addictiveness of the One Ring. Gollum, once a character rather similar to hobbits, is now an abomination. It is both familiar to the characters of hobbits: for example in its usage of language, such as riddles; but also defamiliar, since it is like their corrupted, 'evil twin'.

For the case of hobbits as defamiliar (or even alien) characters in the Middle-earth, the scene in *LotR* where an ent, Treebeard, first encounters two hobbits is also interesting. Treebeard finds it impossible to place hobbits in his long list of the humanoids and animals, saying that: 'you do not seem to fit in anywhere!'

---

18. Op. cit. [3], Letter 190, p. 250.

(*TT*, 'Treebeard', 453).[19] In response, Merry then states that: 'we always seem to have got left out of the old lists, and the old stories' (*TT*, 'Treebeard', 454). They might have been left out of 'the old stories', but in Tolkien's *legendarium* this 'alienness' of hobbits is an important tool of familiarisation.

I also dare to suggest, that without the 'middle-men' of hobbits, without those familiarising characters for the contemporary reading audience, Tolkien's *LotR* would have not became the cornerstone of twentieth-century fantasy, or any fiction, and Tolkien would have not became the 'godfather of fantasy literature', that he is today. For this, we should all hail the hobbits.

---

19. J.R.R. Tolkien, *The Lord of the Rings*, HarperCollins, London, 1995.

# 'White riders and new world orders: Nature and technology in Theodor Storm's Der Schimmelreiter and J.R.R. Tolkien's The Lord of the Rings'

## Larissa Budde

*In this paper I wish to offer a selective reading of Tolkien's The Lord of the Rings and Theodor Storm's Der Schimmelreiter (1888, translated by Denis Jackson in The Dykemaster, 1996) in regards to their different conception of technology and its place in the scheme of things. The two works are very different in scope, genre and time of production, but they are united by their authors' great attention to the natural world as well as by the figure of the Odin-like rider on a white horse. In each case the horse can be seen as expressing a specific view of the world, nature and technology that is presumably based in each author's religious tendency.*

### INTRODUCTION

This paper originates from a personal affection for two apparently very dissimilar works, J.R.R. Tolkien's *The Lord of the Rings* (1954-1955) and Theodor Storm's much earlier novella *Der Schimmelreiter* (1888). I wish to point out in advance that this is a selective and by necessity sometimes simplifying reading, highlighting some similarities and divergences but ignoring others. The events related in *LotR* will be sufficiently known, while those of Storm's novella might not be. *Der Schimmelreiter*, literally, 'The Rider on the Grey Horse', was translated, ironically, as simply *The Dykemaster* in 1996, by Denis Jackson. The tale is set at the north Frisian coast around 1750, and relates how the dykemaster Hauke Haien invents a new, flatter and broader dyke profile, and how he struggles against the resistance of his work-shy, conservative fellows. He acquires a mysterious grey horse that exults in the storms and the sea, and which is linked to a ghostly apparition observed by two farmhands. They see a horse grazing on a moonlit holm before the coast, but when one of the boys goes to investigate and his boat lands there, he finds only the animal's skeleton. However, his companion watches from the dyke and sees him walking straight up to the ghostly animal. Both apparition and skeleton are said to vanish on the day the mysterious Grey appears in the dykemaster's stable. Meanwhile, the new profile is approved despite much hostility from the villagers, and the dykemaster oversees the building of the new dyke from the back of his Grey. However, the new dyke diverts the force of the tides on to the old dyke, which threatens to break during a mighty storm. Hauke furiously prevents the villagers from breaching the new dyke to relieve the pressure on the old one, and the old one breaks. The inrushing flood seizes the carriage of Hauke's wife and child, who had driven out to search for him in the storm, and seeing them drown the dykemaster despairs. Praying to God to take him and have mercy on the others, he urges his horse into the breach of the dyke, and since that night, both apparition and skeleton are back on the holm. Whenever the dykes are threatened by floods, the narrator says, the specter of the dykemaster on his grey horse can be sighted as a warning.[1]

This summary already suggests that the works in question are extremely different in scope, theme, and time of production. Also, Storm and Tolkien probably never read one another's writings. Storm was born in 1817, and he died in 1888, the year the novel was published: he referred to it as a 'Deichsage', thus emphasising its affinity with the 'Sage' or saga as an originally orally performed, place-bound tale that relates an event in which the uncanny, 'das Unheimliche', touches upon the human world. Storm conceived of the 'uncanny' as a parallel world jutting into the ordinary one, and manifesting itself in and through it; he viewed it as a autonomous power whose presence and purpose exceeds human perception, rather than as a mere product of human imagination. Tolkien was born four years after Storm's death, in 1892, and, as he wrote in the well-known letter 131 to Milton Waldman, set out to create a secondary world by writing a vast cycle of interconnected mythological tales, which recount how the spiritual incarnates itself in and through the world.[2] Despite the temporal and geographical distance between them, however, the two writers shared one key experience, the industrialisation.

## MODERATE TECHNOLOGY

Tolkien's disgust with extensive industrialisation is well-documented, as is the role of technology in his Middle-earth. He witnessed the immensely destructive, large-scale political application of 'progress' both abroad and in his own homeland, and he experienced two world wars and the devastating use to which the inventions of the industrialisation could be put. And though Storm experienced only the beginnings of the era in northern Germany, and enjoyed the benefits the railway brought to his region, he was not an enthusiast for modernity either. All his writings are located in rural areas, and technology as such plays no great role in them; rather, the natural world is a strong, (meta)

---

1. Theodor Storm, *The Dykemaster*, trans. Denis Jackson, Angel Books, London, 1996.
2. Humphrey Carpenter, ed., *The Letters of J.R.R. Tolkien*, with the assistance of Christopher Tolkien, 2nd edn, Houghton Mifflin, New York, 2000, Letter 131, pp. 143–61.

# NATURE AND TECHNOLOGY

physically influential presence. Like Tolkien's hobbits, his human population is largely involved in subsistence farming, which supports the local consumption of families and communities, and they rarely engage in factory work or large-scale export. The large-scale dimension of technology's many faces and its destructive power is absent from Storm's writings, possibly because heavy machinery in the sense that Tolkien witnessed it simply did not yet exist.

Tolkien, writing from a Christian perspective, equated industrial technology with magic and the machine, and viewed it as tending towards evil in the sense of domination and static, infertile uniformity. He could give his readers a gloomier picture of extended industrialisation than Storm could presumably have conceived. This is shown most clearly in the industrial, war-scarred wastes of Mordor and post-treason Isengard, both of which are also uniform, absolutist slave-states. They are contrasted to creatures who live without any manipulation of the natural world, like Ents, Woodwoses, and presumably dark Elves, and the agricultural and/or stone-working free peoples, who build larger nations without scouring the land beyond its own powers of self-healing. Moderate, useful technology and its amenities as such are not condemned, but there exists a clear distinction between auxiliary tools that make life easier and industrial machinery that serves excessive gain and centralised power while producing unwarranted waste. Storm, in contrast, was not a devoutly religious person, neither god nor devil are ever explicitly affirmed or denied in his saga, and there is no framework that links technology to evil. In *The Dykemaster*, the term 'progress' is yet definable as an attuning of human works to nature, for Hauke devises his new profile by extensive observation, coming to an understanding of how waves and soil interact and thus constructing a dyke that fits itself to the landscape. The recalcitrant tidal gully and the great flood serve as reminders that human ingenuity has clear limits in the material world, but also prove that the innovative profile is better suited to human goals. The dyke was built without creating desolation around it.

Thus both novels share the advocation of a 'moderate technology' that arises out of and is in contact with the natural world. Human ingenuity is shown as having its place in the scheme of things, as long as it responds to certain rules of conduct. And these rules of conduct are communicated in different ways through the figure of the grey horse and its rider. To elaborate this, I intend to focus on the novels' presentation of the autonomy of the non-human world in terms of a pre-Neolithic, non-agricultural 'mythological consciousness', that is, as a network of powers equal to humans.[3] Thus the horse can be seen as an

---

3. Robert Bringhurst, *A Story As Sharp As A knife: The Classical Haida Mythtellers and Their World*, D and M Publishers, Vancouver, 2011.

agent and a representative of the non-human world, and the figure of the rider on the white horse in both *The Dykemaster* and *LotR* appears as a microcosm of each writer's worldview regarding the relationship between Christian faith and demonic selfhood of the nonhuman world, whether as creation or as autonomous power. Encapsulating a facet of the author's worldview, each rider functions as a crucial mediator between nature and technology, and is involved in facilitating exchange between the human and the nonhuman world as presented in both stories.

## MYTH AND STORIES OF EXCHANGE

Since both novels are indebted to myth, I base the idea of exchange on Sean Kane's concept of myths as stories that provide maps of the human place within a more-than-human universe, an approach that can be found in his book *The wisdom of the mythtellers*. Myths, Kane says, provide rules of conduct for human and nonhuman beings by charting their place in natural patterns and relationships, and the relevant physical and spiritual boundaries.[4] In fact, boundaries are of vital importance in each story: in *The Dykemaster*, they are emphasised by the horse as uniquely suited to and capable of crossing them physically, and embodied in the dyke that separates cultivated human lands from the apparently desolate threat of the nonhuman sea. In Middle-earth, similar boundaries separate the inhabited from the wild regions, but they are permeable, often to an uncomfortable degree if one would ask the Breelanders. The appendices note fierce disputes for them, as when white wolves invade the Shire in the Fell Winter, and the central story presents Isengard's impenetrable fence of rocks: it fulfils a comparable function for Saruman that the dyke fulfils for Hauke, as will be shown in regards to the Odin-like qualities of the white riders.

In *The Dykemaster*, this exchange is a central and driving force, whereas in *LotR* it can be seen as subsumed under the larger issue of dealing with incarnate evil. Storm ascribes demonic qualities to animals and the natural world and thus portrays it as demonic (consider Peischl's argumentation in *Das Dämonische im Werk Theodor Storms*),[5] in the sense that it is a nonhuman, active and sovereign agent: its representative is the grey horse with whom the dykemaster must negotiate. The human being appears as located in this demonic sphere, and must negotiate with it by means of ingenuity. This human ingenuity, I think, can be seen as technology, which seeks to create certain boundaries between the spheres. The personnel of *The Dykemaster* offers characters who believe in the

---

4. Sean Kane, *The Wisdom of the Mythtellers,* Broadview Press, Peterborough ON, 1998.
5. Margaret T. Peischl, *Das Dämonische im Werk Theodor Storms*, Peter Lang Verlag, Frankfurt, 1983.

autonomy of a more or less hostile nature and voice the suspicion that nature is, if not sentient, at least a present power: it can actively deceive humans with its charm, as the schoolmaster says. The rider on the grey horse thus focuses the tension between human control and natural autonomy in Storm's novel, and the demonic horse is at the center of the human/nonhuman interaction, the meeting of human ingenuity with other-than-human power.[6] Similarly, *LotR* does not present 'nature' as diametrically opposed to 'culture' either: almost everything *in* the world *is* also of the world, because all these things were created by one supreme power. However, the natural world reacts to and reflects, but does not actively participate in, or change the course of, central affairs: that seems to be the task of the free and speaking peoples, or of those beings who are 'magically enhanced', like the Eagles and the *mearas*. Further, technology in *LotR* has two distinct faces, for it can be wholesome as well as evil. Shadowfax is central to Gandalf's role here, for the pair of them advocates a kind of domestic communal agrarian technology that is both winning of livelihood and a kind of divinely imposed duty of responsible stewardship. So the White Rider can be seen as one of Tolkien's means of contrasting ingenious technology to pure machinery, the latter of which is merely a means of dominating the natural world for personal gain. Like Hauke and the Grey, Gandalf and Shadowfax serve as a combination of opposites, and signal the interconnection not only of human and nonhuman, but also of created and demonic. This combination of horse and rider as representing human ingenuity in its particular technological incarnation, and as mediating between nature and technology, is achieved through Odinic imagery and qualities, which emphasise ambiguous ingenuity.

## WHITE RIDERS - HAUKE, GANDALF, SARUMAN, AND THE CUNNING MIND

Odin, the primary Norse god, is an essentially capricious power of change, transgression, and transformation, and his name is related to words meaning 'fury' and 'excitation' as well as 'mind' and 'poetry'. His ambiguity is thus inscribed both in his actions and his name(s), therefore it is necessary to take Saruman into account as well. As Marjorie Burns states in *Perilous Realms* Tolkien divorced Odin's destructive aspects from Gandalf and instead applied them to Saruman.[7] Gandalf's ambiguity is thus reduced, and he becomes a creative, transformative character who inspires people to serve a greater cause. In contrast, Saruman in his fallen state embodies Odin's negative, blustering and treacherous side,

---

6. M. Oldfield Howey, *The Horse in Magic and Myth*, William Rider and Son, London, 1923.

7. Marjorie Burns, *Perilous Realms: Celtic and Norse in Tolkien's Middle-earth*, University of Toronto Press, Toronto, 2005, chapter 5.

and he seeks to subject others to his very own, tyrannical 'Knowledge, Rule, Order'. Hauke Haien, whose name derives from *hugo*, meaning 'mind', unites both aspects of Odin into a much more complex and conflict-ridden character, who is both tender husband and feared and ruthless taskmaster. Like Saruman the 'cunning man', he cherishes learning and desires glory, power and mastery. He values firm boundaries between human and nonhuman spheres, and wishes to keep the sea out of the human sphere similar to how Saruman covets the magic-made, impenetrably walled Circle of Isengard. Further, Hauke sometimes has a Sarumannish 'mind of metal and wheels' and in his eagerness to perfect the dyke profile he becomes deaf to the natural world. Because he, like Saruman, feels 'hindered rather than helped by [his] weak or idle friends', he uses the workers' superstitious fear of him and his horse to his advantage. The accomplishment of the new dyke is balm for his ego, but it also underlines his creative side, for it profits the whole community immensely. So, like Gandalf, Hauke inspires people and sets events in motion. Most importantly, however, similar to Gandalf he is also on at least neutral footing with the nonhuman world: Taking his prime inspiration from that sphere, he develops his revolutionary dyke-profile in years of watching the patterns of wave/beach interaction. The new dyke is therefore not so much purely technological ingenuity but rather tailored to natural patterns, made by natural materials and honest manual labour. Both Gandalf and Hauke are characters who see not only the 'human' affairs but take a wider view, and this is where their horses come in.

## HORSES – THE CROSSING OF BORDERS

Like their riders, the horses' conception harks back to Norse templates. Odin the rider functions as transformer and achiever of wisdom by travelling between worlds on his magical, eight-legged steed Sleipnir, the gliding one. This stallion's qualities of fearlessness, endurance and intelligence are reflected in both Shadowfax and the Grey. Like Sleipnir, they are marked as liminal beings by their indeterminate colour (Gandalf the Grey-soon-to-be-White is very careful of making the point to Saruman of many colours, that white/grey escape or fully include the spectrum of other colours), a transgressive state that is stressed by Shadowfax's ability to understand human speech, and the Grey's ominous wariness with which he focuses on the dykemaster and his negotiation with the workers. Unlike Shadowfax, however, the Grey explicitly ranks with the demonic, 'other' quality of the nonhuman world. His intelligence underlines his demonic autonomy, whereas Shadowfax derives his skill from being a descendant of the *mearas*: his special understanding must therefore be seen as a gift, rather than as a mark of his independence. As an in-between creature he is linked to the apparition on the liminal place of the neither-land-nor-sea holm, and he does not only run as fast as Shadowfax, but negotiates the wet, sucking clay of the dyke as if he were running on the firm earth of summer. Further, his demonic selfhood is marked not by speech or the explicit understanding of it, but by silence. The stillness in which the ghostly horse is first encountered, is repeated in the oddly quiet, focused behavior of the Grey, and the deep silence that is often described as underlying and permeating every aspect of life in the marshes. Storm repeatedly invokes the 'widespread silence' that lies over the 'vast landscape'. He actually uses the term 'ungeheuere Ebene', which translates correctly as not only 'immense' or 'tremendous' but also 'uncanny' and 'monstrous', and thus implies a very present, affecting quality.[8]

Thus, while Odin's horse is not truly important as an agent, both Storm and Tolkien endowed their horses with autonomy and the ability to cross borders. But they did so to different degrees, and thus emphasised their 'spiritual' outlook: while Shadowfax's power lies mainly in crossing distances and discerning greater 'good' and 'evil' with his ability to stand before dangers no ordinary horse can endure, the Grey's link to the sea and his effortless running on the dyke's clay stress the conflict embodied in *The Dykemaster* – events take place within the mortal world, on a central, debated boundary, and within the same sphere, they are thoroughly embodied and present. Nonetheless, both writers emphasise the special unity of horse and rider, and this is central for the quality of the new world order that is determined by this unit.

## NEW WORLD ORDERS – AGENTS AND CREATIONS

The Grey is a much more active agent than Shadowfax, and thus appears demonic: he seems to choose Hauke as his master, at a crucial junction in the dyke-project, and in his particular embodiment, and the reaction he excites from the villagers, enables Hauke to eventually build the dyke. Being the only horse Hauke uses when dealing with dyke-matters or riding out to the sea, the Grey thus participates actively in the actual exchange between spheres: returning to the sea, and carrying Hauke with him into the breach, he appears to ensure, given the overall absence of transcendent powers, the observance of an ancient form of proper conduct. He becomes part of the new world order deriving from the new dyke profile, an arrangement that announces that human ingenuity is part of the natural world. At the end of the saga, the dyke still stands, and appears not like the wasted circle of Isengard as abject disfigurement of the natural landscape, a warning, but rather as part of the natural world, a reconciliation: it is lapped

---

8. Op. cit. [1].

by the waves and bathed in golden sunlight. Thus the demonic is instrumental in bringing about the success of a human enterprise. This is given visible form in the composite figure of the 'Schimmelreiter', the dykemaster forever merged with the horse that enabled him to build it. Though he is seen by some characters in the novel as a spectre of ill omen, others view him if not as benign at least as neutral: his appearance is a warning that gives time to prepare, and his presence ensures that the dyke is never only a human pathway, but rather a continually conflicted boundary between sea and land.

Shadowfax and Gandalf are, like the world they inhabit, creations of a supreme god, and subject to a greater plan. They are presented as equals, engaged in the fight against incarnate evil. Though Gandalf says he 'took' and 'tamed' Shadowfax, precluding the horse from having a separate agenda in the way the enigmatic Grey possesses it, he also emphasises that the horse is willing to aid and bear him, and calls him a 'friend' with whom he will 'part not in this world again' (*LotR*, 'The White Rider', 493).[9] Thus, in *LotR* the pair of them serves as contrast to Saruman and his cowed servant Grima Wormtongue: Saruman has come to despise animals and plants beyond their immediate use for him, and Wormtongue is a human who finally crawls 'almost like a dog' (*LotR*, 'The Scouring of the Shire', 995). Unlike the horse for Gandalf, he is a mere tool for Saruman. Thus Shadowfax, as an *animal* in whom Gandalf trusts and whom he respects, underlines the crucial difference between the mentalities of the two Maiar. Interestingly, Shadowfax however, is crucial not in the creation of the new world order of knowledge and rule that Saruman tries to establish, but in the prevention of it. Gandalf's affection for and trust in the hobbits, and his speaking to not only Free Peoples but also to 'bird on bough and beast in den', condemns exploitative, large-scale, industrial machinery in favour of moderate, domestic, land-oriented technology. As Gandalf puts it, his aim is not to create a new world order but to restore an old one, to provide not easy living but 'clean earth to till' (*LotR*, 'The Last Debate', 861). So, just as the intervention of the Grey could be said to ensure balance between human and demonic spheres, the unity of Gandalf and Shadowfax can be seen as contributing to the insurance that enough areas of Middle-earth remain set aside for nonhuman use, such as the Old Forest or Fangorn.

## SUMMARY

To draw the threads together, it can be said that Shadowfax's presence and his relationship to Gandalf serve as a kind of 'still contrast' to Saruman's and

---

9. J.R.R. Tolkien, *The Lord of the Rings*, 50th anniversary edn, HarperCollins, London, 2005. All quotations from *LotR* are taken from this edition.

Wormtongue's destructive new order, which they prevent in order to restore an older order. As Shadowfax subordinates his own freedom to a greater plan, so Gandalf acts only as a servant of higher powers: he and the horse can be seen as representing ideal human/nonhuman interaction, and they are equal in the sense that they belong to the same act of creation. Gandalf's Odin-like qualities are needed to make him the inspiring transformer that can restore a wholesome world order, in which natural and technological sphere interconnect in balance. Shadowfax is an embodied creature, yet his noble *mearas* nature also elevates him above the common animals of Middle-earth. Eventually, Shadowfax and Gandalf embody loyalty and a unity of free will and mastery, mediation between natural and 'supernatural' power, which corresponds to the overall nature of Middle-earth as a creation – the heroes leave for the West, and hope is placed beyond the circles of the world.

The Grey in *The Dykemaster* represents one active side of the bargain between the two spheres that are part of the same world. They are bound by the rhythmic pattern of seasons and tides, which follow the rules of exchange as dynamic balance rather than as permanence: human inventiveness and interference have a firm place in the world. The dykemaster negotiates with the power embodied in the horse itself, a special, but thoroughly incarnate horse. The unit of horse and man is essential for the new world order: here an overall transcendental power is implied by never active or acknowledged. Hauke's fully ambiguous Odin-like qualities reflect that human existence, as well as human/demonic interaction, is never clear-cut but always a shade of grey. The new world order is subject to continuous negotiation, expressed by the circularity of the tidal pattern, the seasons, and the unending ebb and flow of the waves. It ends firmly in this world, where the composite figure of the Schimmelreiter spectre also walks.

Thus, while in both cases the horse functions as a representative of the nonhuman world, each conception is also in keeping with the author's view of the surrounding world. This world is a field of interacting forces, especially those of human ingenuity and demonic – nonhuman – agency. Perhaps for that reason, both authors were drawn to the thoroughly ambiguous figure of Odin, the god not of many colours but certainly many faces. Nonhuman autonomy and human dominion appear in many forms, and the latter can be a sort of creative exchange, as embodied perhaps in the new dyke profile of Hauke Haien's, or a form of ultimate destruction, as can be detected in the battle-fields of Middle-earth. But also, Odin is not transcendental: he may be the chief of the aesir, but he still needs his 'magic' steed to cross between worlds. He can thus be seen also as an emblem of the horse/ rider relationship, which, in the case of both Gandalf and Hauke Haien, is very much dynamic, emphasising how horse and rider are in continual interplay and negotiation. Uniting the two riders in the figure of Odin, more or less thoroughly, suggests that the uncanny – the demonic – in not only, as Storm formulated it, poking into the human world: as an autonomous power, in the form of the grey horse, it rather is part and fabric of the world itself.

## SPECULATIONS

Both Storm and Tolkien had great love for the unconverted natural world and an awareness of its powers, beauties, and dangers. As a devout Christian Tolkien stressed the love uncorrupted people would have for the creation they inhabit,[10] while Storm tended to focus on the darker, unexplained aspects of material existence. Hauke Haien reflects that when he explains the ghostly and frightening figures on the frozen tidal flats to his daughter: 'they are all living creatures, just as we are; there is nothing else; but God is everywhere'.[11] While this actually aligns him very closely with the precepts of Tolkien's mythology, Storm continually allowed for doubt, and for the powers of the demonic as part of, equal to, and sometimes in opposition to the divine power his characters believe in. Most centrally, both were aware of and used the power of language, not only as an authorial art, but also as a marker within their stories. Tolkien conceived of speech as a divine power, with the primal creative speech echoing throughout the mythology: yet his creatures are also separated by worded language, which marks the degree of their agency.

In *The Dykemaster*, the essential function of language seems at first to be similar: it separates the demonic silence and animal voices from the homely human sphere, where spoken words form the world. However, the demonic sounds intertwine with and underlie human life, and human utterances happen only against that background: in the silence of the demonic alone do human words take form, and that which does not talk in words nevertheless makes itself heard. Storm could be said to use language not so much to distinguish between beings, but to underline the demonic as ultimate bearer and source of the human. Hence, the demonic takes the part of the divine creator, and while the sea of middle-earth signifies transcendental hope for those who speak by grace of their maker, in *Dykemaster*, the sea belongs to the more-than-human, wordless sphere which is conditional for human ingenuity and technology. Nonetheless, *LotR* also contains beings that are very close to the Grey in their demonic agency and autonomy, and their earthy, nonhuman 'language': when Old Man Willow is said to spread his thoughts throughout the Old Forest, and to whisper of sleep to drowsy Hobbits, one may think without hesitation of the muffled sound from

---

10. J.R.R. *The Monsters and the Critics and Other Essays*, ed. Christopher Tolkien, George Allen & Unwin, London, 1983.
11. Op. cit. [1].

# NATURE AND TECHNOLOGY

below the earth accompanying Storm's walk over the heath ('Über die Heide') and the mysterious 'voices that are above the deep' ('Meeresstrand') becoming audible on a dusky seashore.[12]

## FINAL THOUGHTS

Returning for a moment to the opening premise, this argument may not be essential for either Tolkien or Storm scholarship since, considering their different nature and the nonexistent connection between the authors, the works can not truly be said to shed light on each other. It shows, however, that mythological structures, and their bearers, survive through different genres. In the end, both stories are united by one important sentiment, one that might be called their authors' conscious or unconscious fascination with the horse: an unknowable animal, whose history is nonetheless closely tied up with the human one. It is not clear how closely Storm experienced horses apart from their function as carriage drawers and field workers; but he saw their displacement beginning with the arrival of the railway and other new technology. It is clear that Tolkien's appreciation for horses was very deep – he worked as hostler in the First World War, and he will have seen horses and soldiers alike falling before the machines of warfare.[13] Both he and Storm seem to have felt that horses are enigmatic beings, whose specialness derives from an odd fact: they sometimes seem to choose human company. In their stories, this choice became central to great schemes, and an expression of hopeful, human and nonhuman cooperation, whether before the backdrop of a grand creation and a central power, or a demonic world full of other-than-human powers.

---

12. Theodor Storm, *Der Schimmelreiter*, Deich Verlag, Wewelsfleth, 2010.
13. John Garth, *Tolkien and the Great War*, HarperCollins, London, 2003, p. 24.

# List Of Contributors

**Robert S. Blackham** conducts tours of Tolkien-related locations in and around Birmingham and Oxford, and has written a number guides and books on these themes as well as contributing regularly to the Tolkien Society's publications, *Amon Hen* and *Mallorn*. He is a member the Birmingham Tolkien Group.

**José Manuel Ferrández Bru** is a Spanish computer science engineer and writer. He has published several articles about Tolkien's often-ignored connections with Spain. The author is a member and the first chairman of the Spanish Tolkien Society. Among his publications are his 2013 book *La Conexion Española de J.R.R. Tolkien* and his essay '"Wingless fluttering": Some Personal Connections in Tolkien's Formative Years', *Tolkien Studies*, 8 (2011).

**Colin Duriez** is author of a number of books on Tolkien, C.S. Lewis, and the Inklings, the latest being the biographies, *J.R.R. Tolkien: The Making of a Legend* and *C.S. Lewis: A Biography of Friendship*.

**John Garth** is a freelance writer, editor and researcher, author of the award-winning *Tolkien and the Great War*, and public speaker.

**LeiLani Hinds** is associate Professor of English at Honolulu Community College, Hawaii.

**Anna E. Thayer (née Slack)** has published a number of essays on the work of J.R.R. Tolkien and regularly contributes to conferences on Tolkien. She is editor of PortalEditions' volume Doors in the Air: C. S. Lewis and the Imaginative World , author of the award winning fantasy trilogy 'The Knight of Eldaran' and co-author to Peter Gladwin's autobiographical apologetic 'Out of the Darkest Place'.

**Sara Brown** teaches English and recently completed a thesis on Tolkien, receiving her doctorate in 2013.

**Franco Manni** is based in Italy and runs the Tolkien fanzine *Endore*. He has written a number of book reviews and articles, contributing to, among others, the magazine Terra di Mezzo. He contributed a paper on Tolkien and the Second World War to The Tolkien Society's 2005 conference.

**Gerard Hynes** is a PhD candidate at Trinity College Dublin, preparing a thesis on creation and sub-creation in Tolkien's works. He has published on Tolkien and geology in *Tolkien Studies* 9 (2012), and, with Helen Conrad-O'Briain, co-edited *Tolkien: The Forest and the City* (Dublin, Four Courts Press, 2013).

**Laura Miller-Purrenhage** is Lecturer in Humanities at Kettering University in Flint, Michigan. She teaches introduction to humanities, world literature, leadership and ethics, and a seminar on J.R.R. Tolkien. A life-long fan of Tolkien, Dr. Miller-Purrenhage hopes to pursue further scholarship relating to the depiction of leadership and ethics in Tolkien's works.

**Claudio Testi** has participated in Tolkien studies in Italy, contributing to seminars and to the 'Tolkien e la filosofia' conference at Modena in 2010. He is the author of a number articles as well as being co-author with Roberto Arduini of *The Broken Scythe: Death and Immortality in the Works of J.R.R. Tolkien*.

**James D. Holt** has degrees from Manchester Metropolitan University, the University of Birmingham, and the University of Chester where he completed his PhD in Mormon theology. His research focussed around an LDS theology of religions and its implications for interfaith dialogue. Deeply involved in forging links between religion and education, he serves on the editorial board of the *International Journal of Mormon Studies* and has also presented papers and written articles on topics such as Tolkien's religious imagery, aspects of Mormon theology and the teaching of religious education.

**Ronald Hutton** is Professor of History at the University of Bristol and is a leading authority on British history in the sixteenth and seventeenth centuries, on ancient and medieval paganism and magic, and on the global context of witchcraft beliefs. He is also the leading historian of the ritual year in Britain and of modern paganism, and has published many books on all these topics.

**Pamina Fernández Camacho** was born in Cádiz, Spain, in 1985. In December 2012 she defended an International PhD in Classical Philology at the University of Cadiz, with a work called 'The image of the city of Cadiz in ancient Greek and Latin sources: a philological and literary analysis'. Long-time Tolkien fan, one of her pastimes is pondering various aspects of Arda – especially, in order to be contrary, pertaining to its Second Age.

**Xavier de la Huerga** is a Spanish musician, writer, and full-spectrum artist, resident in the UK since 1989. He also works in the fields of Low Impact Building and Permaculture Design, applying his wide range of expertise in Archaeoastronomy, Ancient Metrology and Calendrics, Sacred Geometry and Mythology. He is presently writing a book on the metaphysical aspects of Tolkien's work.

**David Doughan** is a prolific writer who has contributed many articles and reviews to the field of Tolkien scholarship. He is an equally active editor, having edited, among other material, the Tolkien Society's scholarly journal *Mallorn* and its linguistic bulletin *Quettar*.

**Zachary A. Rhone** is currently completing a dissertation on J.R.R. Tolkien, C.S. Lewis, G.K. Chesterton, and George MacDonald at the Indiana University of Pennsylvania and is a Visiting Instructor in English at Alfred University.

**Jyrki Korpua** is a lecturer at University of Oulu, Finland, editor of the *Finnish Review of Literary Studies*, and co-editor of the recently-launched *Nordic Journal of Science Fiction and Fantasy Research*.

**Larissa Budde** is a graduate student at the University of Siegen, North Rhine-Westphalia, specialising in English and American Studies, including Animal Studies, English Romanticism, and Old English Literature.

## Index

### A

Abraham 163, 171
academic life 26
Adam and Eve 172
adapted texts 228
Adûnaic 202, 205, 219, 223, 225
Aegean Sea 201
Ælfwine 219, 224, 225, 228
Ahura-Mazda 204
Ainulindalë 115, 146, 169
Ainur 117, 157, 161, 169, 171, 172, 197, 208, 236, 244
alienation 103, 242
Al-Pharazôn 78
ancestral memories 210, 212
Andalusia 17
Andrew Lang Lecture 36, 118
Anduin 16, 17
angels 94, 115, 169, 170, 180, 182, 209
Anglo-Saxon vii, 20, 21, 22, 32, 38, 88, 89, 114, 116, 137, 193, 195, 196, 209, 223, 235, 246
Anglo-Saxon alliterative tradition 89
Anglo-Saxon Literature
  Beowulf 21, 89, 90, 122, 126, 141, 160, 227, 228, 234, 243
  The Ruin 227, 228, 231, 232, 234, 235, 239
  The Seafarer 227, 228, 229, 234, 236, 237, 239
Aquinas, St. Thomas 91, 111, 112, 114, 127, 128, 159, 162
  Summa Theologiae 112, 113
Aragorn 73, 74, 76, 81, 82, 90, 94, 103, 105, 112, 119, 122, 144, 149, 156, 158, 176, 177, 200, 231, 233, 234, 237
Arcos de la Frontera 17
Arda 114, 116, 117, 134, 149, 159, 161, 200, 230, 263
Arda Marred 200
Arda's Theology 159, 161
Arnor 72, 200
Ar-Pharazôn 204
Arundel Lowdham 210

### B

Aslan 180
Atalantie 196
Atlantis ii, vii, 111, 113, 191, 192, 193, 194, 195, 197, 199, 200, 201, 202, 203, 204, 206, 207, 210, 211, 212, 213, 215, 221, 222, 244
Atlantis Complex 211
Atum-Ra 208
Australian Aboriginal Dreamtime 218
Avallonian 191, 223, 225
Avalon 230, 231, 248

### B

Bakhtinian heteroglossia 246
Balrog 74
barbed wire 62, 78, 79, 228
Barfield, Owen 28, 29, 31, 32, 37, 120
Barrow Downs 149, 177
Battle of the Somme 29, 59, 61, 62, 70, 71, 76, 77, 78, 79, 81, 82, 83
Beatles 24
Beleriand 33, 185, 200, 231
Beregond 63
Beren 9, 10, 32, 119, 146, 149
Bible 92, 162, 173, 178, 202, 204, 206
Bilbo (Baggins) 75, 104, 133, 134, 235, 236, 238, 245, 246, 247, 248, 273
Birmingham i, vii, 3, 4, 5, 6, 7, 9, 11, 12, 15, 19, 43, 60, 61, 66, 84, 262, 263
Black Monday 215, 216, 217
Bladorthin 185
Blake, William 243
Bloemfontein 3
Blue Plaque 8
Boethius ii, vii, 111, 113, 116, 125, 126, 128, 131, 133, 134, 135, 136, 137, 138, 139
  De Consolatione Philosophiae 115
  King Alfred's Translation 126, 131, 133, 136, 138
Böhl de Faber, Cecilia 12
bombardment 45, 61, 78, 79
Boromir 74, 103, 104, 116, 144, 147, 149, 177, 181

Bournemouth 24
Brahma 208
Bree 102, 103, 104, 106, 248
Breelanders 254
Bridge of Khazad-dûm 74
Bristol Channel 224
British Expeditionary Forces 77
Brocton Camp 60, 61
Buckingham Palace 77
Bunyan, John 165

C

Cádiz 16, 17, 203, 263
Cannock Chase, Staffordshire 59, 60, 61
Catholic faith 158
Celtic Britain 229
Chaucer (Geoffrey) 22, 111, 116, 133
Christianity 30, 32, 87, 114, 135, 163, 178,
    179, 180, 181, 182, 184, 186, 191
Christian orthodoxy 175, 180
Church of Jesus Christ of Latter-day Saints
    165
Circe 181
Coalbiters 21, 29, 30, 33, 38
coal trucks 5
Coghill, Nevill 31, 33, 38
Coleridge, S.T. 116, 117
Collective Unconscious 218
Collingwood, Robin G. 118, 119, 125, 127,
    128
    The Idea of History 119
communication skills 142
Comparative Philology 20
compassion 75, 76, 81, 82, 158
concentration camps 194
Congregation of the Oratory 5
Corpus Christi College 19
Council of Elrond 73, 74, 104, 134, 139, 144,
    148, 149
Council of Trent 162
counter-culture 24
Crickhollow 4, 102, 103
critical thinking 141, 143
cunning folk 179
Cynewulf 209

D

Dead Marshes 70
defamiliarisation 241, 242, 245, 246
degeneration 10, 195, 196, 198, 203
democracy 73, 196, 197
Denethor 75, 92, 93, 94, 95, 105, 149
de Saussure, Ferdinand 126
diabetes 6
downfall theme 224
dreams 53, 211, 212, 221, 222
Dunlendings 105
Dwarves 75, 105, 185
dyscatastrophe 239
Dyson, Hugo 26, 29, 30, 31, 32, 35, 36, 38,
    219
dystopia 194, 198, 199

E

Eagle and Child 22, 27, 37
Eagles 223, 255
Earendel 209, 210
Earendil 146, 149, 209
Earthsea 86
Edain 230, 231
Edgbaston 5, 6, 7, 61
Egyptians 158
Egyptian traits 204
Eldar 113, 132, 135, 197
Elder Edda 227
Elendil 202, 204, 226
Elf-friend 194
Elohim 170, 171
Elrond 73, 74, 104, 134, 139, 144, 148, 149,
    198
Elros 197, 198
Elven Latin 196, 205
Elves 26, 33, 71, 103, 114, 132, 145, 149, 158,
    161, 176, 183, 185, 200, 202, 212, 231,
    232, 236, 244, 246, 253
Emberü 222
English philosophers 111
En-keladim 223
Ents 103, 121, 158, 253
Éowyn 89, 93, 95, 139, 149
epic language 90
Eru 69, 133, 136, 158, 161, 236, 238
Étaples 61
eucatastrophe 36, 238, 239
evangelium 239

evil as absence 139
Exeter College 3, 13, 19, 20, 22, 59
existentialism 124

F

Faerie Queene, The (see Spenser) 87
fairies 44, 45, 183, 184
fairy story 32, 38, 184
family life 100
Fangorn 103, 258
Fangorn Forest 103
fantasy 32, 38, 85, 86, 87, 88, 93, 106, 116,
        117, 160, 166, 180, 182, 207, 226, 229,
        241, 243, 244, 245, 246, 249
Farmer Maggot 103
fate vii, 75, 76, 131, 132, 133, 134, 135, 137,
        139, 229, 235, 236, 237, 238, 239
Fathers of the Church 162
Fëanor 146, 149
Fields of Arbol 222
financial assistance 13
Fingolfin 146, 149
First Southern Military Hospital 5, 66
Flame Imperishable 169, 173
flat Earth 201
fluvial transport of wine 16
folk-tales 12
free will 115, 131, 132, 133, 135, 139, 146,
        229, 235, 236, 237, 238, 239, 259
Freud, Sigmund 111, 128, 241, 242
Frodo (Baggins) 4, 6, 9, 24, 70, 72, 73, 74, 75,
        80, 83, 84, 90, 91, 94, 95, 96, 102, 103,
        104, 106, 115, 120, 139, 148, 149, 156,
        157, 221, 236, 238, 239, 246, 248, 273

G

Galadriel 74, 96, 103, 106, 139, 149, 157, 181,
        184
Gamgee, Dr Joseph Sampson 6
Gamgee tissue 6
Gandalf 24, 73, 74, 75, 90, 94, 104, 105, 116,
        134, 139, 147, 149, 156, 185, 221, 245,
        255, 256, 258, 259
Genesis 157, 169, 208
geographical upheaval 201
Germanic literature 20
Germanic North 126

Ghân-buri-Ghân 75
giants 229, 230, 231, 235, 239
Gilson, Robert Quilter i, vii, 10, 43, 46, 47,
        48, 49, 62, 70
Gimilkhâd 198
Gimli 103, 122, 233
Gnomish Lexicon 10
goeteia 176, 177
Gollum 23, 24, 75, 83, 116, 120, 149, 238,
        239, 248
Gondor 17, 72, 76, 104, 105, 107, 139, 149,
        200, 204, 229, 246
good leadership 73, 74, 77
Gothic 133, 138, 225, 246
Great Haywood 66
Great Storm 207, 213, 215, 216, 224
Great Wave 210, 226
Greek Gods 126
Gregorian calendar 214
grey horse (the Grey) 251, 252, 253, 254, 255,
        260
Gríma Wormtongue 105
Gualdalquivir 17
guardian 7, 9, 10, 11, 13
Gypsy Green 66

H

Haig, General Douglas 77, 78, 79, 80, 81, 82,
        83
Harmonic Convergence 215, 216, 217
Helm's Deep 72, 90, 103
heroes of ancient Greece 89
heroism of choice 90, 94, 96
HMHS Asturias 65, 66
hobbits viii, 4, 103, 122, 144, 149, 182, 241,
        242, 245, 246, 247, 248, 249, 253, 258
Hollin 232
Hollywood 218
Holy Ghost 167, 168, 170, 171
home 6, 14, 16, 19, 21, 22, 23, 34, 37, 45, 47,
        49, 52, 56, 66, 83, 84, 88, 99, 100, 102,
        103, 104, 105, 106, 107, 114, 122, 132,
        196, 197, 205, 212, 225, 245, 246, 273
Home Guard 99
Homer 90, 196
Hornburg 89
horses 234, 256, 257, 261
Hy Bresail 196

**I**

Icelandic literature  33
Icelandic Sagas  21
Iliad  90
Ilúvatar  146, 169, 170, 171, 172, 199, 231, 236
Imagination  117
Imrahil  93, 94, 139
Indo-European  193
Indo-Germans  193
industrialisation  105, 106, 252, 253
industrial revolution  245
Inklings  i, vii, 21, 22, 25, 26, 27, 28, 29, 30, 31,
    33, 35, 36, 37, 38, 112, 123, 128, 213,
    219, 220, 227, 262
Isengard  30, 70, 91, 103, 253, 254, 256, 257
Ivy Bush  7

**J**

Jackson, Peter  89
Jews  203, 204

**K**

Kant  111, 127
Khazad  74, 105, 202, 231
King Edward's School  4, 19, 43
King Follett  170
King's Heath  3, 4, 5
King Sheave  224, 225
Kortirion  50, 51
Kristevan images  103
Kullervo  196

**L**

Lancashire Fusiliers  7, 48, 59, 60, 61, 63, 83
languages  10, 13, 20, 23, 33, 60, 101, 118, 126,
    191, 193, 196, 202, 208, 209, 210, 212,
    223, 224, 225, 226, 245
leadership and ethics  141, 142, 145, 148, 149,
    150, 263
Leeds  14, 19, 21
legendarium  vii, 102, 103, 192, 200, 206, 208,
    209, 225, 226, 241, 242, 243, 244, 245,
    248, 249
Legolas  103, 122, 231, 232, 233
Lewis, C.S.  19, 21, 22, 25, 26, 27, 28, 29, 30,
    31, 32, 33, 34, 35, 36, 37, 38, 112, 115,

    124, 125, 126, 127, 128, 133, 165, 166,
    180, 181, 183, 213, 219, 220, 222, 224,
    226, 262, 264
lice  64, 65
light of Christ  167, 168
liminal beings  256
Lords of the West  223
Lothlórien  74, 103, 105, 246
Lotho Sackville-Baggins  106
Lugbúrz  72
Luke Skywalker  86
Lúthien  9, 10, 32, 33, 149
Lyonesse  222

**M**

Magdalen College  22, 32, 34, 35, 37
magia  176
magic  vii, 158, 175, 176, 177, 178, 179, 180,
    181, 182, 183, 184, 185, 186, 207, 231,
    253, 256, 259, 263
Maiar  144, 197, 258
Man  10, 53, 70, 78, 79, 80, 118, 121, 155, 160,
    161, 162, 163, 200, 247, 260
Mayan Long Count  207, 214, 215
mearas  255, 256, 259
mechanical devices  247
mechanised war  77, 81
Medea  181
mediaeval romances  87
Mediterranean  178, 183, 199
Melian  33, 161
Melkor  77, 114, 116, 146, 161, 172, 183, 198,
    204, 226, 238
memorial plaque  24
Meneltarma  204
mercy  75, 76, 82, 90, 252
Merry  15, 70, 74, 93, 139, 149, 177, 246, 249
Merton College  21, 22, 23, 24, 37
Mesopotamia  204
Michael Ramer  123
mill  3, 4, 20, 106
Minas Morgul  7
Minas Tirith  7, 17, 63, 70, 72, 75, 93, 105,
    107, 122, 149, 248
Moloch  204
monotheistic beliefs  205
Mordor  9, 61, 72, 73, 74, 76, 82, 84, 88, 93,
    139, 177, 248, 253

Morgan, Father Francis Xavier i, vii, 6, 7, 9, 10, 11, 12, 13, 14, 16
Morgan le Fey 181
Moria 105, 149
Mortality 114, 227, 229, 231, 235, 239
Moseley 3, 4, 5
Mount Doom 73, 80, 83, 95, 156, 238, 239
Music of the Ainur 117, 157, 208, 236, 244
myth vii, 29, 32, 33, 35, 37, 38, 111, 122, 142, 144, 145, 156, 165, 167, 168, 170, 192, 193, 195, 196, 198, 200, 210, 213, 218, 221, 231, 232, 235, 239, 241, 243, 244, 245, 247, 254
mythopoeia 231, 239, 241, 242, 243, 244

## N

Naffarin 13
Napoleonic army 16
Narnia 86, 166, 180, 181
native language 209, 210, 224
natural world 251, 252, 253, 254, 255, 256, 257, 260
Nazgûl 139
Nazi ideologists 193
Newman, John Henry (Cardinal) 5, 11, 15, 16
Newman Society 15, 16
Niebelungenlied 185
Noah 162, 171, 202
Noldor 146, 149, 232
non-violent protagonism 90
Northmoor Road 19, 21, 22, 34
Númenor ii, vii, ix, 71, 76, 105, 111, 113, 122, 191, 194, 195, 197, 198, 199, 200, 202, 203, 204, 205, 211, 212, 215, 219, 223, 225, 226, 231

## O

Odin 251, 254, 255, 256, 257, 259
Officers' Training Corps 59
Old English vii, 20, 34, 114, 131, 133, 136, 139, 223, 224, 225, 227, 228, 229, 230, 231, 233, 234, 236, 237, 239, 246, 264
Old Forest 134, 258, 260
Old Norse 20, 225
One Ring 113, 232, 248
Oratory 5, 6, 7, 9, 11, 15, 61
Oratory School 11

Orientalism 206
Orthanc 221
Ossë 197
Owen, Wilfred 61
Oxford i, vii, 3, 7, 10, 13, 15, 16, 19, 20, 21, 22, 23, 24, 25, 26, 27, 28, 29, 31, 32, 33, 34, 37, 38, 43, 44, 45, 46, 47, 49, 59, 67, 70, 114, 115, 116, 119, 121, 123, 124, 125, 127, 141, 158, 166, 193, 209, 211, 213, 219, 223, 262, 273
Oxford English Dictionary 19, 20

## P

Paganism 137, 161, 162
Pagan perspective 157
pagan saints 162
'Pals' battalions 62
Paradise Lost 44, 87, 247
pastiche 192
Pauline tradition 92
Pearl (poem) 171, 180, 227, 228, 243
Pelennor 92, 149
Pembroke College 19, 21, 22, 32, 37, 118
perennis philosophia 111
Perrott's Folly 7
Persia 203, 204
Pharaoh 204
Philip Frankley 192
Phoenicians 203, 204, 205
Pilgrim's Progress 166
Pippin (Peregrin Took) 4, 61, 70, 74, 149, 177, 246
Plato 111, 113, 114, 116, 125, 127, 128, 161, 178, 191, 192, 193, 195, 196, 197, 198, 199, 200, 201, 202, 203, 204, 205, 206, 222
  Critias 113, 192, 199
  Gorgias 113, 116
  Phaedo 113
  Protagoras 113
  Timaeus 113, 191, 192, 199
Platonic themes 113
Poetic Diction 37
Poseidon 197
Post Traumatic Stress Disorder 81
poverty 4
Precession of the Equinoxes 218
Primitive Eldarin 132

Professor (John) Rashbold  224, 225
Protestant theologians  163
providence  131, 133, 134, 135, 137, 138, 139,
    140, 172
providential cosmology  134, 138

## Q

Quenya  131, 196, 203, 225, 232
Quest  238

## R

Radcliffe Camera  223
Rawlinson and Bosworth Professor of An-
    glo-Saxon  21, 22, 32
reading sessions  26
Realm of Fairy  208, 218
red brick chimney  6
Rednal  5, 6
re-imagining of myths  242
reincarnation  113, 119, 122, 212, 214
retirement  19
Revelation  155, 158, 159, 160, 161, 162, 163
riddles  12, 248
ring bearer  6
Ring of Gyges  244
Rings of Power  232
Rivendell  105, 246, 248
River Cherwell  21, 22, 24
Rohan  75, 76, 82, 88, 93, 103, 105, 107, 149,
    181, 234, 248
Rohirrim  75, 76, 88, 89, 90, 91, 92, 103, 149,
    196, 233, 246
Roman Catholic  5, 32, 37, 167
Roman Catholicism  10, 32, 165
romance  7, 9, 10, 27, 29, 35, 53, 90, 181, 245
Roman Empire  133, 178, 229
Rome  5, 11, 229
Rugeley  60
ruin  199, 201, 223, 229, 231, 232, 233, 234,
    235, 239
runes  185
Russian formalism  241

## S

Sammath Naur  73
Sam (Samwise) Gamgee  4, 6, 24, 62, 70, 72,
    84, 95, 96, 106, 120, 149, 156, 238, 239,

    246
Sandfield Road  23
Sapir, Edward and Benjamin Whorf  120
Sarehole  3, 4, 5
Saruman  91, 92, 105, 116, 148, 149, 247, 254,
    255, 256, 258
Satan  69, 172, 173, 180, 247
Sauron  i, vii, 30, 69, 71, 72, 73, 74, 75, 76, 77,
    78, 79, 80, 81, 83, 84, 86, 104, 105, 106,
    107, 111, 116, 123, 133, 134, 139, 176,
    185, 191, 194, 195, 199, 202, 204, 205,
    207, 219, 221, 224, 226, 232
Sayers, Dorothy L.  28, 29
Schopenauer, Arthur  117, 128
science-fiction  25
sea  70, 128, 197, 201, 203, 204, 205, 221, 231,
    237, 251, 254, 256, 257, 258, 260
sea-power  203, 204, 205
Second Vatican Council  162
Second World War  vii, 5, 22, 26, 27, 30, 99,
    101, 121, 124, 194, 262
Semitic  ii, 191, 193, 202, 203, 204, 226
Semitic group  193
sentiment  229, 233, 234, 237, 261
separation  10, 36, 104, 114
sequel  23, 29, 244, 246
Shadowfax  255, 256, 257, 258, 259
Shakespeare  12, 123, 141
Sharkey  106, 149
Shell Shock  81, 82
Shelob  62, 72, 73
Shield Sheafing  192, 196, 201
silence  257, 260
Sindarin  17, 131, 132
Sir Gawain and the Green Knight  21, 87, 161,
    180, 227, 243
skill-oriented objectives  142
slave-states  253
Smaug  134, 245
Smith, G.B. (or Smith, Geoffrey)  44, 45, 46,
    48, 49, 50, 51, 53, 54, 55, 57, 59, 60, 70
Smith, Joseph  124, 127, 170, 171, 173
social reforms  100
Southampton  65, 66
Spain  9, 11, 12, 15, 16, 262, 263
Spanish language  13
spells  177, 179, 184, 185, 186
Spenser, Edmund (see also Faerie Queene,

The) 87, 243
St. Augustine 91, 111, 113, 115, 116, 127, 128, 159, 162, 179
St. Brendan 192, 196, 224
Stonyhurst 16
straight road 225, 226
sub-creation 94, 208, 209, 231, 263

T

tanks 64
T.C.B.S. i, 29, 32, 33, 35, 43, 44, 46, 49, 50
Tengwar 224, 225
Thames Valley 223
Théoden 73, 74, 75, 76, 88, 89, 90, 91, 92, 93, 105, 149
The Old Forest 134
The Shire 9, 16, 95, 102, 103, 106, 107, 248
Thingol 10, 33, 146, 161
time-travel 207, 210, 214, 215, 218, 220, 222
Tir-nan-Óg 229
Tolkien - Family
    Bratt, Edith (wife) 3, 7, 9, 10, 14, 20, 23, 24, 53, 59, 61, 66
    Tolkien, Arthur (father) 3
    Tolkien, Christopher (son and editor) 10, 11, 23, 25, 30, 32, 33, 50, 71, 85, 88, 111, 112, 115, 121, 146, 147, 156, 157, 160, 169, 176, 191, 192, 193, 194, 196, 197, 200, 205, 207, 208, 212, 219, 220, 225, 230, 231, 238, 242, 252, 260
    Tolkien, Hilary (brother) 3, 4, 6, 7, 59
    Tolkien, Mabel, (mother) 3, 4, 5, 6
    Tolkien, Priscilla (daughter) 15, 23, 70
Tolkien's cosmology
    236
Tolkien's 'philosophy of history'
    121
Tolkien Works
    'Ainulindale' 168, 172
    Akallabêth 191, 196, 197
    'A Secret Vice' 33
    Athrabeth Finrod ah Andreth 111, 113
    Farmer Giles of Ham ix
    'Kortirion among the Trees' 50
    Laws and Customs among the Eldar 113
    Morgoth's Ring 112, 113, 114
    'Of the Flight of the Noldor' 146
    'Of the Ruin of Doriath' 146

'Of the Voyage of Earendil and the War of Wrath' 146, 149
On Fairy Stories 36, 122, 125, 126, 207
    OFS ix, 157, 160, 238, 239
'Perry-the-Winkle' 14
'Tale of Aldarion and Erendis' 205
The Adventures of Tom Bombadil 14
The Book of Lost Tales 50, 236
The Drowning of Anadunë 197
The Fall of Numenor 198
The Fellowship of the Ring ix, 4, 23, 61, 69, 73, 102, 144, 147, 175, 231, 232
    FotR ix, 69, 70, 74, 75, 100, 102, 103, 104, 105, 106, 134, 139, 144, 147, 148, 149, 176, 232
The Hobbit iii, ix, 12, 13, 16, 21, 23, 27, 29, 35, 38, 75, 106, 107, 134, 165, 185, 241, 242, 244, 245, 246, 247, 248
    TH ix, 13, 75
The Homecoming of Beorhtnoth, Beorhthelm's Son 161
The Lord of the Rings iii, ix, 4, 11, 21, 25, 33, 61, 69, 85, 89, 99, 100, 104, 106, 107, 134, 155, 156, 157, 158, 165, 177, 181, 207, 219, 226, 227, 228, 229, 241, 249, 251, 258
    LotR ix, 4, 6, 7, 16, 22, 23, 24, 26, 27, 38, 69, 70, 71, 72, 76, 86, 88, 89, 90, 91, 92, 93, 94, 95, 96, 97, 100, 102, 103, 104, 105, 106, 107, 116, 120, 122, 123, 125, 134, 139, 142, 144, 147, 149, 157, 158, 165, 177, 184, 186, 202, 229, 235, 237, 238, 242, 244, 245, 246, 247, 248, 249, 251, 254, 255, 258, 260
The Lost Road 119, 193, 196, 202, 219, 220, 224, 225, 228, 229, 234, 236
The Monsters and the Critics 157, 160, 165, 227, 238, 260
The Notion Club Papers iii, vii, 28, 111, 119, 122, 191, 193, 195, 196, 197, 202, 207, 208, 219
The Return of the King ix, 23, 62, 72, 73, 144, 238, 247
    RotK ix, 62, 63, 73, 74, 75, 76, 80, 83, 84, 105, 106, 134, 139, 144, 149, 238, 239
'The Sea-Bell' 221
The Silmarillion ix, 33, 34, 71, 113, 116, 117, 141, 144, 145, 146, 165, 168, 169,

172, 183, 197, 198, 230, 231, 242, 244
TSil ix, 71, 72, 146, 149, 169, 172, 197, 198, 201, 230, 231, 232
The Two Towers ix, 7, 23, 62, 72, 89, 147, 148, 233, 234, 247
TT ix, 62, 72, 73, 74, 75, 103, 148, 149, 177, 233, 234, 249
Tom Bombadil 14, 102, 134, 144, 148, 177
tragedy 62, 83, 199, 238
trams 4
translation 12, 89, 115, 116, 133, 137, 163, 198, 225, 227, 228, 233, 234
Treebeard 107, 248, 249
trench fever 5, 59, 64, 65, 83, 84
Tulkas 230
twins 197, 203

## U

ubi sunt 232, 233, 234, 235
Ulmo 230
uncanny 35, 55, 177, 186, 207, 241, 242, 252, 257, 260
Unheimliche 241, 252
University of Louvain 11
Unwin, Rayner 4, 11, 13, 14, 23, 25, 30, 33, 36, 50, 53, 62, 111, 112, 147, 157, 161, 169, 183, 193, 205, 207, 208, 242, 247, 260

## V

Valaquenta 168
Valar 113, 144, 146, 168, 169, 170, 182, 185, 199, 212, 230, 231, 239
Valinor 71, 185, 192, 225, 226, 229, 231, 232, 237
Via Crucis 157
Victorian fantasy 243
virtuous Pagans 162
Völsunga Saga 185

## W

War in Heaven 87, 172, 247
War of Wrath 146, 149, 200
Warwick 20, 59, 61
Wave dream 193
waves 192, 199, 201, 253, 258, 259

Welsh 5, 9, 11, 157, 161, 209, 222, 224
Westernesse 177, 226
Western Front 5, 7, 60, 66, 78
White Rider viii, 255, 258
Whittington Heath Barracks 59
Williams, Charles 22, 27, 28, 29, 30, 38, 224
wolves 173, 254
World War I (One) vii, 5, 7, 9, 20, 22, 26, 27, 29, 30, 61, 69, 70, 71, 72, 76, 77, 81, 82, 83, 84, 99, 101, 121, 124, 194, 195, 261, 262
Wrenn, C.L. 38
Wright, Joseph 20
wyrd 137, 138, 237, 238, 239

## Z

Zeus 199
Zigur 223, 224, 226
Zollern Redoubt 64

# About The Tolkien Society

The Tolkien Society is a literary society and educational charity devoted to promoting the life and works of Professor J.R.R. Tolkien CBE. Founded in 1969 as a fan club in the United Kingdom, today the Tolkien Society has over a thousand members worldwide. We are friendly, fun and passionate in our mission to promote Tolkien to as wide an audience as possible while growing our fellowship of people who consider Middle-earth their home.

Membership include a subscription to the Society's two regular publications. *Amon Hen* is our bi-monthly bulletin which includes news, book reviews, short articles, information about events and much more. *Mallorn* is the journal of the Tolkien Society, featuring scholarly articles and in-depth reviews from scholars supplemented by full-colour artwork from some of the best Tolkien artists. In addition to *Amon Hen* and *Mallorn*, we publish one-off publications such as these proceedings together with our 'Peter Roe' booklets which print papers delivered at our annual events.

As well as our wide range of publications, the Society hosts a series of events each year. On 3 January we celebrate the anniversary of Tolkien's birth in 1892 by encouraging fans all over the world to raise a toast to the Professor at 9pm their local time. 3 March is Tolkien Reading Day, marking the date on which the One Ring was destroyed in *The Lord of the Rings*. In the summer we hold our Seminar for serious Tolkien scholarship, usually in early July in Leeds. But the centrepiece of our calendar is Oxonmoot. Held in an Oxford college on a weekend close to Bilbo and Frodo's birthday on 22 September, we gather for a long weekend of talks, discussions, quizzes, food, partying, masquerading and great company. For any Tolkien fan, Oxonmoot is not to be missed.

To learn more and tobecome a member of the Tolkien Society visit our website at www.tolkiensociety.org.

Milton Keynes UK
Ingram Content Group UK Ltd.
UKHW052337190524
442884UK00011B/555